THE SUPERVISOR'S GUIDEBOOK

EVIDENCE-BASED STRATEGIES FOR PROMOTING WORK QUALITY AND ENJOYMENT AMONG HUMAN SERVICE STAFF

DENNIS H. REID, MARSHA B. PARSONS,
AND CAROLYN W. GREEN

Volume 4
in
The Behavior Analysis Applications in Developmental
Disabilities Series

HABILITATIVE MANAGEMENT CONSULTANTS, INC.

Copyright © 2012 Dennis H. Reid
All Rights Reserved

This book may not be reproduced or transmitted in any form or by any means, electronic, mechanical, including photocopying, recording, or by any information storage and retrieval system, except in the case of reviews, without the expressed written permission of the publisher, except where permitted by law.

ISBN Number 0-9645562-5-1

Library of Congress Catalog Card Number 2011909634

Published by
Habilitative Management Consultants, Inc.
P.O. Box 2295
Morganton, North Carolina 28680

Professional Press
Chapel Hill, NC 27515-4371

Manufactured in the United States of America
12 13 14 15 16   10 9 8 7 6 5 4 3 2 1

DEDICATION

This book is dedicated to our parents: Charles and Margaret Reid, Reece and Rachel Bigham, and Charles and Lavada Worley. If not for their personal devotion and natural abilities to teach and supervise, we would not have been in a position to write this book.

ACKNOWLEDGMENTS

Numerous people have helped us learn about supervision, far too many to recognize individually. However, we have learned most from the dedicated and sincere staff we have been fortunate to supervise over the years. They have greatly facilitated our jobs as supervisors and significantly enhanced our work enjoyment.

ABOUT THE AUTHORS

Dennis Reid, Marsha Parsons, and **Carolyn Green** each have over 30 years of supervisory experience in the human services. Collectively they have consulted with human service agencies in the majority of states across the United States as well as Canada and New Zealand. They have published over 130 applied research articles and seven books. Denny, Marsha, and Carolyn also wrote the highly acclaimed *Supervisor Training Curriculum: Evidence-Based Ways to Promote Work Quality and Enjoyment among Support Staff,* sold internationally by the American Association on Intellectual and Developmental Disabilities (AAIDD). Their work has resulted in awards from local, state, and national organizations, including the North Carolina Department of Human Resources, Association for Behavior Analysis International, AAIDD, TASH (formerly The Association for Persons with Severe Handicaps), and the Organization for Autism Research. Denny is the founder and Director of the Carolina Behavior Analysis and Support Center, Marsha is the Director of Dogwood Resource Center of the J. Iverson Riddle Center, and Carolyn is a Senior Consultant with the Carolina Behavior Analysis and Support Center, all in Morganton, North Carolina.

TO CONTACT THE AUTHORS

Denny Reid, Marsha Parsons, and Carolyn Green can be contacted using the information provided below. Readers are invited to send comments about the book, as well as suggestions regarding future editions in the *Behavior Analysis Applications in Developmental Disabilities Series.*

Habilitative Management Consultants, Inc.
P. O. Box 2295
Morganton, North Carolina 28680
(phone: 828 432 0030)
e-mail: drhmc@vistatech.net

PREFACE

The job of a supervisor of direct support staff in the human services is one of the most important yet unheralded professions. Supervisors are charged with ensuring support staff deliver quality services for people with disabilities whose quality of life is heavily dependent on how well those services are provided. Supervisors must ensure staff receive necessary training in their job duties, are actively supported to stay motivated to work proficiently and at times, effectively assisted to improve their work performance. Supervisors have to overcome many challenges to fulfill these critical duties, often involving frequent changes in their staff work force and varying or limited resources.

Complicating the job of staff supervisors is a lack of formal training necessary to perform their supervisory duties effectively. When supervisors do receive training in how to supervise staff work performance, the training is not always very useful. The training is frequently too general to equip supervisors with knowledge and skills to affect staff work performance on a routine basis. The training also is commonly based on unproven means of promoting quality staff performance, stemming from current fads or ideology that has little if any hard evidence to support the training content.

Over the last four decades, a gradual technology for supervising staff work performance in the human services has been evolving, derived from applied research conducted in many human service agencies. Such research has provided a sound evidence base to support the effectiveness of the supervisory strategies constituting the technology to date. We have been fortunate in participating in research on effective ways to supervise as well as in applying the technology in our work as supervisors in the human services. However, most supervisors have not had opportunities to become aware of these evidence-based means of fulfilling their supervisory duties.

The purpose of **The Supervisor's Guidebook** is to describe the existing evidence-based approach to supervision. It is intended to provide supervisors with detailed information about tried and tested means of promoting diligent and proficient staff performance and to do so in a way that maximizes staff enjoyment with their work. It is sincerely hoped the book fulfills this purpose for the reader.

CONTENTS

SECTION I

INTRODUCTION TO SUPERVISION

Chapter 1

The Importance of Supervision 3

- What is Supervision? 4
- Successful Supervision Involves Promoting Staff Work Enjoyment 5
- Evidence-Based Supervision 7
- Purpose of *The Supervisor's Guidebook* 8
- Intended Audience of *The Supervisor's Guidebook* 9
- Organization of *The Supervisor's Guidebook* 9

Chapter 2

An Evidence-Based Protocol for Supervising Staff Performance 11

- Steps Constituting an Evidence-Based Protocol of Supervision 12
- Implementing Steps of the Supervisory Protocol in Ways to Enhance Work Enjoyment 19

SECTION II

CRITICAL SUPERVISORY SKILLS

Chapter 3

Specifying Staff Work Responsibilities 25

- Three Criteria for Specifying Staff Performance Responsibilities 27
- Strategies for Specifying Performance Responsibilities 36
- Specifying Performance Responsibilities in Ways Acceptable to Staff 42

Chapter 4

Training Work Skills to Staff 47

- Basic Goals of Staff Training 50
- An Evidence-Based Protocol for Staff Training 52
- Two Main Formats for Training Staff 60
- General Considerations when Using Evidence-Based Training Procedures with Staff 68
- Making Training Acceptable to Staff 76
- A Final Note on Staff Training 69

Chapter 5

Monitoring Staff Performance 81

- Formal Monitoring 83
- Informal Monitoring 91
- Special Considerations with Monitoring 94
- Promoting Staff Acceptance of Performance Monitoring by a Supervisor 98

Chapter 6

Supporting Proficient Work Performance: Positive Feedback 109

- The Power of Positive Feedback 114
- An Evidence-Based Protocol for Providing Feedback 114
- Special Considerations when Using the Evidence-Based Feedback Protocol 123
- Different Ways of Providing Feedback 130

Chapter 7

Supporting Proficient Work Performance: Special Recognition Procedures 153

- Special Recognition Awards 156
- Special Recognition Actions 163
- Using Money for Special Recognition 175

Chapter 8

Correcting Nonproficient Work Performance 179

- Prerequisites for Corrective Supervision 179
- A Serious Misconception About How to Correct Nonproficient Performance 181
- Common Reasons for Nonproficient Staff Performance and Supervisor Corrective Actions 183
- Performance Problems Due to Reasons Outside of the Workplace 202

Chapter 9

Promoting Staff Enjoyment: Making Disliked Work Tasks More Enjoyable to Perform 205

- General Considerations for Making Work Tasks More Enjoyable for Staff to Perform 206

- An Evidence-Based Approach for Making Disliked Work Tasks More Enjoyable to Perform: TEMP 212

- An Example of How TEMP Has Been Used to Make a Disliked Work Task More Enjoyable to Perform 217

- Special Considerations for Addressing Highly Disliked Work Tasks 219

SECTION III

RESOLVING COMMON PERFORMANCE PROBLEMS

Chapter 10

Resolving Common Performance Problems: Overview 227

- The Basic Premise of Supervisor Accountability 229

- Supervising in Difficult Situations 233

Chapter 11

Reducing Absenteeism 243

- Reasons for Frequent Absenteeism 245

- Specifying Acceptable and Unacceptable Absenteeism 248

- Absenteeism-Reduction Strategies 251

- Two Final Considerations for Reducing Absenteeism 260

Chapter 12

Resolving Problems with Staff Provision of Consumer-Teaching Services 267

- Improving Formal Teaching Services 270

- Promoting Naturalistic Teaching During Routine Activities .. 285

- Special Considerations for Overcoming Performance Problems with Teaching Services 292

Chapter 13

    Reducing Frequent Nonwork Behavior 301

- Special Considerations in Applying the Evidence-Based Supervision Protocol to Reduce Nonwork Behavior 303

- General Considerations for Reducing Frequent Nonwork Behavior 308

SECTION IV

SELECTED READINGS 317

INDEX 355

SECTION I

INTRODUCTION TO SUPERVISION

CHAPTER 1

THE IMPORTANCE OF SUPERVISION

The most significant determinant of the effectiveness of human service agencies is the quality of work performed by direct support staff. Direct support staff spend more time with agency consumers and provide more services that affect consumer welfare than any other agency personnel. In turn, a major determinant of the proficiency with which support staff fulfill their roles is the quality of supervision they receive.

The importance of supervision on the performance of direct support staff has long been acknowledged in the human services. Such importance is due to a number of factors. Most apparently, the majority of people who begin employment in a direct support capacity have no previous training in how to fulfill their roles. Although newly employed staff usually receive some agency orientation, most of the responsibility for training new staff how to perform daily job duties falls on their immediate supervisors. Relatedly, as new work expectations arise, such as implementing new teaching procedures with clients or programs to reduce challenging behavior, supervisors must ensure staff learn how to perform the new duties.

Because direct support staff have numerous job functions to fulfill, supervisors are also responsible for ensuring staff know what should be done at certain times and that they have the resources to do their jobs. Supervisors must likewise intervene with staff at times to correct problems with work proficiency.

Finally, supervisors must help staff stay motivated to perform their duties proficiently on a day-to-day basis.

WHAT IS SUPERVISION?

As just indicated, supervisors of direct support staff have many responsibilities to fulfill. In addition to the duties illustrated above, supervisors often have a variety of administrative tasks to perform, meetings to attend, work schedules to prepare, and documentation to maintain. However, from the perspective of actually *supervising staff performance*, the job of a supervisor essentially involves two basic responsibilities. First, when staff performance is less than adequate, supervisors must take action to improve that performance. Second, when staff performance is of sufficient quality, supervisors must take action to support and maintain that performance.

Supervisors typically acknowledge the importance of actively working to improve inadequate job performance of their staff. It is usually apparent, for example, that a supervisor must take action to reduce frequent absenteeism by a given staff person, alter inappropriate staff interactions with agency consumers, or resolve problems with inconsistencies with which staff carry out treatment procedures with consumers. In contrast, supervisors are not always cognizant of the importance of actively working to support appropriate staff performance.

Specific supervisory action is needed to support and maintain quality work among staff for a number of reasons. In particular, a rather common phenomenon in human service agencies is what is generally referred to as staff "burnout". Hard working staff can lose their motivation to work diligently and proficiently over time—they "burn out"—due in part to the effortful nature of providing direct services for individuals with disabilities on a daily basis. In other cases, new staff begin their jobs highly motivated but gradually lose their motivation because they are criticized by more experienced and less motivated staff for their work efforts. The latter staff resent the apparent motivation of new staff because it makes their less effortful performance more noticeable. Supervisors can prevent deterioration in the quality of staff work due to these and other reasons by actively supporting staff performance that is of high quality.

> **The essence of supervision is taking action to improve inadequate staff performance and taking action to support and maintain quality performance.**

Taking action to improve inadequate staff performance and taking action to support and maintain quality performance represent the essence of supervision. These are the two supervisory responsibilities that have the most significant effect on what staff do in the workplace and correspondingly, the quality of services provided to agency consumers. However, there is a third component of supervision that also warrants serious attention if supervisors are to successfully fulfill these two responsibilities on a consistent and long-term basis: these responsibilities must be carried out in ways that are acceptable to staff. Staff acceptance of supervisor actions is a key factor affecting staff work enjoyment, which in turn directly impacts staff motivation.

SUCCESSFUL SUPERVISION INVOLVES PROMOTING STAFF WORK ENJOYMENT

Staff enjoyment with their jobs is a primary indicator of a highly motivated and quality work force. It is something that supervisors must actively strive to promote if their supervision is to be successful. Numerous problems exist when direct support staff do not enjoy their work and experience frequent discontent with their work situation.

There are four most important reasons for supervisors to actively promote staff enjoyment with their work. First, when staff are not enjoying their work, they reduce their work effort. Instead of directing their attention and effort to performing quality work, time is spent attempting to resolve the source of their discontent or simply complaining about the job. Second, lack of staff enjoyment can impact life quality of agency consumers. When staff are disgruntled about their work situation, they are less likely to interact in pleasant and positive ways with consumers; their interactions with consumers become more negative in nature. Third, staff discontent with their jobs makes the supervisors' job less desirable. Supervisors, like anybody else, tend to enjoy their workday more if they are interacting with staff who are generally upbeat and pleasant versus staff who are frequently discontented. Fourth, when staff are experiencing frequent discontent with their work, absenteeism tends to increase as does staff turnover.

For the reasons just noted, as well as others to be discussed later, supervisors should go about their jobs of working with staff in ways that are acceptable to staff—ways that promote rather than impede staff work enjoyment. This is not to imply that supervision should emphasize work enjoyment to the detriment of proficient or diligent work performance of staff. Supervisory actions taken to promote staff work enjoyment should occur in conjunction with ongoing actions to promote and maintain quality work performance.

Successful supervision involves supervisors working with staff in ways that are acceptable to staff and promote staff enjoyment with their work.

EVIDENCE-BASED SUPERVISION

In describing supervision to this point, an emphasis has been on *actions* supervisors should take to improve and support staff work performance, as well as to promote work enjoyment. Supervision of staff performance is an active process, requiring consistent effort on the part of supervisors. However, although actively working with staff is necessary for supervision to be successful, it is not sufficient. Supervisory actions must also be *effective*; what supervisors do must have the desired impact on staff work behavior and enjoyment.

The actions supervisors take to affect staff performance and work enjoyment are most likely to be effective if the actions are *evidence-based*. Evidence-based means that a given supervisory strategy has been developed and demonstrated through applied research to effectively impact an area of staff work behavior. For example, if a supervisor is concerned about how a staff person interacts with consumers with intellectual disabilities, an evidence-based approach would involve the supervisor working with the staff person in a way that research has shown to improve staff interactions with consumers. Likewise, if a supervisor is experiencing high absenteeism rates among certain staff, an evidence-based approach would entail using procedures to reduce absenteeism that research has shown to effectively decrease how often staff are absent from work.

When supervisors do not rely on evidence-based strategies for working with staff, their actions are likely to be based on intuition or guess work. Sometimes intuitive actions and guess work are successful but often they are not. The lack of success supervisors experience in such cases is not a reflection of poor intention or effort, only that they have not had opportunities to become knowledgeable about, and skilled in, evidence-based supervisory procedures.

Supervisors in the human services often receive little if any training in how to supervise the performance of direct support staff. Additionally, the training that they may receive usually does not focus on evidence-based supervisory approaches. A common problem inherent in many supervisory training programs is a reliance on current fads, clichés, and someone else's intuition about what constitutes good supervision. Without sound evidence to support these various approaches to supervision, their likelihood of being effectively applied by supervisors is at best unknown and at worst, nonexistent or counterproductive.

> **Supervisory strategies for impacting staff work performance and enjoyment are most likely to be effective if the strategies are evidence-based.**

Reliance on evidence-based strategies to improve and maintain staff work performance or enjoyment represents what is considered *evidence-based supervision*. Because evidence-based supervision consists of supervisory strategies developed through applied research, it is a continuously evolving approach to supervision. As more research is conducted and the results disseminated, the approach becomes further developed and refined. Nonetheless, a considerable amount of research on effective ways to supervise has been completed to date. A very useful technology of supervision currently exists for improving inadequate work performance, supporting and maintaining proficient performance, and to a lesser but still important degree, enhancing staff work enjoyment.

PURPOSE OF *THE SUPERVISOR'S GUIDEBOOK*

The purpose of **The Supervisor's Guidebook** is to describe an evidence-based approach to supervising the work performance of direct support staff in human service settings. Specific strategies developed through applied research in typical human service agencies are presented that supervisors can use to improve inadequate work performance of staff, support and maintain quality performance, and concurrently, promote staff work enjoyment. Step-by-step procedures are described regarding how supervisors can effectively fulfill these essential aspects of supervision, and ensure a quality and highly motivated work force.

INTENDED AUDIENCE OF *THE SUPERVISOR'S GUIDEBOOK*

This book is intended for supervisors of direct support staff, and aspiring supervisors, in human service agencies for people with disabilities. The content presented in this and the following chapters pertains most directly to the supervision of staff in agencies providing supports and services for people with intellectual and related disabilities, including community residential settings (e.g., group homes), center-based programs (e.g., residential agencies), sheltered and supported work settings, and adult day activity and education programs. People who train supervisors in these types of human service agencies also represent a primary audience of the book. The content is likewise relevant for supervisors in agencies overseeing home-based programs for individuals with autism that involve paid staff working in the homes, as well as supervisors in public and private schools.

ORGANIZATION OF *THE SUPERVISOR'S GUIDEBOOK*

This book is organized into four sections. **Section I, *Introduction to Supervision***, consists of this introductory chapter and **Chapter 2** that provides an overview of an evidence-based protocol for supervising staff performance. In **Section II, *Critical Supervisory Skills* (Chapters 3-9)**, elaboration is provided on each respective step of the evidence-based approach to supervision summarized in **Chapter 2**. In **Section III (Chapters 10-13)**, *Resolving Common Performance Problems*, specific examples are provided regarding how the supervisory procedures previously discussed can be applied to resolve some of the most common problems that supervisors encounter with staff performance in the human services. Finally, **Section IV**, *Selected Readings*, provides over 300 references to research on supervisory strategies relating to the performance of direct support staff. The literature referenced in **Section IV** provides a comprehensive listing of what constitutes the evidence-base of the supervisory procedures discussed throughout the book. The articles, chapters, and books referenced provide more detailed information for the interested reader about respective procedures, as well as for applied researchers working in the supervision area.

Chapter Summary: Key Points

1. *The essence of supervision is taking action to improve inadequate staff performance and taking action to support and maintain quality performance.*

2. *To be successful over the long run, supervision must occur in ways that are acceptable to staff and promote work enjoyment.*

3. *Supervisory actions to improve inadequate performance, support and maintain quality performance, and promote work enjoyment are most likely to be effective if the actions are evidence-based.*

CHAPTER 2

AN EVIDENCE-BASED PROTOCOL FOR SUPERVISING STAFF PERFORMANCE

As indicated in **Chapter 1**, a comprehensive set of evidence-based strategies exists for aiding supervisors in promoting quality work among human service staff. The core aspects of these strategies have also been consolidated into an overall protocol for supervising staff performance in the human services. The protocol represents a systematic, step-wise approach to supervision. The protocol has been used to improve many important areas of staff performance in human service agencies, as well as to maintain quality performance over the long run. This chapter summarizes the steps constituting this evidence-based approach to supervision. Subsequent chapters **(Section II)** describe each supervisory step in more detail.

To successfully use an evidence-based approach for supervising staff performance as described in this and the following chapters, a basic premise must be accepted by supervisors: *supervision is an active process*. Successful supervision requires consistent time and effort on the part of supervisors. Contrary to some popularly publicized approaches to supervision, there is no quick and easy way to be an effective supervisor in the human services. Even if a supervisor is fortunate to work with staff who are highly skilled and motivated, a supervisor must still work actively to help maintain their work skills and motivation over time.

> **Successful supervision is an *active* process, requiring consistent time and effort by supervisors.**

In one sense, the time and effort required to successfully practice evidence-based supervision represents a practical disadvantage of this approach to working with staff. Nonetheless, it is the only proven way to effectively impact staff work performance and enjoyment on a consistent basis. On a more encouraging note however, evidence-based supervision has two inherent features that reduce the time and effort required of supervisors when practiced consistently. One feature is that because evidence-based supervision usually results in the desired impact on staff work behavior, over time there are fewer areas of staff performance warranting supervisor action for improvement.

A second feature of evidence-based supervision that reduces supervisor time and effort over the long run is that some areas of staff performance do not always require implementation of each step of the supervisory protocol. Some steps also do not have to be implemented in their entirety to have the desired impact on staff performance. How the steps can be implemented with less time and effort in certain cases will be discussed in respective chapters that describe each supervisory step in more detail.

STEPS CONSTITUTING AN EVIDENCE-BASED PROTOCOL OF SUPERVISION

In **Chapter 1** it was noted that the most significant determinant of the quality of an agency's supports and services for consumers with disabilities is the work performance of direct support staff. Of course, providing quality supports and services for people with disabilities is why most human service agencies exist. It is the quality of supports and services provided that determines if agency consumers attain the desired outcomes that an agency is intended to help them attain.

Consumer outcomes that should result from an agency's supports and services are determined by the mission of a respective human service agency and the desires of individual consumers (as well as their involved family members and/or guardians). In educationally related agencies for example, desired outcomes usually focus on consumer attainment of designated skills and knowledge. In residential agencies, consumer outcomes are often more varied, ranging from living safely and happily to increased independence in daily functioning. Vocational agencies focus on outcomes associated with obtainment of real jobs and successful work in those jobs to allow for continued and productive employment.

Because the primary mission of human service agencies is to provide supports and services necessary for consumers to attain desired outcomes, the first step in supervision is to identify desired consumer outcomes. Subsequently, the second step is to carefully specify what staff must do to assist consumers in attaining the targeted outcomes. The third step then entails training staff in the skills to perform their designated duties. The fourth step involves development and implementation of a system for routinely monitoring staff performance of their respective duties. The fifth and sixth steps involve using information obtained from the monitoring to support proficient staff performance and correct nonproficient performance. Finally, the seventh step involves continuously evaluating how well staff perform respective job duties and consumers attain desired outcomes, again based on results of systematic monitoring.

A Protocol for Evidence-Based Supervision

Step 1: Identify desired consumer outcomes.

Step 2: Specify what staff must do to assist consumers in attaining desired outcomes.

Step 3: Train staff in the performance skills specified in Step 2.

Step 4: Monitor staff performance.

Step 5: Support proficient staff performance.

Step 6: Correct nonproficient staff performance.

Step 7: Continuously evaluate staff performance and consumer outcome attainment.

STEP 1: IDENTIFY CONSUMER OUTCOMES

Beginning the supervisory process by identifying outcomes that are desired to be attained among an agency's consumers represents an *outcome management* approach to supervision. Successful supervision centers on identifying those outcomes and then promoting and maintaining staff performance necessary to assist consumers in actually attaining the outcomes. Most human service agencies have established procedures for identifying desired consumer outcomes, usually involving an interdisciplinary or transdisciplinary team process. The outcomes are usually reflected in targeted goals for consumers to attain (e.g., secure a supported job, acquire functional living skills, overcome challenging behavior), supplemented with specific behavioral objectives that must be met in sequence to attain the overall goals.

Because most human service agencies have mechanisms for determining desired consumer outcomes, this initial step of evidence-based supervision will not be covered in-depth. It is noted however due to its importance. Supervisors should never lose sight of the main mission of their agency, which again is to help consumers attain desired outcomes.

STEP 2: SPECIFY STAFF PERFORMANCE

Once desired outcomes of respective consumers are identified, then what staff should do to assist the consumers in attaining the outcomes must be precisely specified. The focus should be on those areas of staff work performance that directly impact consumer attainment of the outcomes. To illustrate, if desired outcomes involve consumers learning certain skills, then the related staff performance usually pertains to how, and how often, staff carry out teaching programs with consumers. If desired outcomes relate to prevention or reduction of challenging behavior, then the related staff performance usually involves how staff interact with consumers and implement formal behavior support plans.

Areas of staff performance that are likely to impede consumer outcome attainment also require specification in many cases. For example, if staff are frequently late in arriving at designated classrooms or other teaching settings, then their assigned arrival times must be specified in order to address the tardiness. Such tardiness can impact consumer skill attainment because staff time devoted to teaching is reduced relative to what should be occurring. Similarly, if staff are doing activities for consumers in contrast to teaching the consumers to perform the activities themselves, then how staff can incorporate teaching procedures into daily activities must be specified to increase teaching opportunities with consumers.

Although human service agencies are often adept at specifying desired outcomes for consumers as indicated previously, specifying related areas of staff performance often is not accomplished very well. Many supervisors have difficulties specifying precisely what staff should do to fulfill various performance expectations. Unless performance expectations of staff are indeed carefully specified, the likelihood staff will perform their duties proficiently decreases substantially. Likewise, the probability that supervisors will be able to help staff perform in a proficient manner also decreases significantly.

> **Human service agencies must clearly specify outcomes intended to be attained by consumers as a result of agency supports and services, and supervisors must clearly specify staff duties necessary to assist consumers in attaining the desired outcomes.**

STEP 3: TRAIN WORK SKILLS TO STAFF

Once it is determined what staff should do to help consumers attain desired outcomes, then a supervisor must ensure staff have the necessary work skills to perform those duties proficiently. Staff should not be held accountable for performing work tasks if they have not been trained how to perform them. The importance of staff training is well recognized within most human service agencies. However, *how* staff training is conducted often leaves much to be desired.

If staff training programs are to effectively equip staff with the skills to perform their expected duties, the programs must be *performance-* and *competency-based*. Performance-based means staff are both shown how to perform a respective duty and required to demonstrate the relevant skills as part of the training process. Competency-based means the training does not stop until staff are observed to perform the skills competently. Hence, the third step of the evidence-based supervisory protocol is provision of performance- and competency-based staff training.

STEP 4: MONITOR STAFF PERFORMANCE

To effectively supervise staff performance, supervisors must have up-to-date, accurate information about how well staff are performing their job duties. Information on the quality of staff performance is necessary for a supervisor to determine if actions are required to improve the performance of respective staff or to support and maintain ongoing performance of a quality nature. Such information is also necessary for a supervisor to evaluate whether supervisory actions are having the desired effect on staff work behavior.

The best way to obtain accurate information about the quality of staff performance is to objectively and systematically monitor day-to-day work behavior of staff. Monitoring of staff performance in this regard should be an ongoing part of a supervisor's job routine. Systematically and objectively monitoring staff work performance represents the fourth step of the supervision protocol.

STEP 5: SUPPORT PROFICIENT STAFF PERFORMANCE

The supervisory steps summarized to this point set the occasion for staff to perform their job duties in a quality manner. Identifying staff work duties that impact consumer outcome attainment, ensuring staff are effectively trained to perform the duties, and routinely monitoring how staff carry out their work activities are necessary components of evidence-based supervision. However, these supervisory steps usually are not sufficient to ensure proficient staff performance. Once staff are trained in relevant work skills and their application of the skills during the daily routine is regularly monitored, supervisors must *actively respond* in certain ways to how staff are performing.

One way supervisors should respond to staff performance involves actively supporting performance that is observed to meet expected levels of proficiency. This represents the fifth step in the supervisory protocol, which is often referred to as *supportive supervision*. This is the step that promotes maintenance of quality work among staff over time. Supportive supervision is also the component within an evidence-based supervisory approach that most readily lends itself to promoting work enjoyment among staff. A supervisor who actively works with staff to support their quality work almost always has the added benefit of enhancing staff enjoyment with their work.

STEP 6: CORRECT NONPROFICIENT STAFF PERFORMANCE

In addition to responding to proficient staff performance in ways that support and maintain such performance, supervisors must respond in certain ways to performance that is nonproficient. Supervisors must be able to effectively correct work performance that is not of sufficient quality. This represents the sixth step of the evidence-based supervisory protocol, or what is generally referred to as *corrective supervision*.

How supervisors respond to inadequacies in staff performance must be based on the reasons for the inadequacies. If staff lack some key skills for performing a given work duty adequately, for example, supervisors must ensure that staff receive additional training in how to perform those work skills. Alternatively, if certain staff lack the motivation to consistently exert the effort to perform various duties proficiently, then supervisors must find ways to effectively motivate those staff. Consequently, supervisors must not only be aware of when staff are not performing in an acceptable manner, they must be knowledgeable about why performance is not adequate in respective situations.

Maintaining an awareness of when staff are not performing certain job duties adequately and the reasons for such performance is one reason why regularly monitoring staff performance is a key part of supervision (i.e., **Step 4** of the supervisory protocol). Routinely monitoring staff performance in an objective and systematic fashion results in supervisors having up-to-date information about problems with staff performance and the reasons for the problems. Supervisors can then base corrective actions on the information resulting from their monitoring.

STEP 7: EVALUATE STAFF PERFORMANCE

The seventh, and final, step in the evidence-based supervisory protocol is to evaluate the effects of whatever action supervisors have taken. The evaluation focuses on the proficiency of day-to-day staff performance as well as the degree to which consumers are attaining the outcomes expected as a result of staff performance. Actually, this step within the supervision process is not a final step that terminates the supervision process but rather an ongoing action on the part of supervisors.

Evaluating the effects of supervisory action is another reason why monitoring of staff performance (and consumer outcome attainment) is a critical part of supervision. In this case, information stemming from monitoring allows supervisors to determine whether the action they have taken has had the desired effect on staff performance. Such information also informs supervisors regarding how they should then respond to staff performance. If, for example, staff performance improves following a specific supervisory action, then supervisors can actively support that performance. In contrast, if staff performance does not improve, supervisors can take other corrective action to bring about necessary improvement.

IMPLEMENTING STEPS OF THE SUPERVISORY PROTOCOL IN WAYS TO ENHANCE WORK ENJOYMENT

When implementing the evidence-based supervisory protocol, it is important for supervisors to carry out each supervisory step in ways that are acceptable to staff. Staff acceptance of supervisory actions has a considerable impact on staff work enjoyment, and especially in terms of their enjoyment associated with working for a particular supervisor. As will be discussed in subsequent chapters, there are specific ways certain steps can be carried out to enhance staff acceptance of respective supervisory actions. For example, when specifying performance expectations or assignments of staff in terms of expected work behavior, staff acceptance of their assignments is usually enhanced if they have input into how the assignments are determined by the supervisor.

There are also certain ways that steps of the supervisory protocol are sometimes carried out that are not well accepted by staff, and seriously decrease staff enjoyment with their work (and working for a particular supervisor). A common example is when the supervisor monitors staff performance but does not inform them about what is being monitored or why their performance is being monitored. The latter action often results in varying degrees of staff discontent.

Again, each step of the supervisory protocol should be carried out by supervisors in ways acceptable to staff. Supervisors should also actively avoid specific ways of implementing respective steps that staff typically find unacceptable. The latter supervisory actions are also discussed in subsequent chapters that describe each step of the supervisory protocol in more detail.

Supervisors should strive to implement each step of the evidence-based supervisory protocol in ways that are acceptable to staff, and generally avoid ways that are unacceptable.

When supervisors consistently follow the guidelines to be presented regarding supervising in ways staff find acceptable and generally avoiding ways staff find unacceptable, they will usually be helping staff enjoy their work routine. Often, however, these actions will not be sufficient to *maximize* staff work enjoyment. Additional supervisory actions beyond carrying out the evidence-based supervisory steps in specific ways are usually needed to maximize staff enjoyment with their work. Actions supervisors can take to maximize staff enjoyment with their daily work routine, while also maximizing work diligence and proficiency, are also discussed in subsequent chapters.

Chapter Summary: Key Points

1. *Supervision is an active process, requiring consistent time and effort by supervisors.*

2. *A protocol for evidence-based supervision consists of seven basic steps: (1) identifying desired consumer outcomes, (2) specifying staff duties necessary to assist consumers in attaining desired outcomes, (3) training staff in the skills to perform specified duties, (4) regularly monitoring staff performance, (5) actively supporting proficient staff performance, (6) correcting nonproficient staff performance and, (7) routinely evaluating staff performance and consumer outcome attainment.*

3. *To promote staff enjoyment with their work, supervisors should act in ways that are acceptable to staff and generally avoid ways that are unacceptable.*

SECTION II

CRITICAL SUPERVISORY SKILLS

CHAPTER 3

SPECIFYING STAFF WORK RESPONSIBILITIES

As indicated in **Chapter 2**, evidence-based supervision from an outcome management perspective begins with identifying outcomes for consumers to attain. It was also noted that human service agencies usually have established means to identify consumer outcomes. Again, the most common ways are through goals for individual consumers and corresponding behavioral objectives developed by each consumer's support team. The mission statements of human service agencies likewise help establish goals for the agencies' consumer populations.

Because agencies typically have ways to identify outcomes for consumers, the supervisory process can then proceed with the next step of evidence-based supervision: specifying staff performance responsibilities. The focus should be on specifying what staff need to do to ensure consumers attain the desired outcomes. Attention should also be directed to specifying workplace behavior that at any point in time interferes with staff completion of the former duties.

Clear specification of staff performance responsibilities is critical in the supervisory process for two primary reasons. First, staff cannot be expected to fulfill job responsibilities if they are not certain what those responsibilities entail; staff must know precisely what they are expected *to do* to complete their duties satisfactorily. Second, it is essentially impossible to supervise staff performance in a way that consistently promotes diligent and quality work if performance expectations have not been clearly specified.

Previously it was indicated that specifying performance responsibilities of staff can be difficult for some supervisors. To illustrate, agencies serving older individuals with disabilities usually stress the importance of interacting with consumers in a dignified manner appropriate for older adults. In turn, supervisors are charged with ensuring staff interact with consumers in a dignified manner. However, what it means—or what staff should *actually do*—to treat older consumers with dignity is not always specified.

To some staff, treating older consumers with dignity means that because of their age, consumers should be allowed to spend leisure time doing whatever they want even if some consumers engage in behavior likely to be detrimental to their well being. For other staff, treating with dignity means they should treat agency consumers the same way they treat their own family members. However, how staff interact with their family at times may be considered inappropriate when interacting with older consumers who have disabilities.

Similar concerns sometimes exist when specification is not provided regarding what should *not be done* by staff to avoid interacting with consumers in ways that are not dignified. For example, some staff refer to adult consumers as "their kids", even though the consumers are not children. Relatedly, some staff interact with adults in ways appropriate for children but not for adults, which can cast the adult consumers in an undignified light. Although these ways of interacting with adults who have disabilities may seem rather natural for some staff, they are often inappropriate. Staff need to be clearly informed when these ways of interacting are not acceptable.

In short, if an agency and its supervisors value staff interacting with older consumers with dignity, then they must make it clear specifically what it means to interact in dignified versus undignified ways. It may be specified, for example, that staff should refer to adult consumers as adults and not children, and staff should not actively encourage child-like activities among adult consumers. The point is that dignity and interacting with dignity mean different things to different people. What an agency means by dignity should be clearly specified for staff in terms of interactive behaviors they should and should not engage in while at work.

The purpose of this chapter is to describe how supervisors can specify performance responsibilities in a clear manner for staff. Again, without such specification, staff are often uncertain regarding precisely what they should and should not do during the daily work routine. Lack of clear performance expectations also makes it highly unlikely that supervisors will be successful in promoting quality staff performance on a day-to-day basis.

> **Clear specification of performance responsibilities helps ensure staff know exactly what they are expected to do on the job and facilitates a supervisor's job of promoting quality work.**

THREE CRITERIA FOR SPECIFYING STAFF PERFORMANCE RESPONSIBILITIES

Clear specification of staff performance responsibilities can occur if three criteria are met when delineating work duties for staff. First, each performance responsibility of concern must be specified in terms of staff *work behavior,* or what staff should actually *do* to fulfill the responsibility (and at times, what staff should *not do*). Second, each performance responsibility must be specified such that it can be readily *observed*. Third, the responsibility must be defined as work behavior that can be observed to the degree that two people *consistently agree* when the designated staff behavior is occurring and not occurring.

CRITERION 1: PERFORMANCE RESPONSIBILITIES MUST BE DESCRIBED IN TERMS OF STAFF WORK BEHAVIOR

Specifying performance responsibilities for staff begins by delineating each responsibility of concern as work *behavior* in which staff must engage to fulfill the responsibilities. To illustrate, it is usually desired for staff to show initiative with their work. Most people have a general understanding of what "showing initiative" means. However, such understanding often differs across supervisors and staff to varying degrees. Unless "showing initiative" is specified in terms of what staff should actually do, there will be disagreement regarding whether respective staff are showing initiative or not.

Disagreement among agency personnel due to lack of specification of performance responsibilities as work behavior can occur in a variety of situations. For example, a shift supervisor who works weekdays in a group home may believe that staff show initiative because they usually report to work at the scheduled shift time and when they will be absent from work they always inform the supervisor. However, another supervisor, who may supervise the staff on weekends at times, believes staff do not show initiative because they rarely begin certain duties until specifically requested to do so by the supervisor. In this case, the two supervisors will have differing opinions about staff initiative with work, and will go about various supervisory duties (e.g., attempting to support or correct the performance) in differing and possibly conflicting ways.

To avoid the situation just illustrated, a rather general performance expectation such as "showing initiative" must be specified as work behavior. Supervisors must exert the effort in their particular work setting to specify the types of work behavior that reflect initiative and at times, a lack of initiative. For something as general as "work initiative", supervisors usually must identify for staff a variety of work behaviors such as beginning duties without being instructed to do so, asking supervisors questions about a duty when they are not sure what to do, reporting problems to a supervisor as soon as they become aware of the problems, and persisting with a job duty beyond expected time periods if more time is needed to complete the duty.

Specifying performance responsibilities as work behavior is also important when supervisors are concerned about job-related problems staff may be experiencing that interfere with quality work. To illustrate, many supervisors have been concerned at times that certain staff have a bad attitude about work. Everyone has an idea regarding what constitutes a bad attitude, but everyone's idea may not be the same. Some supervisors may believe staff have a bad attitude because they frequently complain about work assignments. Other supervisors may believe staff have a bad attitude because they rarely interact with a supervisor unless specifically addressed by the supervisor.

In the situations just summarized, staff are likely to be given different directions about their attitude, and what should be done to change or improve it. Staff themselves also may have conflicting views regarding what constitutes a good attitude about work and believe their attitude is just fine. Such differences result in confusion for both supervisors and staff, and impede the likelihood that any supervisor action to improve the bad attitude will be successful. Again though, if supervisors specify what is meant by a good or bad attitude as work-related behavior when there are concerns about staff attitude, the occasion is set for supervisors to help staff improve their attitude.

Specifying general performance responsibilities like work initiative and a good attitude as work behavior takes time and effort by supervisors. Like doing many things though, it becomes easier with practice. Presented below are some general performance areas that supervisors have delineated as specific work behavior. The examples are not hard and fast rules regarding behaviors that represent each performance responsibility, only some illustrations that have proven helpful in certain situations. Each supervisor, perhaps with the assistance of upper management, must decide what specific work behaviors are most relevant for given situations and staff.

EXAMPLES OF PERFORMANCE RESPONSIBILITIES SPECIFIED AS STAFF WORK BEHAVIOR

Performance Area	Work Behavior Specification
Requesting vacation	complete "Leave Request Form" and put in supervisor inbox on office door at least 2 weeks prior to requested time off
Securing house at night	when consumers are in bed, lock all outside doors, activate alarm system, turn on outside motion detector, turn off all indoor lights except bathroom night lights and staff office light
Preparing consumer work table	place four chairs around table (one per consumer), place work materials on table in front of each chair, place work-period timer on table, place box for completed materials beside door
Returning phone messages promptly	return all phone messages before end of work shift

Specification of performance responsibilities as work behavior is also important for job duties that are more discrete or circumscribed than general performance expectations such as showing initiative or a good attitude. To illustrate, in residential centers many supervisors spend considerable time arranging staff work schedules to ensure required numbers of staff are on duty across a 24-hour day. If a staff person unexpectedly fails to report to work, the supervisor must spend extra time re-arranging the work schedule. In such situations it is usually critical that staff notify the supervisor *prior to* when they will not be reporting to work (due to illness, lack of transportation to get to work, etc.). Generally though, simply informing staff that they should notify the supervisor prior to an absence is not sufficient. Rather, the supervisor should specify that such notification must occur, for example, at least two hours before the beginning of a staff person's work shift.

At this point the importance of specifying performance expectations as work behavior should be apparent. It may also be apparent though that clearly specifying all performance expectations of staff as work behavior can be overwhelming. Indeed, in most human service agencies direct support staff have many responsibilities to fulfill. It is usually unrealistic for supervisors to specify all duties expected of staff as work behavior. Supervisors should nonetheless attempt to specify as many of the responsibilities as they can.

There are also two helpful guidelines for determining which performance responsibilities should be a priority for specification as staff work behavior. The first guideline is that work duties relating most directly to consumer attainment of identified outcomes should be a priority for specification. If a desired outcome is to help a consumer overcome challenging behavior such as aggression, for example, then it should be specified precisely what staff should do to prevent and reduce aggression—usually represented by staff carrying out the steps of a behavior support plan exactly the way each step is written in the plan. If a desired outcome is to decrease a consumer's dislike of performing certain activities of daily living, then what staff should do to reduce such dislike must be specified as work behavior (e.g., giving the consumer a choice regarding how to do an activity, incorporating specific consumer preferences into the activity).

The second guideline is that performance responsibilities should be specified as work behavior if fulfillment of those responsibilities is interfering with other duties related to consumer outcome attainment. A common situation in some agencies is when staff spend so much time completing paper work that direct contact time with consumers for teaching or providing support with personal care, for example, is hindered. Hence, the latter duties are not completed satisfactorily. In such a case, precisely when paperwork duties should be completed should be specified to avoid interference with direct contact time with consumers (and perhaps with specification of the amount of time that should be devoted to various types of paper work). Of course in this situation, supervisors must ensure the paper work is organized such that it can be completed in the allotted amount of time.

> **The most important performance responsibilities to specify as work behavior for staff are those that: (1) relate most directly to consumer outcome attainment and, (2) are interfering with staff completion of duties relating to consumer outcome attainment.**

CRITERION 2: PERFORMANCE RESPONSIBILITIES MUST BE DESCRIBED IN TERMS OF WORK BEHAVIOR THAT CAN BE DIRECTLY OBSERVED

The second criterion for specifying performance responsibilities is that they should be presented as work behavior that can be directly observed. A supervisor should be able to watch staff and readily see that they are *doing* what needs to be done to fulfill a performance responsibility. Describing performance responsibilities as work behavior that can be directly observed ensures that the responsibilities have been adequately specified. If a supervisor has difficulty determining if what staff are doing represents fulfillment of a performance responsibility in a given situation, then the responsibility has not been adequately specified.

Specifying performance responsibilities as work behavior that can be easily observed is also critical for implementing the other steps of evidence-based supervision. A key part of supervision in this respect is monitoring staff work performance, and responding to how staff are performing based on results of the monitoring. Performance responsibilities must be described as observable work behavior for a supervisor to objectively evaluate if the work is being performed by staff, and being performed correctly. If performance responsibilities have not been specified as work behavior that can be readily observed, a supervisor will be unable to adequately monitor staff work activities. Correspondingly, the supervisor will be unable to respond appropriately to either support or correct staff performance.

A supervisor can be confident that a performance responsibility has been sufficiently specified as observable work behavior if the supervisor can walk into the staff work area and immediately determine if staff are doing what they should be doing. Of course, making such a determination also requires that the supervisor know the exact situations in which the specified responsibility should be met (see later chapter section on **Work**

Activity Schedules). If a supervisor cannot immediately determine if staff are fulfilling performance expectations in a given situation by quickly observing what staff are doing, then the responsibilities usually have not been adequately specified as observable work behavior.

An illustrative situation of the benefits of specifying performance responsibilities as observable work behavior is staff provision of choices in agencies serving people with severe disabilities. Making choices as part of daily activities increases the control a consumer has during ongoing routines, and promotes enjoyment during daily activities. Individuals with severe disabilities often need specific support from staff to have choice opportunities and make meaningful choices. Hence, staff must know how to provide choices during everyday activities for individuals who lack skills to tell staff what they prefer. Supervisors could specify for staff how to provide choices during mealtime, for example, by presenting two types of condiments in arm's reach of a consumer during the meal and requesting the consumer to choose one of the items. It could be further specified that staff should watch what the consumer points to, reaches for, or touches as an indication of the consumer's choice for one of the items and then provide the chosen item.

In the situation just referred to, it would be easy for a supervisor to walk in the dining room and observe to see if staff were providing choices. In contrast, if the supervisor merely told staff to give choices during meals without specifying how to provide choices, the supervisor may observe various staff activities but be uncertain if staff were providing true choice opportunities. The supervisor may observe staff ask a consumer what type of condiment was desired, for example, and then see no corresponding response by the consumer (due perhaps to the consumer lacking the skills to respond meaningfully to what staff asked). The supervisor is likely to be in a quandary over whether that represented a choice opportunity presented by staff, even if staff believed a choice opportunity was provided. In contrast, in the former situation that specified staff behaviors for providing consumer choices, there would be no difficulty determining whether a choice opportunity was presented.

> **Performance expectations of staff should be specified to the degree that a supervisor can enter a staff work area and immediately determine if staff are fulfilling the expectations or not.**

CRITERION 3: PERFORMANCE RESPONSIBILITIES MUST BE SPECIFIED AS OBSERVABLE WORK BEHAVIOR SUCH THAT PEOPLE AGREE WHEN THE BEHAVIOR OCCURS

In essence, the bottom-line indicator of whether a performance responsibility has been sufficiently specified as observable work behavior is that two people can readily agree when the behavior occurs and does not occur. This represents the third criterion for specifying performance responsibilities.

In the situation just referred to, if two supervisors agreed when they saw provision of choice opportunities by staff and consumer choices being made, then staff choice provision has been appropriately specified as observable behavior. If they do not agree, then more specification would be needed. Efforts to further specify providing consumer choices as observable work behavior should continue until the supervisors consistently agree on the occurrence of that particular work behavior.

STRATEGIES FOR SPECIFYING PERFORMANCE RESPONSIBILITIES

The examples in the preceding section illustrate how performance responsibilities can be specified in terms of staff work behavior. There are also more specific strategies supervisors can use to accomplish this key component of an evidence-based approach to supervision. Two of the most helpful are developing *performance checklists* and *work activity schedules*.

PERFORMANCE CHECKLISTS

A performance checklist is a written listing of all the key actions or staff behaviors necessary to perform a respective duty. A performance checklist is analogous to a *task analysis* often used when teaching a learner with disabilities how to complete a task that has a number of steps. In this case however, the list refers to *staff actions* necessary to perform a work duty.

An example of a performance checklist is provided in the following illustration. This particular checklist specifies necessary steps for cleaning the front porch of a group home in a residential neighborhood. This type of checklist was developed because an agency's management was receiving complaints from the home's neighbors that the porch was often in disarray and detracted from the neighborhood's appearance. The process for cleaning the porch as indicated by the sequence of actions to be completed by staff does not represent a universally accepted means of cleaning a porch. It is simply how one home's supervisors decided that their porch could be adequately cleaned. In this regard, performance checklists are almost always situation specific; each supervisor will have to determine what type of checklist is most helpful for a given area of staff responsibility.

EXAMPLE OF A CHECKLIST FOR
CLEANING THE FRONT PORCH OF A GROUP HOME

1. Remove all trash from porch.
2. Remove all non-furniture items from porch.
3. Arrange porch chairs to face front yard.
4. Sweep porch.
5. Water all hanging plants.

Checklists are especially helpful when there are many actions to complete such that performing a respective duty represents a rather complex task for staff. Generally, the more complex the duty or task, the more helpful a checklist will be for staff. Some typical performance responsibilities for which supervisors have found it helpful to prepare performance checklists are presented below.

EXAMPLES OF MORE COMPLEX STAFF DUTIES FOR WHICH
SUPERVISORS HAVE FOUND IT HELPFUL TO DEVELOP
PERFORMANCE CHECKLISTS

1. Conducting shift change meetings in residential settings.
2. Dispensing medications to consumers who do not administer their own medications.
3. Organizing/cleaning a van following a community outing.
4. Conducting a discrete-trial teaching session with a learner who has autism.
5. Conducting a leisure activity with a group of consumers.
6. Implementing a consumer's behavior support plan.
7. Preparing a recreational outing with an overnight stay.

Performance checklists are likewise helpful when staff actions must occur in a certain sequence to complete a job task, even if the task is not very complex. To illustrate, a consumer with severe disabilities at a sheltered workshop may have trouble managing the transition involved in going home at the end of the workday. A checklist could be prepared based on an assessment of procedures likely to facilitate the consumer's transition and to ensure the transition process occurs the same way every day.

The checklist for assisting a consumer's transition should identify specific steps for staff to follow during the transition period. Such steps may include, for example, to: 1) tell the consumer that in 15 minutes it will be time to get on the van to go home, 2) make sure the consumer has all personal possessions (e.g., eye glasses, jacket, voice output communication device), 3) watch and make sure the consumer goes to the correct place to meet the van and, 4) make sure the consumer gets on the correct van. In this case, each of the steps must occur in the designated sequence to effectively assist the consumer in transitioning from the workshop to the home.

Performance checklists can be developed by a supervisor in several ways. One way is for the supervisor to perform the staff duty and write down each action involved in completing the duty as it is performed. Often this process has to be completed several times to make sure the checklist is accurate and complete. Another way to develop a checklist is for a supervisor to watch a competent staff person complete a job duty and write down each action as the staff person completes it. However, it is usually also helpful if the supervisor then completes the duty using the developed checklist to ensure all relevant actions were written down in the correct sequence.

WORK ACTIVITY SCHEDULES

Another strategy that can help supervisors specify performance responsibilities to make work duties very clear for staff is *work activity schedules*. Work activity schedules provide specification in addition to delineating a work duty as staff behavior. Activity schedules precisely indicate in writing when, where, and often with whom, the duty is expected to be performed by staff.

The following illustration indicates how an activity schedule can be used to precisely specify a given work duty for staff. In this situation, the performance responsibility pertains to conducting a group instruction session with six consumers. The schedule specifies that the duty should be fulfilled by staff Hilary (to be the lead instructor) and Carlos (to be the co-instructor) at 9:00 in Classroom 1 at the work table. It further specifies that Hilary should be in front of the table facing the consumers along with the instructional duties she should perform. It likewise specifies that Carlos should stand behind the consumers and what constitute his expected duties. The consumers to participate in the session are also listed. In this manner, the duties that each staff person should perform to carry out the instructional session are specified. Such a schedule can be much more useful for the staff relative to simply informing them that they should conduct a group instruction session in the morning with a group of consumers.

ACTIVITY SCHEDULE FOR GROUP INSTRUCTION
LEARNING ACTIVITY: <u>FOLDING A TABLE NAPKIN (10 TRIALS)</u>

Responsible staff: *Hilary, Carlos*   **Time:** *9:00 am*

Place: *Classroom 1 work table*

Lead instructor: *Hilary*   **Co-instructor:** *Carlos*

Consumers: *John, Vivian, Yolanda, Sampson, Hector, Michael*

Lead instructor duties (facing front of consumers at table):

1) **Demonstrate and describe for consumers at the table each step required to fold the napkin.**

2) **Vocally instruct all consumers to fold their napkin.**

3) **Provide additional vocal prompts to individual consumers as needed.**

4) **Praise correct consumer responses and attempts.**

Co-instructor duties (standing behind consumers at table):

1) **Following lead instructor's initial instruction, provide physical prompts to individual consumers as needed.**

2) **Praise correct consumer responses and attempts.**

The activity schedule just illustrated also facilitates the supervisor's job of monitoring staff fulfillment of the assigned duty of conducting a group instruction session. The supervisor could complete the schedule on a daily or weekly basis and then observe during a sample of the scheduled sessions. Using the developed activity schedule, it would be easy for the supervisor to determine if staff are carrying out the necessary duties for completing the group instruction session.

Work activity schedules have several advantages. As just indicated, they help make performance expectations clear for staff and facilitate the supervisor's job of monitoring staff fulfillment of the assignment. Additionally, when a supervisor develops an activity schedule, it helps ensure that the supervisor is acutely aware of what needs to be done by staff to complete a given duty.

In some cases, as a supervisor prepares an activity schedule it becomes apparent to the supervisor that various obstacles exist that can interfere with staff completing the specified duty. For example, the supervisor may find there is not sufficient time allotted to perform the duty or certain materials need to be acquired for staff use that otherwise would not have been available. The obstacles might not have been apparent if the supervisor simply informed staff about a respective duty relative to specifying what needs to be done with an activity schedule.

Another advantage of work activity schedules pertains to agencies in which staff who are unfamiliar with a particular setting are assigned temporarily to work in that setting. This often occurs in residential agencies when staff are temporarily assigned or "pulled" from one home to another to cover for a staff person who is absent from the latter setting. The situation also occurs in educational programs with substitute teachers. A work activity schedule can facilitate the unfamiliar staff person's understanding of what needs to be done during the work routine in the setting in which the staff person does not regularly work.

> **Work activity schedules are especially helpful for staff in terms of expected job duties when staff are temporarily assigned to work in an unfamiliar job setting.**

Specifying Performance Responsibilities In Ways Acceptable to Staff

The time and effort a supervisor exerts to make sure performance expectations are clearly specified for staff is often well received by many staff. It becomes apparent to staff that a supervisor is trying to help them do their jobs well and they appreciate the supervisor's efforts in this regard. Additionally, having a good understanding regarding what they should do on the job reduces confusion and possible apprehension or anxiety staff may experience when they are not sure what needs to be done to complete a job duty.

There are also certain things a supervisor can do within the process of specifying performance responsibilities that further enhance staff acceptance of this supervisory action. The most important thing a supervisor can do is to *involve staff in the process.* Involving staff in the process of specifying their expected job duties represents a type of *participative supervision;* staff participate in the supervision process. More specifically, a supervisor should try to take the time to solicit staff input into precisely how various performance responsibilities should be specified as work behavior expected of staff.

The essence of participative supervision is that staff have input into decisions affecting their job. There is a good evidence base indicating that staff prefer working for a supervisor who solicits and values their input relative to a supervisor who makes all supervisory decisions without staff input. Of course, by the nature of supervision, a supervisor should still have the final say regarding what should happen on the job. However, supervisory decisions can be made after supervisors have listened to staff opinions about what the supervisor is considering.

Involving staff in specifying their expected performance duties has some unique benefits for enhancing staff enjoyment with their work relative to involving staff in other areas of supervisor decision making. First, as already indicated, many staff are appreciative of a supervisor who listens to their opinion about how to complete a particular job duty. Second, staff often can provide valuable information about the best way to complete a given work task, and especially staff who are experienced with the respective duty. When a supervisor obtains such information from staff, it is more likely that how the expectation is delineated into specific work behavior will allow staff to complete the work activities efficiently (and thereby make it easier for staff to complete).

As with specifying performance responsibilities in general, involving staff in the specification process takes time and effort on the supervisor's part. Hence, it is unrealistic for a supervisor to solicit staff input into every decision the supervisor has to make regarding delineation of performance responsibilities. The same guidelines discussed earlier regarding specification of performance responsibilities in general are also relevant for determining when to involve staff in the specification process. That is, supervisors should strive to involve staff in specifying performance responsibilities that relate most directly to consumer outcome attainment, and relate to problem areas that interfere with consumer outcome attainment.

Another priority for staff involvement in the process of specifying performance responsibilities pertains to those aspects of the work routine that are *most important to staff*. In every job situation there are certain things that are very important to staff. When a supervisor addresses those aspects of the job as part of the performance specification process, it is especially beneficial to actively solicit staff input. What is particularly important to staff will vary from agency to agency, but there are several areas that are almost always among the most important for staff. Provided below are some of these areas.

> **TYPICAL ASPECTS OF JOBS THAT ARE VERY IMPORTANT TO STAFF AND WARRANT STAFF INPUT WHEN SUPERVISORS SPECIFY DUTIES ASSOCIATED WITH THOSE ASPECTS**
>
> **Work schedules (e.g., when work days and days off are assigned)**
>
> **Consumer teaching and behavior-support assignments**
>
> **Work-break and lunch schedules**
>
> **Temporary reassignment to other work locations (e.g., being "pulled" to cover for an absent staff person)**
>
> **Mandatory overtime**
>
> **Special assignments that represent periodic, extra duties relative to the usual work routine**

Whenever a supervisor must alter any of the job aspects just illustrated, staff acceptance of the supervisory action is likely to be significantly enhanced if the supervisor involves staff in the process. Conversely, work enjoyment is less likely to be negatively impacted by the supervisor's actions if the supervisor involves staff in the process. To illustrate, many agencies experience staffing issues from time to time such that it is necessary to require someone to work overtime. Staff will usually be more accepting about working overtime if they have been involved in developing the process of how it will be determined which staff will be required for overtime when needed.

In contrast to the participative process just summarized, if a supervisor decides how overtime assignments will be determined without staff input, staff are more likely to be displeased when they are unexpectedly assigned to work overtime. In the latter situation, staff may believe, for example, that the supervisor is "picking on them" or showing favoritism to certain staff. These types of reactions are much less likely if staff had input into determining the process the supervisor uses to decide who will work overtime.

Chapter Summary: Key Points

1. *Performance responsibilities should be clearly specified for staff to ensure they know exactly what they are expected to do on the job and to facilitate a supervisor's job of promoting quality work.*

2. *To ensure performance responsibilities are clear for staff, they should be specified as work behavior that can be directly observed such that two people can readily agree when the behavior is occurring or not.*

3. *Two helpful strategies for specifying performance responsibilities as observable work behavior are performance checklists and work activity schedules.*

4. *Staff acceptance of having their performance responsibilities specified as precise work behavior can be enhanced if staff have input into the specification process.*

CHAPTER 4

TRAINING WORK SKILLS TO STAFF

Once performance responsibilities have been specified as discussed in **Chapter 3**, the next step in evidence-based supervision is to train staff in the skills to perform the designated duties. Training is critical for ensuring staff know how to do what is expected of them on the job. In this regard, essentially every human service agency has some type of staff training component. In larger agencies, there is often a staff training department, or at least one person identified as being responsible for staff training. In smaller agencies, different personnel share staff training responsibilities in addition to their more routine work duties. Regardless of how staff training services are formally organized within an agency however, staff training is still an essential part of a supervisor's job.

Staff training is a critical part of supervision for several key reasons. A primary reason pertains to characteristics of the typical work force in human service agencies. As indicated in **Chapter 1**, when people are hired into direct support positions they usually have no prior training or formal education specifically related to their newly acquired jobs. Hence, they must have opportunities to be trained in relevant work skills once they are hired within a human service agency. In those relatively few cases where newly hired staff have previous experience in providing direct support, often that experience is not sufficient to equip them with certain skills needed in their new job setting.

It is well recognized across human service agencies that newly employed support staff require training in the skills to perform their jobs. Agencies usually address the immediate training needs of new staff through orientation-training programs. Orientation programs are clearly a necessary part of an agency's training services. However, they are insufficient for providing all the training needed by new staff. Orientation training often focuses on presenting information that new staff need to function within an agency on a general basis, but has little specific bearing on how to provide direct-support services needed by agency consumers. Information presented in orientation classes typically pertains to such things as, for example, how to complete time sheets to receive one's pay, where and when to report to work, agency policies regarding abuse and neglect, and learning the names and roles of key agency personnel.

The information provided in orientation programs for new staff is of course important, but again, usually does not pertain directly to fulfilling specific job duties on a daily basis. Additionally, the amount of time agencies can devote to training newly employed staff in orientation programs is limited. When people are hired into direct support roles, they are almost always needed quickly in their new jobs. Agencies typically do not have sufficient numbers of direct support staff to allow vacant positions to remain unfilled for very long. This relates to the second reason that staff training must be a key part of a supervisor's job: orientation programs simply cannot devote sufficient time to train all the work skills that new staff need to fulfill their job responsibilities. Consequently, supervisors must provide additional training to new staff after they complete orientation.

Even when agencies can devote large amounts of time to orientation training for new staff, such training is still not sufficient for equipping staff with certain work skills. In particular, what staff learn in orientation may not be what they need to function satisfactorily in a specific job setting. Every setting in a human service agency, such as different group homes or classrooms, is a little bit different. The skills required of staff to work effectively in one setting are not always the same as skills needed to work in another setting. It is usually the responsibility of the staff supervisor to provide training that is relevant to each staff person's specific work area.

Additionally, regardless of how well orientation-training programs are conducted, some staff do not transfer what they learn in orientation to their day-to-day job site. Many supervisors have experienced situations in which a newly employed staff person appears to have forgotten seemingly everything taught in orientation as soon as the orientation is completed. These latter features relate to the third reason staff training must be a critical part of a supervisor's job: orientation training is not always directly relevant to the skills staff need on the job, and staff do not always maintain the skills learned in orientation that are relevant once they report to their specific job site.

The fourth reason a supervisor must function in part as a staff trainer is that new skills are periodically required of human service staff over time. Ways to provide quality support for people with disabilities are continuously evolving and improving. Unless direct support staff have opportunities to be trained in new developments they cannot be held accountable for providing up-to-date, quality services. Relatedly, individual consumers require different types of support from time to time, such as new behavior support plans for challenging behavior or new teaching programs for acquiring useful skills. Supervisors must ensure staff are trained in the new or revised ways of providing such support.

For all the reasons just summarized, supervisors must be willing and able to train their staff in relevant work skills if staff are to provide quality supports and services. This chapter describes how supervisors can provide effective staff training. In accordance with a continuing theme throughout all chapters, how staff training can be provided in a way that is acceptable to staff and enhances their work enjoyment is also described.

Staff training is a fundamental part of a supervisor's job, regardless of other staff training services provided by an agency.

Basic Goals of Staff Training

Effective staff training involves providing staff with the knowledge and skills to perform their jobs in a quality manner. Although providing staff with job-related knowledge and specific work skills are both critical goals of staff training, the focus here is on training work *skills* necessary to perform job duties. The rationale for the focus on training specific work skills is several-fold. First, it is what staff *do* on the job, or the skills they demonstrate while performing job duties, that has the most significant impact on consumer welfare and attainment of desired outcomes. Second, most agencies have established procedures for providing relevant knowledge or information that staff need, as represented in the types of information addressed in orientation-training programs summarized earlier.

A third reason for focusing on training of actual work skills is that human service agencies typically are better at providing staff with relevant knowledge about their jobs than training them how to perform their jobs. Providing information to staff involves what is technically considered as *verbal training*. Verbal training involves providing lectures about relevant issues and written information, often supplemented with video or other visual media presentations. For example, in an agency serving consumers with autism, information may be provided in orientation lectures and handouts about the diagnostic characteristics of the disability of autism, and perhaps videos of how people with autism often act in various situations. Such information and presentation formats are important parts of training for direct support staff, but rarely train staff how to actually perform their jobs.

Effectively training staff how to do the things necessary to fulfill their performance responsibilities involves what is technically considered as *performance training*. Performance training involves showing staff how to perform various job duties and having staff practice performing the duties under supervision of the staff trainer. This type of training is not provided very well in staff training programs such as orientation training in many human service agencies. It is usually the supervisor's job to provide effective performance training for direct support staff.

Before describing what supervisors should do to effectively train staff how to perform their work duties, a caution is warranted about the success of agencies in providing relevant job knowledge for staff. In **Chapter 2**, it was noted that to be consistently successful, staff training programs should have a performance basis and a *competency* basis. Competency-based staff training means that the training is not complete until staff demonstrate competence in the area addressed by the training.

In regard to presenting relevant information to staff such as that often provided during orientation training, the competency part is sometimes lacking. For example, newly hired staff may listen to a presentation or lecture, receive some handouts, and perhaps watch a video. Staff trainees may also be required to sign a form indicating they have completed the training. To be truly competency-based though, another step must be added. Staff must demonstrate that they have acquired the knowledge that the training is intended to provide.

Any training program that focuses on providing staff with certain types of knowledge should include a way of assessing staff knowledge following training. Such assessment can be accomplished by having staff trainees complete written quizzes or exams, or simply answering questions posed to each trainee by the trainer. If staff answer the questions accurately, they can be considered to have demonstrated competence in acquiring the knowledge that the training is intended to provide. If staff do not answer the questions accurately, then they have not demonstrated competence and re-training should be provided. Training should continue until each staff trainee demonstrates competence in having acquired the necessary knowledge. Again, this step is sometimes lacking in training programs offered by human service agencies, and warrants more attention to ensure staff become sufficiently knowledgeable as a result of agency training programs.

AN EVIDENCE-BASED PROTOCOL FOR STAFF TRAINING

There is a basic, step-by-step protocol for training staff how to perform specified job skills. Although variations can be made in how the protocol is used to suit certain situations as will be described later, every supervisor should be skilled in applying the protocol in its entirety. The steps constituting the protocol are presented in the illustration on the following page.

There is a very strong evidence base supporting the effectiveness of this staff training protocol. It represents both a performance- and competency-based approach to staff training (also referred to at times as *behavior skills training*). The steps constituting the protocol have been used in research and application to train a wide variety of important job skills to support staff, including how to teach people with disabilities, provide choices, lift and transfer individuals who are nonambulatory, carry out behavior support plans, and adapt electronic devices for use by people with physical and intellectual challenges, to name a few. The training steps constituting the protocol represent a very valuable tool for supervisors when needing to train job skills to staff.

EVIDENCE-BASED PROTOCOL FOR TRAINING STAFF HOW TO PERFORM SPECIFIED JOB DUTIES

Step 1: Describe the skills to be trained.

Step 2: Provide staff trainees with a written summary of the skills to be trained.

Step 3: Demonstrate the target skills for staff.

Step 4: Have staff practice performing the target skills and provide feedback.

Step 5: Repeat Steps 1, 3, and 4 until staff demonstrate competence in performing the target skills.

TRAINING STEP 1: DESCRIBE TARGET SKILLS TO BE TRAINED

When beginning the staff training process, what is going to be trained should be described in detail for the staff trainees. This is one reason that performance responsibilities should be delineated into specific work behaviors of staff as discussed in the preceding chapter. Each behavior that a staff person needs to perform to complete the job duty being trained should be described by the supervisor for staff. For rather complex skills that require a staff person to perform many behaviors to complete a job duty, the description process is greatly facilitated if a performance checklist has been prepared (again, see **Chapter 3**).

Training Step 2: Provide Written Summary of the Target Skills

After the target skills to be trained to staff have been described, a written summary of the target skills should be given to each staff member being trained. In many cases, this step can entail providing staff with the performance checklist that the supervisor has prepared as part of the process of specifying performance responsibilities. Providing a written summary of the target skills has several benefits. One particular benefit is that some staff learn more readily from reading about how to do a job task relative to hearing a trainer describe how to do the task.

A second benefit of providing a written summary of the necessary skills to perform a work duty is that the summary provides staff with a permanent reminder of how to perform the task. When staff need to perform the job task at a later time, they can review the summary if they are not certain what should be done to complete the designated task. It should also be noted though that some supervisors question the utility of this step because they have experienced situations in which staff lose or discard the written summary shortly after the training session. In other cases, supervisors have experienced staff who have difficulty reading such that the written summary is of little use. These situations will likely occur from time to time. However, there are also many staff who will be motivated to perform the designated task (and can read adequately) and will benefit from having the written summary to use as a reminder.

It is important that the written summary of the target skills be provided to *each* staff person who is being trained. Sometimes, supervisors and other agency personnel prepare one summary of what needs to be done that is filed in a central location for staff to review as needed. This often occurs with copies of behavior support plans for challenging behavior of consumers as well as written copies of instructional plans for use when teaching consumers. The latter approach, though common, is not as effective as providing each trainee with a summary. When trainees have their own written summary, it is easier for them to quickly access the information when needed relative to having to go to another location to obtain the information. Because of the ready access to their own written copy, the likelihood that staff will review the information when needed is increased relative to the situation in which they have to go to another place to access the information.

The situation just referred to relates to a common obstacle to effective staff training. A number of skills that supervisors need to train to direct support staff are derived from information prepared by other personnel, such as clinicians (e.g., behavior specialists) and executives. A common example is when a supervisor is charged with training staff how to carry out a behavior support plan developed by a psychologist. Often the plan is quite lengthy, consisting of a number of typed pages of information. Documents such as behavior plans frequently need to include a lot of information (e.g., about the consumer, assessments that were completed) beyond what staff need to do to carry out the plan. The inclusion of such information, though necessary, often detracts from the staff training process as well as subsequent on-the-job performance.

Too much written information, such as that often included in behavior plans, makes it difficult for staff to quickly look at the document and find information that tells them specifically what to do on the job. The increased time and effort required to read through all the information to glean what is relevant for completing a task also results in some staff not bothering to search for the information. The latter staff will not spend the time and effort searching for needed information.

It is recommended that when a supervisor needs to train staff in a job task that was developed and written by someone else, the supervisor do one of two things. The most efficient action by the supervisor is to request the person who wrote the information to prepare a succinct, written summary pertaining only to what staff need to do to complete the given task. This should be the summary that is provided to staff. The complete document that contains other information can still be filed in a central location for staff to review if necessary. The other thing a supervisor can do is review all of the written information that someone else has provided and then prepare a precise summary of action steps to give to staff. The essential point is that staff need a concise, written summary of the skills being targeted by the training.

> **A supervisor should always provide *each staff person* with a concise, written summary of the skills the supervisor is training to the staff.**

Training Step 3: Demonstrate How to Perform the Target Skills

After the supervisor describes the target skills for staff and provides each trainee with a written summary, the next step in the training process is for the supervisor to demonstrate how to perform the skills. Often the most efficient way to demonstrate how to perform a work duty, and especially if it involves interacting with a consumer, is in a *role-play* situation. The supervisor role plays the part of a staff person, and another individual (e.g., another supervisor or staff person) role plays the part of a consumer. The supervisor then carefully demonstrates each aspect of the target skills as they are listed on the written summary while the staff who are being trained observe the demonstration.

Demonstrating how to perform a job task for staff is one of the best ways to help staff learn how to perform the task themselves. It also is a key component of performance-based training as referred to earlier—the supervisor *performs* the task for staff to see how to do the task. Adequately demonstrating a work task for staff requires some skill on the part of the supervisor. Most notably, the supervisor has to know how to actually perform the task accurately that is being trained to the staff. In one sense, noting the importance of a supervisor knowing how to do what the supervisor is training staff seems quite obvious. However, such is not always the case.

The situation in which a supervisor is expected to train staff in a job task that the supervisor is not sure how to perform usually occurs when the supervisor is training something that someone else developed as discussed previously. This situation occurs most frequently when an agency clinician develops a consumer program and expects the supervisor to train staff how to implement the program, but the clinician does not adequately train the supervisor in all aspects of the program. Either the clinician does not take the time to train the supervisor, or basically does not know how to train the supervisor (e.g., the clinician is not skilled in the evidence-based training protocol). The same situation can occur when an agency executive directs a supervisor to train staff in a new job duty, but does not provide the supervisor with adequate training regarding how to perform the duty.

When a supervisor is expected to train staff but the supervisor is not certain how to perform the target skills to be trained, corrective action must be taken by the supervisor. If the supervisor does not take corrective action and attempts to train staff to do something that the supervisor is not competent in doing, multiple problems result. In particular, it is essentially impossible for a supervisor to adequately train staff if the supervisor cannot perform the target skills proficiently; the staff training will not be effective. Additionally, staff usually become aware rather quickly that the supervisor is instructing them to do something that the supervisor does not know how to perform. Such awareness tends to cause staff to question the competence of the supervisor and subsequently, to lose respect for the supervisor.

What a supervisor does to avoid attempting to train staff in skills that the supervisor is not competent in performing will depend on each specific situation. However, the most common corrective action is to make sure whoever is expecting the supervisor to conduct the training is aware of the problem and can offer assistance. Such assistance can involve initially training the supervisor prior to the supervisor training the staff. Assistance can also be provided by the person who prepared the information helping to conduct the staff training while the supervisor is present. In the latter case, the supervisor is essentially trained along with the staff.

> **Supervisors should avoid situations in which they are expected to train staff in work skills that the supervisors themselves are not sure how to perform proficiently.**

Earlier it was noted that demonstrating work skills as part of the training process is usually accomplished most efficiently in a role-play activity. Target skills can also be demonstrated *in vivo* in terms of the supervisor performing the task with staff in the actual work site. How to provide in vivo demonstrations as part of the training process will be discussed later in the section on **Training Staff Individually**.

TRAINING STEP 4: TRAINEE PRACTICE OF TARGET SKILLS WITH SUPERVISOR FEEDBACK

Immediately after a supervisor has demonstrated how to perform the target skills being trained, staff should be required to demonstrate the skills themselves. This represents the second key component of performance-based training: staff *perform* the target skills as part of the training process. If the supervisor's demonstration occurred in a role-play situation, then staff should also perform the task in a role play. If the supervisor demonstrated the target skills in vivo, then that demonstration should be followed by staff performing the skills in the actual work site as well (again, in vivo training procedures will be discussed more in-depth later).

As staff practice performing the target skills, the supervisor should watch the performance and then immediately provide feedback to staff based on the accuracy with which they performed the target skills. Providing feedback is another critical supervisory skill, and will be discussed in much more detail in subsequent chapters. In regard to training staff though, providing feedback means that the supervisor informs staff what they performed accurately and if applicable, not accurately. If staff did not perform each aspect of the target skills correctly, the supervisor should also inform the staff what they need to do differently to perform the skills correctly (see next step in the training protocol).

TRAINING STEP 5: REPEAT STEPS 1, 3, AND 4 UNTIL STAFF PERFORM THE TARGET SKILLS PROFICIENTLY

As indicated previously, the approach to staff training described here is not only performance-based, it is also *competency-based*. Again, competency-based means that the training continues until each staff trainee demonstrates competence in performing the target job skills. To ensure staff demonstrate competence, **Training Steps 1, 3,** and **4** should be repeated until the staff trainer observes each staff trainee perform the target skills correctly.

Competency-based training as referred to here also means that staff demonstrate competence in performing newly trained work skills during their daily job routine. Hence, if all trainee demonstrations occur in a role-play situation, the supervisor must then observe staff in their regular job setting. The intent is to document that the staff carry over what they learned during training to the actual job site in which they are expected to apply the skills. Such on-the-job observation by the supervisor should also be followed by feedback as just described with **Step 4**. Likewise, **Steps 1, 3,** and **4** should be repeated in the routine work site of staff until they demonstrate competence. It is only when the supervisor observes staff perform the target skills proficiently as part of their regular work situation that the supervisor's training can be considered complete.

> **Staff training should never be considered complete until the supervisor observes staff perform the skills targeted in training proficiently during their routine work situation.**

Two Main Formats for Training Staff

There are two main formats for training staff in specified work skills. One format, which is more formal in nature, pertains to training a group of staff. The second format, which is more informal in nature, involves training an individual staff member. Supervisors should be well skilled in using both types of training formats. Within both the group- and individual-training formats, the same evidence-based staff training protocol as just described should be used by supervisors. However, there are also variations in how the protocol is implemented when conducting group versus individual staff training.

Training Staff in A Group

Conducting staff training in a group format is necessary when several or all of a supervisor's staff contingent require training in a specified set of work skills. This occurs, for example, when all staff need to be trained in a new behavior support plan for a respective consumer. It is much more efficient in regard to the supervisor's time to conduct training in a group format relative to training each staff member in the same work skills on an individual basis.

The first thing a supervisor should do when training a group of staff in designated work skills actually occurs before the group training session: the supervisor should carefully *prepare* for the upcoming training. Initially, the supervisor should outline how the training will occur, using the steps of the evidence-based training protocol as a guide. The training should then proceed according to the protocol (see subsequent discussion regarding additional preparation procedures associated with various steps of the protocol).

A group training session should be initiated with staff by explaining the rationale for why the training session is being conducted. The rationale should consist of providing an overview of the skills to be taught, and why it is important that staff learn to perform the new job duty. For example, it may be that a consumer has just secured a supported work placement in a community job and it is desired that the consumer be taught certain work skills prior to beginning the job. The supervisor could explain that it would help the consumer's likelihood of success in the new job if staff conducted teaching sessions to prepare the consumer for the new work assignments. It could be further explained that each staff member needs to be trained how to conduct the teaching sessions in order for all sessions to be conducted in a consistent and effective manner with the consumer.

Following presentation of the rationale for why the training session will be conducted, the supervisor should describe all work behaviors that the staff need to be able to perform (**Step 1** of the evidence-based training protocol). Subsequently, each staff member should be provided with a written summary of the skills they will need to perform (**Step 2**). To prepare for these two steps, the supervisor must become proficient in the skills to be trained. In the example provided above, the supervisor would need to be very familiar with the consumer's teaching plan. The supervisor would likewise need to have prepared, prior to the training session, the written summary of the consumer-teaching procedures to distribute to each staff person.

After staff have had the opportunity to read the written summary of the target skills, the supervisor should then demonstrate how to perform the skills in a role-play situation (**Step 3**). To ensure adequate demonstration, some additional preparatory actions need to occur before the actual training session. These actions include deciding who will help the supervisor perform the demonstrations (e.g., soliciting assistance of another supervisor or one of the staff trainees to perform a part in the role play, such as the consumer's part), and specifying what each person should do within the demonstrations. It is also helpful if the supervisor practices the role-play demonstrations with whomever is helping the supervisor prior to the training session. The practice is necessary to ensure the demonstrations are sufficiently thorough and accurate to allow staff to observe precisely how to perform the targeted work skills.

The importance of practicing role-play demonstrations prior to a group training session with staff is a critical but often overlooked preparatory step. Without such practice, it is common for the demonstrations to occur in a manner that either does not include all the key skills for staff to observe, or that illustrates incorrect ways to perform certain skills. Practicing the demonstrations beforehand also makes it more likely that the demonstrations during the actual training will require less training time (i.e., the supervisor and "helper" will be more accurate in the demonstrations and will not have to repeat parts of the demonstrations in which something may have been omitted or performed incorrectly).

Supervisors should prepare for conducting a group training session with staff: be well versed in the skills to be trained, develop written summaries of the skills to give to staff trainees, and practice the role-play demonstrations to ensure accuracy.

Following demonstration of the target skills, supervisors should instruct staff to practice the skills themselves in a role play with each other (**Step 4**). To ensure each staff member participates appropriately in the practice activities, supervisors should specify the roles in which the staff should engage (e.g., one trainee should role play the part of a staff person performing the target skills and one trainee should role play the part of the consumer). It should likewise be stressed that each staff person must practice the target skills and that the other staff should observe and give feedback to the staff person. The feedback should be based on how well the staff person performed the target skills using the written summary and the supervisor's previous demonstration as a guide. If there is a large number of staff trainees in a group, usually meaning more than four or five staff, then the supervisor should divide all the staff into two or more subgroups for their practice activities.

The supervisor should also inform staff that in addition to giving feedback to each other, the supervisor will be circulating among the group to give feedback to each staff person. The feedback should be provided as described previously, specifying what a respective staff person demonstrated correctly and if applicable, incorrectly. In the latter case, the feedback should include specification about what the staff person needs to do differently to correct the demonstrated performance. It is critical for the supervisor to observe each staff person demonstrate the target skills correctly during the training session, which may require some staff to repeat the demonstrations (**Step 5** of the training protocol).

After each staff person has performed the target skills proficiently, the training session should be concluded by the supervisor informing staff when they will be expected to perform the newly trained job skills during their work routine. In many situations this final step can be facilitated if the supervisor provides a work activity schedule regarding the new job duty (refer back to **Chapter 3** for a summary of work activity schedules). The supervisor should also inform staff that their performance involving the target skills will be observed as they implement the skills on the job. It should be explained that such observations are actually a continuation of the training process to ensure everyone has mastered the target work skills. As discussed in the next chapter, informing staff that their performance will be observed and why it will be observed helps reduce apprehension among staff that often occurs when a supervisor formally observes their work performance.

Special Considerations for Conducting Group Training Sessions. In addition to following the evidence-based training protocol when conducting a group training session with staff, there are some special considerations to enhance effectiveness of the training. One consideration is for the supervisor to solicit the assistance of someone to help conduct the training. This is especially relevant if training focuses on work duties designed by someone other than the supervisor.

To illustrate, again considering the example in which staff are being trained to teach supported-work skills to a consumer, the teaching program that the staff are expected to carry out was developed by a clinician. Because the clinician is the most informed person regarding the teaching program, it would be helpful if the clinician assisted the supervisor in conducting the training session. It such situations, the supervisor should also be assertive in soliciting the clinician's participation in the preparatory activities described earlier prior to the training session with staff.

Another consideration with group training sessions pertains to ensuring that the training focuses on the *performance* of staff trainees. There is a tendency among staff trainers (including supervisors) to spend too much time talking during a training session and not enough time demonstrating target skills and having staff practice the skills. Trainers must remember that the key to effective training of job skills stems from the performance aspects: staff seeing how the work duty is performed and then practicing it themselves. Hence, the majority of the staff training session should be spent on the trainer demonstrations and trainee practice activities with the role plays.

When staff trainers spend more time talking to staff relative to demonstrating and staff practicing, there is another detrimental effect on training effectiveness (beyond staff not having sufficient opportunities to actually see and practice the target skill). Specifically, when trainers spend large amounts of time talking during a training session, staff attentiveness directed to the trainer diminishes significantly. As a result, the staff trainees do not sufficiently hear or comprehend what the trainer is talking about, which erodes the trainer's effectiveness.

As a general rule, a staff trainer should not spend more than 15 to 20 minutes talking without a demonstration or trainee practice activity. Adult learning research as well as the experience of skilled trainers suggests that trainees lose their attentiveness if required to listen to a trainer talk for more than 15 to 20 continuous minutes. Consequently, as supervisors prepare the group training session, they should outline their training process such that they always have a demonstration or trainee practice activity at least every 20 minutes.

To maintain staff attentiveness during a training session, trainers should not talk continuously for more than 15 or 20 minutes without a demonstration or trainee practice activity.

TRAINING STAFF INDIVIDUALLY

Training individual staff in expected work duties is a responsibility that many supervisors encounter frequently. A supervisor often needs to train individual staff when, for example, a new staff person is hired and assigned to work within a supervisor's area, a staff person is temporarily assigned to a supervisor's area due to the absence of a regular staff person, and a given staff person is expected to perform a new duty that other staff may not be expected to perform. In these situations, the recommended way to train a staff person is through application of the evidence-based training protocol as discussed throughout this chapter. However, there are also a few variations and considerations when using the protocol with an individual staff member relative to training staff in a group.

One variation with individual staff training is that it is generally less formal than when conducting a group training session. The training usually can occur in the staff person's regular work setting by taking the staff person aside for a relatively brief period of time. Alternatively, if other work demands make it unlikely that a staff person could attend to the staff trainer in the work setting, the training can occur in the supervisor's office or any other available room. Regardless of where the training occurs, the supervisor should go through the five steps of the evidence-base training protocol in a systematic manner.

Another variation pertains to the demonstration and trainee practice steps of the training protocol. Often, the supervisor can ask the staff person to play a certain role, such as that of a consumer if the target skill involves interacting with a consumer, while the supervisor demonstrates the skill. Next, the supervisor and staff person should exchange roles so that the staff person can demonstrate the skill. In some cases though, and particularly with work skills that are rather complex or involve a number of behavioral steps to complete, it is more effective and efficient if a supervisor solicits the help of someone else to assist with the role-play demonstration (e.g., another supervisor, a clinician, an experienced staff person).

Training a staff person in vivo within the staff person's routine work setting is the most efficient way to train staff on an individual basis. Once the staff person demonstrates the target skill correctly, the training is completed. That is, the supervisor does not have to go to the staff person's work site at a later time, as when training occurs in a different location, to ensure the staff person can perform the skill in the regular job setting (i.e., because the training is conducted in the actual job site). However, if the target skill being trained involves interacting with consumers, then the supervisor has to be sufficiently familiar with the consumers to accurately demonstrate the target skill. This is not always the case when a supervisor works with a large number of staff who in turn work with a large number of consumers. In the latter case, in which the supervisor may not be very familiar with a respective consumer, the initial demonstration should probably be conducted in a role-play manner.

Again, the essence of effectively training staff on an individual basis is to systematically follow the steps of the evidence-based training protocol. The supervisor meets with the staff person, explains the target skills to be trained (and why the skills are important), provides a written summary of the skills, demonstrates the skills, observes and provides feedback while the staff person practices the skills, and repeats the steps as often as necessary until the staff person demonstrates competence in performing the skills.

General Considerations When Using Evidence-Based Training Procedures with Staff

The evidence-based approach to training discussed to this point has been used effectively with groups of staff and with individual staff members in many human service agencies. However, there are also some practical issues when using this method to train staff with which supervisors should be familiar.

Time and Effort Considerations When Using Evidence-Based Training Procedures

One of the most significant considerations when conducting performance- and competency-based training, and especially from a practical perspective, is the time and effort required of the supervisor. This approach to staff training usually requires more time, and often more effort, to conduct than what typically occurs in human service agencies. As indicated earlier, much of staff training in human service agencies is verbal-based, consisting of trainer lectures or presentations supplemented with written handouts or other visual material. Again, these training procedures are often helpful to some degree but are usually not sufficiently effective for training staff how to perform specific work skills. Because the latter training procedures do not involve trainer demonstrations and trainee practice though, they often require less time than performance- and competency-based training.

The reduced time and effort when relying exclusively on a verbal-based training format is one reason this approach to training is so common in the human services. Reliance on training procedures that require less supervisor time is understandable when considering the numerous job duties supervisors are expected to fulfill on a daily basis. However, on closer examination, it is counterproductive to invest time on training programs with staff when the programs are not likely to be effective. Consequently, consideration is warranted on how effective, evidence-based training procedures can be conducted more efficiently.

Before describing potential ways to reduce supervisor time spent in staff training, it should be noted that in some situations verbal-based training is used even though it is apparent the training will not be very effective. One rather common situation is when a service-delivery problem is identified by senior management or some external regulatory or survey body (e.g., surveys conducted within agencies receiving funding through the Federal Medicaid Program for Intermediate Care Facilities—ICFs). Staff training, usually involving a group session in which the trainer presents information about staff doing some aspect of their job differently, is proposed as the corrective action to solve the problem. The purpose in this situation, though not always recognized officially, is to demonstrate to the regulatory or survey body that the agency has done something to resolve the problematic issue.

Conducting a training session for the purpose just noted may be necessary in some cases, but should not be mistakenly considered as an effective way to train staff. The concern here is with training for the primary purpose of ensuring staff learn to perform specified work skills. If performance- and competency-based training also serves another purpose such as that just illustrated, that purpose should be considered secondary.

Ensure Staff Competence During Role-Play Practice Activities. One means for a supervisor to minimize the amount of time to conduct performance- and competency-based training pertains to the trainee practice activities, and particularly when training a group of staff. As previously described, trainee practice of the target skills (accompanied by trainer feedback) should first occur during the group training session and then individually with staff while they are in their work setting. One aspect of this training approach that often involves a considerable amount of supervisor time is when respective staff do not perform the target skills competently on the job. When this occurs, the supervisor has to conduct repeated on-the-job training interactions with a staff person that sometimes entail going to the staff person's work site on several occasions to complete the training.

One way to reduce a supervisor's time due to a staff person not demonstrating competence on the job is to ensure each staff member attending the group training session demonstrates competence during the role-play practice. When possible, it is helpful to have each staff person perform the target skills competently at least twice during separate role plays within the group training session. Typically, the better the competence displayed by staff during role plays, the better they will perform the target skills later on the job.

Sometimes trainers become rushed and hurry through a group training session such that they do not sufficiently observe all staff members perform the target skills correctly. When this occurs, there is increased likelihood that certain staff members will have difficulty performing the skills competently on the job (which then requires additional time by the supervisor to complete the training). In short, the more time spent ensuring staff are competent during the initial role plays, the less time will usually be needed to ensure their competence on the job.

On-the-job competence of staff following group training sessions is enhanced if each staff trainee is required to demonstrate skill competence in role-play activities during the group sessions.

Use Visual Media as Part of Training. Another consideration for reducing supervisor time required to effectively train staff is to incorporate visual media components within the training process (see the **Staff Training** sections in the **Selected Readings** that refer to use of visual media for more in-depth information). Access to visual media is becoming increasingly available to many human service agencies, including use of videos, computer-based training packages, and web-based or on-line training. For example, staff may be scheduled to watch a training video related to a specified work skill or complete a training session on-line. These processes usually require minimal supervisor time during the actual training.

Some research suggests that visually based media can be effective in certain situations for training work skills to staff. For example, there are several videos and DVDs that have been shown to increase the teaching proficiency of support staff when working with individuals who have autism. However, at this point there is not enough research to provide a strong evidence base to support the effectiveness of these approaches for training many work skills to staff.

One concern with visual media is the performance components that need to be included if the training is to be effective. Visual media can present one performance-based component of training, that involving demonstrations of how to perform a target skill. Sole reliance on visual media though does not include the trainee practice-with-feedback component that is a critical part of performance- and competency-based training.

One approach that has some supportive research for using visual media within training while also providing the performance practice components is to use a video or DVD only for selected parts of the training. To illustrate, in a situation in which a behavior analyst needed to train support staff in a residential center regarding a new behavior support plan for a consumer with challenging behavior, the behavior analyst developed a DVD to provide some of the training. Staff could watch the DVD as their schedule permitted within a designated time period. The DVD explained the rationale for the plan, described the component parts, and showed how to perform some duties associated with implementing the plan. Subsequently, the behavior analyst met with individual staff on the job for demonstration and practice-with-feedback purposes. In this manner, all components of the evidence-based training protocol were implemented. However, the behavior analyst did not have to meet with the group of staff to initiate the training process because this was accomplished by staff viewing the DVD.

Use of a DVD as just summarized reduced the amount of behavior analyst time required to train staff relative to the usual process of conducting a group training session followed by individual staff training on the job. One reason the DVD component successfully reduced trainer time was because when conducting group training with staff, it is common that several sessions are required to make sure all staff receive the training. Often supervisors and other trainers have to schedule several group training sessions because not all staff can attend a given session due to different work schedules, absences from work, or competing assignments. By using a DVD for the group training component, the staff trainer's presence is not required for repeated training sessions with different groups of staff. However, when considering using visual media in such a manner, the amount of time to develop the DVD must also be taken into account.

Until more research is conducted on the use of visual media for training staff to thoroughly determine its effectiveness, reasonable caution should be taken by supervisors when considering visual media for training purposes. A logical guideline would be that visual media could be used for training purposes as long as staff are still required to demonstrate competence in performing the target work skills on the job. As indicated previously, training should never be considered complete—regardless of whether visual media are used or not—until staff trainees are observed to perform the target work skills competently on the job.

Pyramidal Training. Another means of reducing the amount of time required of a supervisor to train staff is through a *pyramidal training* approach. Pyramidal training involves a supervisor training work skills to a small number of staff who in turn train the skills to a larger number of staff. The pyramidal feature of this training process is represented by the following. One trainer (the supervisor) is at the top of the "pyramid" and trains two or three staff to function as trainers who represent the middle of the "pyramid". The latter staff then train the remaining staff members who are at the bottom of the "pyramid". Because this process involves staff training other staff, it is also referred to as a *peer training* model.

For pyramidal training to be effective, a supervisor must train two sets of work skills to the staff who will serve as peer trainers with other staff. First, the supervisor must train the staff trainers in the target work skill. For example, a target skill to be trained to all staff may be how to use a least-to-most assistive prompting strategy to teach self-help skills to consumers with severe disabilities. The supervisor would use the evidence-based training protocol in a group format to train the peer trainers how to use the targeted prompting strategy. Second, the supervisor must train the peer trainers how to use the evidence-based training protocol to train the rest of the staff in the prompting strategy. The latter process involves training the peer trainers how to apply the same steps of the protocol that the supervisor used when training the trainers in the target prompting strategy.

Once peer trainers are prepared to train the target skill to the remaining staff, it is helpful if a supervisor develops a work activity schedule regarding how and when the peer training will take place. This step is necessary to make sure the training proceeds in an organized manner. A work activity schedule is also necessary to ensure that the peer trainers have sufficient time built into their more routine assignments to allow them opportunities to conduct peer training sessions.

There are two primary advantages to using a pyramidal approach to staff training. The most apparent advantage is that it usually reduces the amount of time required of a supervisor to train all staff in a designated work skill. This is particularly the case when a supervisor has a large number of staff, perhaps involving different work shifts across the day, who need to be trained. It should also be noted, however, that the *total* amount of time devoted to staff training is not reduced. Only the supervisor's time is reduced; time is still required of peer trainers to conduct training.

A second advantage of pyramidal training pertains to the work skills of staff who function as peers trainers. The process of training other staff helps maintain the peer trainers' proficient application of the skills that they are training. With the example of peer trainers training other staff how to use least-to-most assistive prompting with consumers, the trainers' proficiency in using the prompting strategy will likely maintain at a high level due to their peer training activities. The trainers' skill maintenance is enhanced due to their review of the prompting strategy and increased practice using the strategy that occurs as they train the other staff.

There are also some disadvantages in using a pyramidal training approach. One disadvantage is that it requires additional duties of peer trainers beyond their regularly scheduled work tasks. A second disadvantage is that some staff do not enjoy functioning as a peer trainer. Their dislike of having to train other staff is due at times to the increased work required of them to conduct the peer training. This is especially the case if supervisors do not relieve the peer trainers of other work responsibilities in order to train staff. Hence, it is recommended that supervisors ensure peer trainers are relieved of certain duties to train other staff, instead of expecting them to function as peer trainers *in addition to* performing all their other job duties.

Another reason some staff do not like to function as trainers of other staff is due to the specific *peer training* feature. Some staff are uncomfortable instructing their peers, much less giving their peers feedback, which is a necessary part of the training process. In essence, the act of training staff places the peer trainers in a temporarily elevated role relative to their usual side-by-side working relationship with the other staff. Relatedly, some staff trainees do not like having their peers assume a seemingly elevated role with them. The trainees' dislike is often apparent to the peer trainers, which makes the trainers even more uncomfortable with their peer-training duties.

Because of the advantages and disadvantages of pyramidal training, supervisors should decide on a situation-by-situation basis whether this approach to staff training is desirable. A few guidelines can help in this respect. First, supervisors should strive to involve staff as peer trainers only if the selected staff express a willingness to function in a peer-training capacity; staff should not be required to train their peers if they express serious concern or discontent about being a peer trainer. Second, as indicated previously, supervisors generally should involve staff as peer trainers only when they can relieve those staff from some of their other work duties.

A final note on pyramidal training pertains to how a supervisor works with staff who are selected to train other staff. The peer trainers' training responsibilities should be addressed by the supervisor as with any other important job duty of staff. The supervisors should not only train the selected peer trainers how to train other staff, they should also periodically monitor the trainers' subsequent staff training and provide supportive and corrective feedback as needed. If supervisors do not use the steps of evidence-based supervision with the training duties of the peer trainers, then it is unlikely the trainers will carry out the duties sufficiently to train other staff in a consistently effective manner.

Pyramidal training involves using evidence-based procedures to: (1) train peer trainers in the work skill that they will then train to other staff, (2) train the peer trainers how to train other staff and, (3) follow up the training with monitoring and feedback.

MAKING TRAINING ACCEPTABLE TO STAFF

When a supervisor trains staff using the performance- and competency-based approach discussed throughout this chapter, the training is usually well received by staff. Staff acceptance of the training process is due to several factors inherent in evidence-based training. One factor is that the training is quite effective; staff usually become competent in performing the work skills targeted in the training. When staff feel competent performing a given work duty, they generally enjoy performing that duty relative to duties with which they do not feel competent. Relatedly, acquiring competence with performing a new task as a result of effective training reduces anxiety and apprehension staff often experience when assigned a new task without being effectively trained to perform the task.

Staff are also usually appreciative of a supervisor who takes the time to ensure they know how to perform their job duties. When a supervisor takes the time to provide performance- and competency-based training, it indicates that the supervisor is sincerely concerned about staff being able to perform their duties proficiently. Staff typically enjoy working for a supervisor who they believe is truly concerned about the quality of their work performance relative to a supervisor who exerts minimal effort to help them complete their duties in a proficient manner.

There are also several more specific aspects of this approach to staff training that tend to enhance its acceptance among staff. For example, the initial rationale provided by the supervisor about why it is important that staff be trained in the designated work skills promotes staff acceptance of the training. Staff are usually more accepting of assigned duties when they have an understanding of the reason for their assignments.

Additionally, the act of the supervisor demonstrating the work skills that are being trained tends to enhance staff acceptance. When the supervisor performs the work skills expected of staff, it shows staff that the supervisor knows how to do what is expected of staff to perform on the job. As indicated previously, staff often respect a supervisor more when they know the supervisor can do what is required of staff. In turn, staff tend to enjoy working more for a supervisor they respect than a supervisor whom they do not respect.

Another aspect of the evidence-based training protocol that helps increase staff acceptance pertains to when using a group-training format. Earlier it was noted that to maintain staff attentiveness during a group session, the trainer should not talk more than 15 to 20 minutes at a time without some type of demonstration or trainee-practice activity. This strategy also tends to make the training more enjoyable for staff trainees. Staff often become bored when they have to listen to a trainer talk for long periods of time. Such boredom causes many staff to become discontented with having to participate in the training session. In contrast, when the training involves frequent breaks from having to listen to the trainer talk—and especially breaks that include the trainees becoming active such as by practicing the targeted work skills—boredom and general discontent are reduced or avoided.

Staff practice in performing the work skills being trained can also increase staff enjoyment in many cases due to the nature of role playing. Role-play activities often become somewhat humorous as staff fulfill various roles while interacting with their peers during the training. However, staff enjoyment with role-play activities should not be taken for granted; supervisors must take specific steps to promote enjoyment with the role plays. Otherwise the role plays can actually decrease staff enjoyment.

Many staff are likely to feel awkward or uncomfortable when requested to participate in role-play activities. Supervisors can help staff avoid the latter experiences by letting them know prior to role plays that they may be a little uneasy when initially participating in the role plays. Supervisors should likewise inform staff that such feelings are common and they should not be surprised or bothered by feeling awkward or uncomfortable.

Supervisors should further explain that as the role plays continue, staff are more likely to feel comfortable with the activities. This is also one reason supervisors should always follow staff practice activities with feedback that includes letting them know what they performed well. Receiving positive feedback from the supervisor helps staff enjoy the role-play activities and be more comfortable during subsequent role plays.

A Final Note on Staff Training

At the beginning of this chapter, the importance of supervisors being willing and able to train work skills to staff was emphasized. If supervisors follow the steps of evidence-based training, their training should be effective and well received by staff. However, supervisors should be selective in deciding when to provide training for their staff. There is a tendency in many human service agencies to provide staff training whenever there is a problematic situation with the performance of one or more staff. This tendency was illustrated earlier when staff training is provided in an attempt to resolve a poor review of an agency's services by an external regulatory body (even if the way the training is provided is not likely to be effective).

When issues arise with problematic performance, staff training is necessary if and only if the problem is due to staff not knowing how to perform a work duty of concern. There are many other reasons why problems occur with staff performance, ranging from lack of time for staff to perform a duty adequately to insufficient motivation to complete the task. Providing staff training in these cases will not resolve the problems with work performance. As will be discussed in subsequent chapters, other evidence-based strategies should be used by supervisors to resolve problematic work performance in the latter situations.

Chapter Summary: Key Points

1. *Staff training is a critical part of every supervisor's job.*

2. *Evidence-based training of work skills to staff involves: (1) describing the skills to be trained, (2) providing trainees with a written summary of the skills, (3) demonstrating the skills, (4) having staff practice the skills and providing feedback and, (5) repeating steps 1, 3, and 4 until staff demonstrate competence in performing the skills.*

3. *Staff training is most successful if supervisors prepare for the training by being well versed in the work skills to be trained, preparing a written summary of the work skills to distribute to staff trainees, and practicing the demonstrations that will be performed.*

4. *When conducting staff training in a group format, supervisors should limit their talking to no more than 15 or 20 continuous minutes without a demonstration or trainee-practice activity.*

5. *Ways to consider reducing a supervisor's time to conduct staff training include being well prepared prior to the training, ensuring staff competence in performing target skills during initial role plays, incorporating visual media for part of the training, and pyramidal training.*

6. *Staff acceptance of training activities can be enhanced by a supervisor explaining the rationale for the training, adhering to the steps of evidence-based training, limiting the amount of time talking in lieu of demonstrations and practice activities, preparing staff for role play activities, and always following staff practice activities with positive feedback.*

7. *Staff training should not be used as a means of resolving problematic performance unless the problems are due to staff not knowing how to perform specific duties of concern.*

CHAPTER 5

MONITORING STAFF PERFORMANCE

The fourth step in evidence-based supervision consists of monitoring staff job performance. Monitoring involves systematically and objectively observing the quality of staff work, and represents a critical part of every supervisor's job. Information obtained through monitoring provides the basis for almost every action a supervisor should take to ensure quality staff performance. Most importantly, routine monitoring provides supervisors with information about the quality of staff performance and whether they should act to support or improve ongoing performance.

In preceding chapters the importance of an evidence base was emphasized in regard to supervisors relying on strategies for working with staff that have been demonstrated through research to be effective. Routine monitoring by supervisors provides another type of evidence base that is also important. The data obtained through monitoring, when conducted appropriately, provides evidence regarding the degree to which supervisory actions have had the intended effect on day-to-day staff performance. Evidence obtained by supervisors in this manner is not as scientific or thorough as the evidence base supporting the supervisory protocol discussed throughout this text, but is nonetheless critical for supervisors to perform their jobs successfully.

Although monitoring is presented as the fourth step in the supervisory protocol, it is not a singular step within a sequence of steps. Rather, monitoring should be an ongoing responsibility of supervisors. Monitoring helps inform a supervisor when, for example, staff require training in certain job skills, whether the training has been effective, and when other supportive or corrective supervisory action is needed. In each of these ways monitoring provides an information-gathering and evaluation function for supervisors. In this manner monitoring also represents the basis for **Step 7** of the supervisory protocol: **Evaluating Staff Performance**.

As with monitoring, evaluating staff performance should be an ongoing activity of supervisors. Evaluating staff performance involves reviewing the results of monitoring to assess the quality of staff performance and whether supervisor actions have had the desired impact on staff fulfillment of their duties. Evaluating is listed as the final step in the protocol only to indicate that it should follow every action a supervisor takes to affect staff work performance.

> **Monitoring staff work performance should be an ongoing activity of every supervisor; it provides information regarding the quality of staff performance and how supervisory actions are affecting staff performance.**

The purpose of this chapter is to describe how supervisors should monitor staff work performance as part of their routine supervisory responsibilities. Two general ways supervisors should monitor staff performance will be described: *formal monitoring* and *informal monitoring*.

Formal Monitoring

Formal monitoring refers to a supervisor entering a staff work area for the explicit purpose of systematically observing a designated aspect of staff work performance. Formal monitoring also involves collecting specified information on the quality of that performance. To illustrate, a supervisor may have specified a desired responsibility of staff in an adult activity program that pertains to promoting a client's use of a voice output communication aid (VOCA) for communication. The client's support team had determined the VOCA was the most effective means for the client (who is nonvocal) to communicate. The performance specification indicated staff should act in certain ways with the client that included making sure the VOCA was in arm's reach of the client at all times, ensuring the VOCA was operative (i.e., the batteries were charged), and prompting the client to use the VOCA when the client attempted to communicate through gestures. Subsequently, the supervisor had trained staff how to provide the VOCA, check the batteries, and prompt the client's use of the VOCA. The supervisor could then periodically enter the adult activity site and observe staff behavior to evaluate how well they performed the specified duties necessary to promote the client's VOCA use.

The purpose of formally monitoring staff work behavior in the illustration just provided would be to determine how well staff were performing each of the designated actions necessary to help the client use the VOCA. If respective staff were appropriately completing the targeted duties, then the supervisor could actively support their behavior. In contrast, if certain staff were not adequately performing the designated work behaviors to promote the client's VOCA use, the supervisor could take corrective action to improve their work performance. Specifically how the supervisor might support or correct work behavior will be described in subsequent chapters. The point of concern here is that the supervisor must formally monitor staff performance to know how well they are performing and consequently, what further action should be taken.

Before discussing the intricacies of formally monitoring staff performance, a qualification is warranted regarding how results of formal monitoring should and should not be used. One outcome of formally monitoring staff performance is the collection of data or written information regarding the quality of the observed performance. Many human service agencies have formal monitoring systems in place for use by supervisors. Some larger agencies also have certain personnel whose primary job is to frequently monitor staff performance, such as individuals working within the agencies' quality assurance or improvement departments. The availability of data obtained through such monitoring is a highly useful resource for supervisors—*if used appropriately.*

The qualification warranting attention is that data collected on the quality of staff work activities must be used by supervisors to either support or correct staff performance. Often what happens is that collection of data on staff performance becomes rather institutionalized within an agency and over time, the obtained information is not used for its intended purpose. The information is stored in a central location, and perhaps summarized periodically for various personnel, but then essentially ignored or discarded. When this situation occurs, the monitoring serves no useful purpose for the supervisor. Additionally, as will be discussed later, such a process can have detrimental effects on staff acceptance of the monitoring and reduce their work enjoyment whenever the monitoring is taking place. In short, from a supervisory perspective, collecting data on staff performance through monitoring is only useful to the degree that it is used by supervisors to support or correct the monitored performance.

> **Information obtained on staff work performance through formal monitoring should be used by supervisors to actively support or correct staff performance; otherwise the monitoring usually should not be conducted.**

Formally monitoring staff work performance must be conducted in certain ways if it is to result in information that will assist supervisors in promoting quality performance. First, the monitoring must be *focused.* Formal monitoring by supervisors should focus on a specified area of staff work performance. This is another reason why supervisors must specify performance responsibilities in terms of specific work behavior of staff. Without such specification, it is essentially impossible to adequately monitor staff performance on a formal basis.

Formal monitoring also needs to occur in an *objective* fashion by supervisors. It must be very clear to supervisors when they formally monitor staff performance whether the designated work behaviors are occurring or not. If monitoring is not objective, usually due to lack of clear specification of the work behavior to be monitored, then inaccurate information on the quality of staff performance is likely to be obtained.

Without an objective basis for formally monitoring staff performance, supervisors must make subjective evaluations about the quality of staff work. Subjective evaluations tend to vary over time, such that a true picture of the quality of staff work will not result from the monitoring. This is particularly the case when several supervisors or other agency personnel are monitoring staff performance in a subjective manner. Evaluations of the quality of staff performance will usually vary significantly across the different monitors, resulting in inconsistent and often conflicting information about the quality of staff performance.

When formal monitoring is conducted objectively on focused areas of staff work performance, it is more likely that the monitoring will occur in a *consistent* manner. Formally monitoring staff performance must be conducted using a consistent method to obtain accurate information on the quality of staff performance over time. If supervisors conduct monitoring inconsistently across monitoring sessions, the information resulting from the monitoring will be of little use to supervisors.

When monitoring is done inconsistently, supervisors tend to look at different aspects of what staff are doing during various monitoring sessions. Consequently, supervisors will have inconsistent information about the quality of staff work because the supervisors are not looking at the same work behavior. Supervisors also will not be able to objectively determine if their efforts to support or correct an area of staff performance are effective; the monitoring will not be consistently focused on the area of concern.

> **Formal monitoring of staff work performance should focus on a specified area of staff behavior and be conducted in an objective and consistent manner.**

To ensure that formal monitoring of staff work behavior is conducted in a focused, objective, and consistent manner, supervisors should have prepared monitoring forms or tools to guide their observations. Often, performance checklists and work activity schedules prepared during the performance specification process can serve this purpose. A supervisor can use a checklist or work activity schedule and observe to see if a respective staff person is doing everything identified on the checklist or activity schedule. It is also important to use the checklist or activity schedule the same way during each monitoring session. For example, the supervisor should observe staff performance of each target behavior identified on a checklist or activity schedule in the same sequence during each monitoring session.

Other types of monitoring forms in addition to performance checklists and work activity schedules can also be used to formally monitor staff performance. The most common type is a form developed to count how often a designated work behavior occurs within a specified time period. For example, a supervisor may have instructed (and trained) staff in a group home for individuals with severe disabilities to provide frequent attention to one client in particular. In this case, the client's support team determined that the client acted inappropriately to gain staff attention. The team also determined the client's inappropriate attention-seeking behavior often occurred during unstructured times, such as in the evening before supper. It was decided that to reduce the client's inappropriate behavior, staff should provide frequent attention to the client. Hence, it was determined the client should receive an attentive interaction from staff at least once every 10 minutes on average. In this manner the client would be receiving frequent attention such that the client would not need to act out to obtain staff attention.

The supervisor could use a form such as that on the following page to monitor and count how often the client (B.T. on the form) received interactions from the staff person working in the home. The supervisor could use the form during a 20-minute period before supper and count how many interactions were provided by the staff person. It would also be assessed if at least one interaction was provided every 10 minutes on average (i.e., there would be at least two interactions observed within the 20-minute observation period). What constituted an interaction would have been previously specified before training the staff person (e.g., speaking directly to the client and beginning each interaction by saying the client's name).

MONITORING FORM: STAFF INTERACTIONS WITH B.T.

Date: _____

Time of observation (must continue for 20 minutes): _____

Interactions <u>(mark each occurrence with a slash "/" on the following line)</u>:

_____

Monitoring Summary: _____

Total number of interactions: _____

Formally monitoring staff performance with checklists, work activity schedules, and forms for counting staff work behavior provides highly useful information for supervisors to promote quality work performance. Every supervisor should be skilled in, and routinely use, formal monitoring procedures as part of their supervisory duties. When considering formal monitoring in this regard, an initial decision supervisors must make is how often to monitor a designated area of staff performance.

Generally, monitoring should occur as often as necessary to obtain an adequate sample of the performance of concern to accurately evaluate the work quality. Following this guideline means that the supervisor will usually have to determine how often to monitor work performance on a situation-by-situation basis. There are also several more specific guidelines a supervisor can use to determine how often a particular area of staff work performance should be formally monitored.

One guideline is that staff performance pertaining to job skills that have been recently trained to staff should be monitored frequently, usually at least several times per week. Frequently monitoring staff performance is important in this situation to ensure staff are appropriately performing the recently trained work skills during the daily job routine. Often supervisors will have to provide some corrective feedback when staff initially apply newly acquired work skills to help them perform the targeted duty proficiently. After staff have demonstrated proficient performance during several monitoring sessions, the frequency of monitoring can then be reduced to, for example, weekly and perhaps eventually to every other week or monthly (provided staff continue to demonstrate proficient performance involving the target skills).

A second guideline regarding when formal monitoring should occur frequently is when a supervisor has just taken corrective action to improve an area of staff performance. The rationale for frequent monitoring in this case is similar to that with the first guideline. In contrast to ensuring that staff are appropriately performing recently trained work skills though, the purpose here is to ensure the corrective action taken by the supervisor resulted in improved staff performance. As with evaluating staff performance of newly trained work skills, supervisors will often need to conduct several monitoring sessions with feedback to adequately improve an area of staff performance and subsequently, to provide supportive feedback for their improvement.

A third guideline is that formal monitoring should occur frequently when a supervisor has concerns that staff are not performing a certain job duty proficiently. Monitoring is needed frequently in this case to help the supervisor determine the reasons for the problematic performance (more detailed information on assessing reasons for problematic staff performance will be provided in subsequent chapters). Monitoring is also needed frequently when there are suspected problems with staff performance because a supervisor may need to take corrective action to improve the performance. As indicated with the second guideline, increased monitoring is needed in the latter situation to determine if the supervisory action resulted in improved performance.

A fourth guideline pertains more to *what* a supervisor should monitor than how often to monitor, though the latter issue is still relevant. As with specifying performance responsibilities as observable work behavior (which, again, is a prerequisite for formal monitoring), there are limits to how many areas of staff performance can be formally monitored on a regular basis. The same guideline regarding what performance areas are priorities for precise specification applies to what areas should be formally monitored: staff completion of job duties that relate most directly to consumer attainment of desired outcomes and work behavior that interferes with adequate completion of those duties. The former areas, relating to staff performance most necessary to help consumers attain identified outcomes, should always be monitored on a regular basis and certainly at least monthly. The latter areas should be monitored formally on an as-needed basis, using the first three guidelines to help decide exactly how often.

FORMAL MONITORING OF STAFF PERFORMANCE SHOULD OCCUR MOST FREQUENTLY WHEN:

1. **Staff are expected to perform new work skills that were recently trained.**

2. **Corrective action has just been taken by a supervisor to improve an area of staff work activity.**

3. **A supervisor has concerns about the quality of an area of staff performance.**

4. **Staff perform duties most directly related to assisting clients in attaining desired outcomes or engage in activities that interfere with completion of those duties.**

INFORMAL MONITORING

In contrast to formal monitoring that requires a prepared observation tool (e.g., checklist, activity schedule, form for counting a work behavior) and occurs during set time periods, *informal* monitoring requires no prepared tool and can occur at any time of the staff work day. Informal monitoring involves a supervisor making quick observations of ongoing staff performance and immediately determining if staff are performing their job duties appropriately. Informal monitoring usually occurs while a supervisor is present in the staff workplace to perform other supervisory duties. The supervisor simply looks at what staff are doing and makes a mental note regarding the adequacy of their performance. No written recordings are made during informal monitoring, although a supervisor may make notes about observed work activities at a later time. Informal monitoring in this manner should occur essentially every day a supervisor is at work.

The general purpose of informal monitoring is the same as that with formal monitoring: to assess the quality of staff performance to determine whether to support or correct the performance, and to determine if previous supervisor actions have had the desired impact on staff work activities. If informal monitoring indicates an area of staff performance is not of sufficient quality, then one of two supervisory actions is usually needed depending on the severity and prevalence of the problem across staff persons. If the performance problem is relatively minor and involves only one or two staff, the usual supervisory action is to intervene immediately to improve the performance. If the problem is more serious or involves a larger number of staff, supervisory action should involve developing a formal monitoring system to begin to assess the reasons for the problematic performance (both of these types of supervisor action will be discussed later).

If informal monitoring indicates staff are performing ongoing duties in a quality fashion, a supervisor should take immediate action to support such performance—usually by providing impromptu feedback that indicates to staff how well they are performing the observed duties. The latter action represents the most important reason a supervisor should routinely observe staff performance on an informal basis: it provides the supervisor opportunities to provide positive feedback to staff on a frequent and regular basis. As discussed in-depth later, frequent provision of positive feedback is a critical supervisory action for both promoting quality staff performance and helping staff enjoy their work.

There are also other important benefits of frequent, informal monitoring of staff behavior. One noted benefit is that it makes the supervisor *visible* to staff. That is, because informal monitoring requires the supervisor to be in the staff workplace, staff frequently see their supervisor. When a supervisor is frequently visible to staff on the job, staff tend to view the supervisor as being sincerely concerned about their work. This view helps make it apparent to staff that their work is important and appreciated. Additionally, by being in the staff workplace frequently, it makes it easy for staff to pose questions to the supervisor if they are unsure about an assignment or how to do a work task.

Supervisors should strive to be highly visible to staff by being present in their workplace frequently. If a supervisor is not present and visible, staff have to seek out the supervisor in another location (e.g., the supervisor's office) when needing assistance. When staff have to leave their workplace to find the supervisor, the likelihood that they will seek the supervisor is reduced and their concerns will not be resolved. In this regard, some staff are reluctant go to the supervisor's office because they are concerned they will be bothering the supervisor. Other staff simply will not exert the time and effort to seek out the supervisor. Still other staff may be concerned that if their peers see them go to the supervisor's office, they may be viewed as trying to gain special favor with the supervisor (or what is often referred to as "buttering up", "sucking up" or "brown nosing"). There is also the concern that if staff have to leave their workplace to seek the supervisor's assistance, clients may be left unattended and completion of ongoing duties will be impeded.

Concerns regarding visibility of a supervisor are most relevant when a supervisor works with staff in a variety of different locations such that the supervisor is not continuously present in a respective staff member's workplace. If a supervisor's workplace is the same as that of the staff being supervised, such as in a classroom or a group home, visibility is usually not much of a concern. However, even in the latter situation, a supervisor should still be informally monitoring staff performance essentially every day the supervisor is at work.

> **Frequent informal monitoring increases a supervisor's opportunities to support proficient staff performance and increases the supervisor's availability to staff.**

Special Considerations with Monitoring

There are two special considerations when monitoring staff performance beyond the issues discussed to this point. The first consideration pertains to staff *reactivity* to the monitoring. The second involves issues associated with *overt* versus *covert* monitoring of staff performance.

Staff Reactivity to Monitoring

Reactivity refers to staff changing their ongoing work behavior upon becoming aware that their behavior is being monitored—the staff *react* to the monitoring. Reactivity to supervisory monitoring is a frequent concern in human service agencies. When staff change what they are doing and act differently when aware of being monitored, the supervisor will not be observing typical staff performance. Hence, the supervisor may not be obtaining accurate information regarding the quality of routine work performance.

Staff reactivity is especially a concern during formal monitoring by a supervisor. Many supervisors have experienced the situation in which some staff members appear to change their work behavior when the supervisor begins to formally monitor their performance. A common example pertains to living units in residential centers when a group of consumers is present in a room during leisure time along with several staff persons. When a supervisor initially enters the room, the supervisor notices that the staff persons are all sitting down, perhaps talking to each other. When the staff members see the supervisor though, they immediately get up and begin interacting with consumers. In this type of situation, the staff members are reacting to the supervisor's presence and alter what they are doing.

Staff reactivity to having their performance observed by a supervisor is a rather natural phenomenon. Nonetheless, it can interfere with a supervisor's attempts to obtain an accurate evaluation of the quality of typical work behavior. Hence, special concern is warranted by supervisors to conduct their monitoring in ways that reduce or eliminate reactivity. There are several key ways that supervisors can prevent reactivity.

The best way to reduce reactivity associated with monitoring is to monitor staff performance *frequently*. A primary reason that staff react to a supervisor's formal monitoring is that the act of monitoring represents a novel event in the workplace. The novelty essentially creates an unusual situation that attracts staff attention and evokes various responses by staff, many of which result in them changing what they are currently doing.

By monitoring frequently though, the novelty tends to erode over time and staff stop responding to the monitoring. In essence, staff get used to the supervisor's monitoring because it becomes a common occurrence.

Another way to reduce or overcome reactivity in some cases is for a supervisor to begin monitoring quickly when entering the staff workplace. In essence, the supervisor begins monitoring before staff have time to change what they are doing. This is especially the case when staff are expected to be performing a work duty that requires preparation on their part. For instance, if a supervisor enters the staff workplace at a time when staff are assigned to conduct teaching sessions with clients, staff would be expected to be interacting with clients with certain materials present. If, upon entering the staff workplace, the supervisor observes staff doing something else such as completing paper work, it would take the staff some time to begin teaching clients. In such a case, the supervisor usually could be certain that what is initially observed represents what staff were doing prior to the supervisor's presence, thereby giving an accurate (though not necessarily desirable) account of typical staff performance at that time.

A third way for a supervisor to overcome reactivity is to conduct unexpected, return visits to the staff workplace relatively quickly after conducting a formal monitoring session. To illustrate, after completing a monitoring session, the supervisor could leave the workplace but then return unannounced within 10 or 15 minutes to conduct another monitoring session (provided the work activity that is to be monitored is expected to be occurring over that time span). If the supervisor observes staff doing the same work activity that they were doing during the initial monitoring session, then the supervisor can usually be confident that what is observed is an accurate representation of what staff are usually doing within that time period.

A final way to reduce reactivity in some cases is to formally monitor staff work performance on an unpredictable schedule. In this manner, staff are unlikely to change what they are doing prior to the supervisor's arrival to monitor because the supervisor's presence in the staff workplace is unexpected. However, this does not mean that a supervisor should not inform staff about forthcoming monitoring sessions. As indicated later when addressing staff acceptance of a supervisor's monitoring, staff should always be informed beforehand that formal monitoring will occur. In this case though, the exact time of forthcoming monitoring is not provided, just that monitoring will be conducted. For example, staff may be informed that the supervisor will be coming around on a number of occasions during the week to watch certain work activities, but not informed specifically on which days or times of day the monitoring will occur.

Ways to Reduce Reactivity to Formal Monitoring by a Supervisor

1. **Monitor frequently.**
2. **Begin monitoring immediately upon entering the staff workplace.**
3. **Conduct unexpected, "return" monitoring sessions.**
4. **Monitor on a generally unpredictable schedule.**

Overt Versus Covert Monitoring

One way some supervisors attempt to overcome staff reactivity to the supervisors' monitoring is to monitor *covertly*. Covert monitoring involves observing staff performance without staff being aware that their performance is being observed. The reasoning behind covert monitoring is that if staff are not aware that the supervisor is monitoring their work activities, then they will not change their ongoing work behavior during the monitoring. Covert monitoring can successfully overcome reactivity in many cases, but it also causes serious problems among staff.

The main problem associated with covert monitoring is that it rarely remains covert; staff almost always become aware that a supervisor is monitoring their work behavior. In particular, because monitoring is followed by a supervisor responding to observed staff behavior (i.e., when the supervisor acts to support or correct the performance), staff will then become aware that the supervisor has been formally monitoring their performance. In other cases, staff quickly become aware when a supervisor begins to monitor their work performance due to other various actions (e.g., the supervisor making recordings on a monitoring form in front of staff), despite the supervisor's attempts to keep the monitoring covert.

When staff become aware that a supervisor is attempting to covertly or secretly monitor their work behavior, their respect for the supervisor begins to seriously erode. Covert monitoring tends to give staff the impression that the supervisor does not trust what they are doing and in essence, does not value the honesty or professionalism with which they approach their work. Consequently, staff acceptance of the supervisor and their enjoyment associated with working for that supervisor is decreased substantially.

For the reasons just noted, covert monitoring *should not be a part of the usual supervision process.* Supervisors should not hide the fact that part of their job is to regularly monitor the quality of staff work performance. There is one exception though. If a supervisor has reasonable evidence that something highly unacceptable is occurring in the workplace, such as client abuse or neglect, staff sleeping on the job, stealing agency or client property, or consuming illegal substances or alcohol at work, then covert monitoring may be needed. However, in such cases the purpose of monitoring is not to work with staff from a supervisory perspective to support or correct their performance. Rather, the purpose in these situations is to catch staff in the suspected act and remove them from the agency work force. This is the only type of situation in which covert monitoring should be conducted.

Promoting Staff Acceptance of Performance Monitoring by a Supervisor

Monitoring of staff work performance is one of the steps of evidence-based supervision that warrants particular attention by a supervisor in regard to staff acceptance. Staff are often displeased when a supervisor monitors their work activities, and particularly when monitoring is done on a formal basis. Staff dislike of monitoring is prevalent across many human service agencies due to a number of reasons.

The most common reason staff dislike having their performance formally monitored is a rather natural one. Most people simply feel uncomfortable or anxious when they are aware that someone is systematically watching what they are doing. Another reason pertains to previous experiences staff may have had when their performance was formally monitored within a given agency. In many agencies, monitoring is not conducted for the purposes described to this point. Rather, formal monitoring of staff performance occurs primarily when senior management has concerns with the quality of staff performance. Monitoring is conducted to substantiate the concerns and then to impose negative sanctions with staff (e.g., supervisor criticism, disciplinary action). Consequently, when monitoring occurs in these situations, it serves as a signal to staff that negative actions are forthcoming.

In short, supervisors need to be aware that staff are likely to experience discontent or apprehension with having their work activities formally observed. Such feelings by staff can have a negative effect on their daily work enjoyment. Hence, supervisors should make special efforts to formally monitor staff performance in ways acceptable to staff.

Follow Specific Guidelines When Formally Monitoring Staff Performance

The following guidelines have been shown to enhance staff acceptance of having their work performance formally monitored by a supervisor.

Guidelines For Making Formal Monitoring Acceptable To Staff

1. **Inform staff prior to monitoring what will be monitored and why it will be monitored.**

2. **Upon entering the staff workplace to monitor work performance, greet all staff present.**

3. **Discontinue monitoring if a potentially harmful or embarrassing situation is apparent.**

4. **Provide feedback to staff soon after monitoring.**

5. **Acknowledge staff upon completion of the monitoring prior to departing the staff workplace.**

The first guideline for enhancing staff acceptance of monitoring is for the supervisor to inform staff about the monitoring before initiating formal monitoring procedures. Staff should be informed about the aspect of their work performance that will be observed along with the rationale for why it will be observed.

The most advantageous time to provide such information is either when the expected duty is specified for staff as work behavior, or when they are being trained in the expected duty. It can simply be explained that part of the supervisor's job is to have first-hand information regarding how performance expectations are being fulfilled. It can also be explained that monitoring is necessary to acquire information to help support staff with their work. As indicated previously, the exact time when monitoring will occur does not have to be specified, only that it will occur within a general time frame.

If staff are informed that a specific aspect of their performance will be formally observed along with the rationale for the monitoring, then misconceptions staff may have when the supervisor arrives to monitor can be prevented. This is especially important in cases described previously in which staff have experienced monitoring to signal that management has concerns with staff work activities and negative sanctions are likely to be forthcoming. Staff should be aware that is not the reason why the supervisor will monitor their performance. Additionally, often staff simply appreciate a supervisor who lets them know about future events on the job—in this case that monitoring will be taking place.

The second guideline for enhancing staff acceptance of supervisory monitoring is of a social courtesy nature. Often when supervisors and other agency personnel enter the staff work area to monitor, they attempt to be as inconspicuous as possible and do not interact with staff in any way. The intent is to avoid drawing attention to themselves as a means of reducing potential staff reactivity to their observations. Though well intended, this strategy is usually counterproductive. The mere act of a monitor entering the staff work area will usually make staff aware of the monitor's presence such that potential reactive effects could still occur. More importantly, it is basically rude and even disrespectful to staff to enter their workplace without any form of social greeting.

It is generally considered common social courtesy that when a person enters a room with other people present, that person will greet the people already there. The same courtesy applies to when supervisors enter the staff workplace for monitoring purposes: the supervisor should socially acknowledge staff. This simple act of greeting staff who are present can make the monitoring experience more pleasant for staff, and beneficially impact their acceptance of the monitoring.

The third guideline pertains to when monitoring should not occur, even though the supervisor has entered the staff workplace with the intent of formally monitoring their performance. If it is apparent that an unusual situation is occurring that involves staff or clients who are present, then generally the supervisor should abandon the planned monitoring. This is especially the case if a situation is occurring in which somebody, either staff or clients, could be potentially harmed such as an aggressive or disruptive act by a client. It is also the case if the situation is one in which someone is likely to be embarrassed, such as a toileting accident involving a certain client.

In the situations just illustrated, a supervisor should do one of two things. First, if possible, the supervisor should attempt to help resolve the potentially harmful or embarrassing situation, such as by helping to calm a client who has become upset or aggressive. Second, if the supervisor is not able to help resolve the situation or the supervisor's presence is likely to make the situation worse (e.g., the presence of a new person in the immediate area is likely to upset the client even more), the supervisor should acknowledge the situation and leave the area. The supervisor could also indicate that observations of work performance can simply occur later when things are settled down.

It can be quite frustrating and unpleasant for staff in the types of situations just noted if a supervisor does not help resolve the problem and begins to formally monitor staff activities. Additionally, the monitoring is not likely to result in the supervisor obtaining intended information in regard to evaluating routine staff performance. The supervisor is not likely to be able to monitor the intended performance of staff because it is an unusual situation and staff are required to forego their usual tasks to resolve the problematic situation.

One concern that arises at times in the type of situations just noted is that a supervisor may be interested or concerned about how staff respond to problematic situations and hence, desire to observe their performance. This concern is certainly valid in some cases. However, if a supervisor believes it is important to observe how staff perform in problematic situations, the supervisor should still attempt to help resolve the ongoing situation and only monitor on an *informal* basis while providing assistance. For reasons just summarized, the supervisor usually should not engage in formally monitoring staff performance without attempting to help resolve the problem.

The fourth guideline for enhancing staff acceptance of formal monitoring is for the supervisor to inform staff about the evaluation of their performance that resulted from the monitoring. When a staff member's work activities are observed, the staff person often experiences a degree of anxiety regarding the supervisor's evaluation of the performance. Such anxiety can be relieved if the supervisor provides information, and especially some positive feedback, immediately after the monitoring. If the staff person is very busy with a given duty and the supervisor does not want to interfere with completion of the duty, the supervisor should briefly inform the staff member that they can meet later when things are not so busy to discuss the monitoring results. It is also helpful if the supervisor briefly provides at least some positive feedback concerning an aspect of the observed performance before departing the staff workplace.

The final guideline is similar to the second guideline and pertains to social courtesy. The supervisor should acknowledge staff prior to departing their work area upon completion of the monitoring. Sometimes monitors simply leave the staff work area as soon as they are through with the monitoring without saying anything to staff. This occurs because, for example, the monitors are in a rush to complete variously expected work tasks or they do not want to interrupt ongoing staff work. However, it does not take much time or interruption to simply acknowledge staff in a pleasant manner upon departing the workplace such as thanking them for putting up with the monitoring. This seemingly simple act, just as with initially greeting staff upon entering their workplace, can help make the monitoring experience more acceptable to staff.

> **Supervisors should always practice common social courtesy when formally monitoring staff work performance: greet staff when entering their workplace and acknowledge staff when leaving.**

USE A PARTICIPATIVE APPROACH WHEN INITIATING A FORMAL MONITORING SYSTEM

Earlier it was mentioned that to enhance staff acceptance of formal monitoring, supervisors should inform staff that their performance will be monitored prior to initiating a monitoring session. Such acceptance can be enhanced further if supervisors take a participative approach as described in the previous chapter when initiating a formal monitoring system. Specifically, a useful process when staff are being trained in work skills that subsequently will be monitored is for the supervisor to thoroughly familiarize staff with the monitoring tool and how it will be used. In this manner, staff will have a good understanding about what the supervisor is doing when monitoring eventually occurs, such that anxiety can be prevented that often arises over not knowing what or why the supervisor is monitoring.

One highly useful way to familiarize staff with a supervisor's monitoring system involves the following. First, as the staff training process is winding down, the supervisor should show staff the monitoring form that will be used. Second, the supervisor should explain how the form will be used to assess staff proficiency in performing the designated work skills. Third, the supervisor should have staff use the form to observe the supervisor's performance of the target skills either in a role-play or in-vivo situation (depending on how the training is conducted) and then discuss the staff observations.

The process just described has several beneficial effects on staff acceptance of the supervisor's forthcoming monitoring of their work performance. Most importantly, it thoroughly familiarizes staff with what the monitoring involves. As previously indicated, such familiarity can prevent staff misconceptions and apprehension when their performance is subsequently observed. Additionally, when staff monitor the supervisor's performance of the work skills that the staff are being trained in and expected to perform, it helps reduce the "we versus they" view that some staff develop in human service agencies.

Sometimes direct support staff form the perception that they are considered a devalued component of an agency's work force, due in part to being at the bottom of the management hierarchy in the agency. They view themselves as the "we" and everybody in a supervisory or executive position as "they". This view often develops when a predominant management approach in an agency appears to staff as one in which they are usually blamed for problematic issues that arise. A common illustration is when staff rarely receive special attention from agency executives, and perhaps their supervisor, unless there is a problem in the workplace. The perception is presented to staff that the problem is the fault of the staff; they are considered by management to be doing something inappropriately or not performing tasks that should be performed.

The situation just described represents a serious concern within a human service agency from several perspectives. This will be discussed more in-depth later along with what supervisors should do to avoid such an atmosphere from developing in an agency. The point of concern here is that how formal monitoring is conducted can play a small but important part in either fostering or preventing a "we versus they" view among staff.

When staff have opportunities to observe and evaluate supervisors performing what the staff are expected to do, it tends to show that it is not just the performance of staff that is of concern; supervisors are expected to be proficient in the same work skills as staff. As a result, staff are less likely to believe that it is only their performance being singled out. It becomes apparent that concerns for quality work pertain to supervisors as well as staff themselves such that the "we versus they" perception is reduced. Additionally, the act of the supervisor performing the duty expected of staff (while the staff observe with the monitoring tool) helps diminish the "we versus they" perception because everybody—the staff and the supervisor—are doing the same thing at least in part. As noted earlier, staff tend to be more accepting of supervisor actions when they observe the supervisor proficiently perform what the supervisor expects them to perform.

ENSURE PERSONNEL WHO OBSERVE FOR SUPERVISORS MONITOR IN A WAY ACCEPTABLE TO STAFF

Previously it was noted that in larger agencies sometimes designated personnel are assigned to monitor staff work performance in addition to staff supervisors. This should not be interpreted to mean that supervisors themselves should not formally monitor staff performance. Again, monitoring should be a routine part of every supervisor's job. However, when a supervisor has responsibilities over large numbers of staff, often the assistance of others must be solicited to ensure the performance of all staff is formally monitored sufficiently frequently to obtain necessary information about the quality of staff performance.

When other agency personnel assist a supervisor in formally monitoring staff performance, those personnel should follow the same guidelines discussed to this point regarding the supervisor's own monitoring of staff performance. This is particularly the case in regard to how a formal monitoring session should be conducted. Again, those guidelines involve informing staff about upcoming monitoring prior to the monitoring, greeting staff upon entering and departing the staff workplace, discontinuing monitoring if a situation arises in which someone could be harmed or embarrassed, and providing at least some positive feedback soon after the monitoring is completed.

Agency personnel who formally monitor staff performance should monitor in a way that is acceptable to staff for the same reasons that supervisors need to be concerned about staff acceptance of monitoring. Additionally, when someone other than the supervisor monitors staff performance, that person's actions are often viewed by staff as an extension of the supervisor. Staff are aware that the monitoring is occurring with the supervisor's knowledge and the supervisor will be aware of results of the monitoring. If the monitoring is conducted in a way that is not acceptable to staff, then staff will likely view the monitor in a less than approving nature. Such a view will also be extended to the supervisor who is at least partially responsible for the actions of the monitor.

Chapter Summary: Key Points

1. Monitoring staff performance should be an ongoing supervisor responsibility; it provides information on the quality of staff work and how supervisory actions affect staff performance.

2. Monitoring should be conducted formally and informally. Formal monitoring requires use of a prepared monitoring tool and occurs on a periodic, scheduled basis by a supervisor. Informal monitoring occurs while a supervisor is present in the staff workplace for other purposes and requires no formally prepared tool or recording of information.

3. Monitoring of staff performance should be conducted exclusively for evaluating staff work activities and assessing how supervisory actions have impacted staff performance.

4. Formal monitoring must be focused on a specified area of staff work behavior and be conducted in an objective and consistent manner.

5. Formal monitoring should occur most frequently when: (1) staff are expected to perform recently trained work skills, (2) corrective action has recently been taken with a specified area of work performance, (3) a supervisor has concerns over insufficient work quality and, (4) staff perform duties most directly related to consumer attainment of desired outcomes or engage in activities interfering with completion of those duties.

6. Staff reactivity to formal monitoring can be reduced by monitoring frequently, beginning monitoring immediately upon entering the staff workplace, conducting unexpected "return"

monitoring sessions, and monitoring on a generally unpredictable schedule.

7. Covert monitoring should not be routinely used by supervisors; staff should be informed about forthcoming monitoring and why it is being conducted, and familiarized with the monitoring process.

8. Staff acceptance of a formal monitoring session can be enhanced by: (1) informing staff about the monitoring prior to initiating the session, (2) greeting staff upon entering their workplace, (3) discontinuing monitoring if a potentially harmful or embarrassing situation is apparent, (4) providing feedback to staff soon after monitoring and, (5) acknowledging staff upon completion of monitoring prior to departing their workplace.

CHAPTER 6

SUPPORTING PROFICIENT WORK PERFORMANCE: POSITIVE FEEDBACK

The steps constituting evidence-based supervision described to this point will often result in staff performing their work in a quality manner. Once performance expectations have been specified as staff work behavior, expected work skills have been trained to staff using performance- and competency-based procedures, and staff work activities are routinely monitored by the supervisor, many staff will demonstrate proficient work performance. However, although these supervisory steps are critical, they represent only part of what constitutes effective supervision.

Supervisors must also respond in certain ways to ongoing staff performance to ensure job duties are consistently completed in a proficient manner. As indicated in previous chapters, supervisors must actively respond to quality work behavior in ways to support and maintain that behavior. Supervisors likewise must actively respond to work behavior that is not of acceptable quality in ways that correct and improve such behavior. This and the subsequent chapter focus on how supervisors can act to support and maintain proficient work behavior of staff. **Chapter 8** focuses on how supervisors can improve nonproficient work performance.

In the introductory comments to this text the importance of supervisors actively supporting quality performance was noted for helping motivate staff to perform their duties proficiently on a routine basis. It was also noted that if quality staff performance is not well supported, staff motivation often diminishes over time and staff appear "burned out" with their jobs. There are also other reasons why supervisor support is important for motivating staff to work diligently and proficiently.

One fundamental reason why active supervisor support is necessary pertains to why many people seek employment in a direct support position. There is a common view that people who enter the direct support profession do so because of an inherent desire to help individuals who have disabilities. This is certainly a reason why some people seek employment in a human service setting. However, it is not the most common reason. Most people who take a job in the human services do so because it is the best available job they can find at the time. As indicated in **Chapter 4**, they usually have no prior experience working with people who have disabilities. As such, they do not necessarily have a pre-established motivation specifically for working in a direct support capacity.

Hopefully people who obtain jobs in the direct support area develop a special concern for individuals with disabilities upon gaining experience in a human service agency. Undoubtedly this happens with many support staff. Again though, this usually is not why they took the job in the first place. Consequently, it cannot be assumed that an inherent concern for the welfare of individuals with disabilities will motivate all staff to perform their job duties diligently and proficiently.

Another reason supervisors need to actively promote staff motivation and quality performance pertains to features of the direct support job. Providing direct support for individuals with developmental and related disabilities can be demanding. The work may be physically challenging due, for example, to having to repeatedly lift and transfer consumers who are nonambulatory. In other cases the work is demanding because of having to physically intercede with aggressive or disruptive behavior that some consumers display. Additionally, direct support work may not be very pleasant at times, such as when having to help bathe consumers who have frequent toileting accidents. For many staff, aspects of the job can also become rather monotonous in regard to having to do many of the same things every day. Each of these job features can reduce staff enjoyment with their work, and impede day-to-day work motivation.

Still another feature of the job of providing direct support that can reduce work motivation pertains to how staff are treated by management in some agencies. In the preceding chapter the effects of working in an agency with a predominantly negative or punitive management style were noted, often resulting in a "we versus they" atmosphere. As will be discussed later, a serious effect of working in a situation in which management imposes frequent negative action with staff is a reduction in staff motivation to work diligently. Staff tend to do only what is necessary to avoid receiving criticism and other negative sanctions.

The effect on staff motivation of working in an agency with a negative management style is further compounded by another common feature of direct support jobs. Human service agencies typically have a number of clinical personnel who interact with direct support staff on a frequent basis, such as nurses, psychologists, speech and language pathologists, and behavior specialists. Clinicians generally develop client programs and other services that direct support staff are expected to implement. Clinicians likewise provide directives to staff about carrying out duties associated with the programs and services. This places direct support staff in a rather difficult situation: they are often receiving directives about what they should do on the job not only from their supervisors but also from several clinicians.

Being directed to perform various duties by a number of agency personnel often is not an enjoyable experience. Many people do not particularly like being repeatedly told what to do, and even less so when being told what to do by multiple individuals. Receiving repeated directives from different agency personnel, some of which are conflicting at times, contributes to the "we versus they" phenomenon described earlier. It can also lead to situations in which staff simply become frustrated or overwhelmed and essentially give up trying to please everyone—they reduce their motivation to work proficiently.

> **Supervisors should not assume all staff are inherently motivated to work with people who have disabilities; supervisors should actively strive to promote staff motivation to work diligently and proficiently.**

The importance of supervisors actively supporting proficient staff performance is due to all of the features associated with direct support jobs just presented. There are also more proactive reasons for supervisors to support quality work performance. When supervisors actively support quality work among staff, not only is quality performance likely to continue but staff are more likely to feel good about their work. As emphasized later, the process of supporting staff performance involves a supervisor letting staff know when they are doing a good job. When the good work of staff is acknowledged by their supervisor, it helps staff feel good about their work efforts. In turn, when staff feel good about their work, they are more likely to enjoy their jobs.

Another proactive reason for supporting quality staff performance is that it helps promote staff retention. Staff are much more likely to want to continue a job if they are actively supported in fulfilling their job duties and feel good about their work. In one sense, the work behavior of staff who do consistently perform their jobs diligently and proficiently should be especially supported by supervisors. Staff who perform in a quality manner are usually the individuals who have the most opportunities to seek employment elsewhere. Employers desire staff with good work histories relative to staff who have histories of problematic work performance.

The importance of actively supporting staff who regularly perform their duties in a quality fashion is will illustrated in situations in which such support is lacking. This often happens in those agencies characterized by a predominantly negative management style. When a negative management style is used with staff, proficient work of staff generally goes unrecognized whereas frequent attention (of a negative nature) is directed to staff whose performance is problematic. Hence, there is minimal if any support for the actions of staff who perform proficiently. Unless the performance of the latter staff is actively supported and they feel good about their work, they are more likely to seek other jobs. The result is that over time the remaining work force within an agency is represented in large part by staff whose performance is often less than desirable because the agency is not able to retain staff who perform proficiently.

Due to the noted importance of supervisors actively supporting good work performance of staff, a considerable amount of research has focused on developing ways to provide effective support. Such research has resulted in a number of evidence-based strategies supervisors can use to effectively support quality work among human service staff. Essentially all of the strategies involve providing positive feedback to staff in some manner regarding the proficiency of their work.

THE POWER OF POSITIVE FEEDBACK

In its purest form, feedback involves providing information about the quality of a specific aspect of staff work behavior. Information is presented to staff regarding what was performed correctly and if applicable, incorrectly. Feedback is most helpful for supporting proficient performance if it is accompanied by explicit expressions of approval or commendation for work performed appropriately. Information about the quality of work that includes approval or praise is referred to as *positive* or *supportive feedback*.

Providing positive feedback is the most readily available, effective means for a supervisor to support proficient staff performance. There has been more research demonstrating the supportive effects of positive feedback on the work performance of human service staff than any other supervisory strategy. Routinely providing positive feedback is also the most readily available means for a supervisor to enhance staff enjoyment with their day-to-day work activities.

Providing positive feedback is straightforward in concept. Supervisors observe staff perform a given job duty and determine if their performance meets the previously specified criteria for completing the work task. Subsequently, the supervisor informs staff what they performed appropriately accompanied by expressions of approval for the good work performance. However, providing feedback in a way that truly supports staff in continuing to perform a task proficiently and feeling good about their work also requires certain skills. Skills in providing positive feedback are essential for supervisors to acquire and practice if their supervision is to be successful.

AN EVIDENCE-BASED PROTOCOL FOR PROVIDING FEEDBACK

There are many ways to provide positive feedback. Due to recognition that providing feedback also requires a specific set of skills by supervisors, a significant amount of research has been conducted on *how* supervisors should provide feedback. Such research has resulted in a basic protocol for providing feedback to staff about the quality of their work. The steps constituting this evidence-based means of providing feedback are summarized below.

EVIDENCE-BASED PROTOCOL FOR PROVIDING FEEDBACK TO STAFF

Step 1. **Begin feedback with a positive or empathetic statement.**

Step 2. **Specify what staff performed correctly.**

Step 3. **Specify what staff performed incorrectly, if applicable.**

Step 4. **Specify what staff need to do to correct the work behavior identified in Step 3.**

Step 5. **Solicit questions from staff about the information provided.**

Step 6. **Inform staff about subsequent supervisory actions regarding the target work behavior.**

Step 7. **End feedback with a positive or empathetic statement.**

Before discussing the steps involved in providing feedback, it should be noted that the protocol represents a comprehensive feedback process. It is comprehensive in that it involves a means of not only supporting proficient staff performance, but also correcting or improving nonproficient performance. The protocol is also comprehensive in terms of promoting staff acceptance of the manner in which feedback is provided. Each of these features will be highlighted as the steps constituting the protocol are described. Subsequently, this and the following chapter focus on those steps of the protocol that are specifically designed to support proficient performance and work enjoyment. **Chapter 8** then focuses on the steps that supervisors can use to improve nonproficient staff performance.

The evidence-based protocol for providing feedback is intended primarily for formal feedback sessions involving a supervisor and an individual staff member. It was designed as a guide for when a supervisor meets with a staff person for the explicit purpose of providing feedback, such as following formal monitoring of a staff person's work performance. The protocol is also useful when providing feedback on a more impromptu or informal basis, and particularly after a supervisor has informally observed staff performance. In the latter case though, a supervisor does not always have to include each step of the protocol. When the various steps are and are not needed is discussed in subsequent chapter sections.

STEP 1: BEGIN FEEDBACK WITH A POSITIVE OR EMPATHETIC STATEMENT

Supervisors should initiate formal feedback sessions with a positive tone for the staff person. This can usually be accomplished by saying something complimentary about the person's observed performance in a general sense (e.g., "Things seem to be going well.", "You are getting the hang of this.") or something more empathetic in nature (e.g., "I know this is a tough part of the job."). Precisely what supervisors say will have to be determined based on what they are comfortable with and each specific situation. The primary point is to say something that is likely to begin the feedback session on a pleasant note for the staff person.

Beginning a formal feedback session in a pleasant manner is important for several reasons. First, many staff are likely to be somewhat anxious about having their work performance formally evaluated by their supervisor. Beginning the feedback session in a pleasant manner can help reduce the anxiety. Second, as indicated in the preceding chapter, some staff have had negative experiences with having their performance formally observed and evaluated. Consequently, they are likely to expect the supervisor's feedback session to be negative as well. Beginning in a pleasant fashion can help change this type of expectation. Finally, beginning the feedback on a positive or upbeat note simply helps make the feedback session more acceptable overall for the staff person.

STEP 2: SPECIFY WHAT STAFF PERFORMED CORRECTLY

Immediately after initiating the feedback session in a positive or empathetic manner, the supervisor should specify each aspect of the observed work duty that was performed correctly. This information lets the staff person know exactly what was performed appropriately and how the staff person should continue to perform specified aspects of a task. To effectively serve these purposes, the feedback must be very specific in terms of describing appropriate work behavior of the staff person.

Often supervisors tend to be more general when providing feedback to staff about their appropriate work performance. For example, when giving feedback to a staff person regarding carrying out a client's teaching program, a supervisor may say something like "You did a nice job with the teaching program.", or "Well done!". These types of rather broad statements can be helpful in certain situations as will be discussed later. For the purposes of this step of the feedback protocol however, such statements are too general. Information related to the staff person's teaching should be much more specific to the staff person's actual teaching behavior. More specific information would be represented by statements such as "When the client did not respond to your first prompt you always provided more assistance on the next prompt.", and "You always provided a reinforcer at the end of each teaching trial.". The specificity of the latter statements is much more helpful for ensuring the staff person knows precisely what was performed correctly, and what should be continued.

STEP 3: SPECIFY WHAT STAFF PERFORMED INCORRECTLY, IF APPLICABLE

After informing the staff person what was performed correctly, the supervisor should describe in detail what was performed incorrectly or what was not performed that should have been completed. If the staff person performed all aspects of the job duty proficiently, then this step of the feedback protocol can be omitted. Alternatively, the supervisor could inform the staff person that there were no aspects of the job task that were performed incorrectly.

As with informing the staff person what was performed correctly, when indicating those aspects of a work task that were not performed correctly the supervisor should be very specific. The exact behaviors that were incorrect should be described. Using the client-teaching example again, such statements could be something like, "There was one instructional trial to which the client responded independently but you did not provide a reinforcer." or "On two occasions you repeated the same prompt on a given trial without providing the client with more assistance.". Such specificity is warranted to ensure the staff person knows exactly what was not performed correctly.

STEP 4: SPECIFY WHAT NEEDS TO BE DONE TO CORRECT THE BEHAVIOR IDENTIFIED IN STEP 3

Following identification of what was not performed correctly, the supervisor should specify what the staff person needs to do differently to correct the performance (if the staff person did not perform anything incorrectly, then this step is not applicable and can be omitted). In this regard, there is little value in informing staff that their performance is not correct or appropriate without specifying how to improve that performance. As with the preceding two steps of the protocol, the information provided to the staff person should be very specific. To illustrate, for those client-teaching behaviors exemplified above in **Step 3**, the staff person could be told something like "Remember that the teaching program calls for providing a reinforcer following each of the client's independent responses to instructional trials." and "Make sure that if the client does not respond correctly to a prompt, the next prompt provides more assistance for the client—just like we practiced in our training session.".

Sometimes supervisors inform a staff person what was not performed correctly and then provide only general information that improvement is warranted (e.g., "You need to be more consistent with your teaching."). Such information may indicate to the staff person that a change is needed but not exactly what or how to change the teaching activities. One reason general information is provided by some supervisors is they are not sure what the staff person should do to improve the performance, only that there are problems with the way the staff person is currently performing a task.

To avoid the situation just illustrated, supervisors must make sure they are well skilled in performing the job duty themselves for which they are providing feedback to the staff person. When a supervisor is not so skilled and cannot specifically instruct the staff person how to improve the performance, the feedback session will be of minimal benefit. More pointedly, the feedback will probably not help the staff person perform the given duty more proficiently. Additionally, staff quickly become frustrated and potentially discontented when their supervisor points out problems with their performance but cannot tell them precisely what to do to improve the performance.

> **Supervisors should not give feedback to staff about performing a job task if the supervisors are not skilled themselves in performing the task.**

STEP 5: SOLICIT QUESTIONS ABOUT THE INFORMATION PROVIDED

The fifth step of the feedback protocol involves soliciting questions from the staff person about what the supervisor has described. The intent is to provide the staff person with an explicit opportunity to seek additional information or clarify what was said by the supervisor. Sometimes a staff person is unsure about something that was described, but feels uneasy questioning the supervisor. When the supervisor specifically solicits questions, it becomes easier for the staff person to seek clarification. Additionally, prompting questions gives the staff person the opportunity to explain what was done in case there were mitigating circumstances that may have affected the observed performance. In short, this step helps make sure the staff person and supervisor are both very clear about the content of the feedback that has been presented to this point.

Providing the staff person with opportunities to seek clarification or explain why something was performed in a certain manner also makes the feedback session more participative. When staff are actively encouraged to participate in a feedback session, it tends to make the session more acceptable to the staff. In contrast, if a supervisor provides feedback without encouraging staff input in the process, a feedback session is usually less well received by staff (see discussion in previous chapters on the beneficial effects of staff participation on their acceptance of supervisory activities).

STEP 6: INFORM STAFF ABOUT SUBSEQUENT SUPERVISORY ACTIONS

After answering any questions posed by the staff person, the next step is for the supervisor to inform the staff person about when another feedback session will be conducted. The supervisor should make a decision about how soon the performance of concern needs to be monitored again, followed by giving feedback, based on how well the staff person performed the duty of concern. The guidelines previously presented in **Chapter 5** regarding how often formal monitoring should occur can be used as a basis for the decision. To review briefly, if the staff person is having difficulty performing the duty proficiently, then monitoring and feedback should occur again soon, generally within a few days at most. If the staff person's performance is of acceptable quality, then monitoring and feedback will not need to occur as quickly. Whatever time period is determined by the supervisor, this information should be given to the staff person.

Informing staff when feedback will be provided again serves several useful purposes. On a general basis, it is just good practice from a staff-acceptability standpoint to let staff know about forthcoming supervisory actions. Additionally, for many staff, knowing the supervisor will be formally monitoring a specific aspect of their performance in the near future will motivate them to attempt to perfect their performance. When a supervisor follows the guidelines for conducting monitoring and providing feedback in ways that are acceptable to staff, many staff will also begin to look forward to future monitoring and feedback sessions. Staff will want to demonstrate their proficient work skills because they know the supervisor will recognize their good work.

In other cases, staff will attempt to improve their performance because they know their work will be formally observed less often once they demonstrate work proficiency. This occurs when, despite a supervisor's best attempts, some staff still feel somewhat anxious or uncomfortable when their supervisor formally monitors their performance. From a staff acceptance perspective, avoiding future monitoring by the supervisor is not the most desired reason for staff being motivated to improve their performance. However, it is a relatively common phenomenon in many agencies such that it warrants mention.

There is also another important reason for supervisors to inform staff about forthcoming monitoring and feedback sessions. In a lot of agencies, staff become accustomed to a particular area of their performance being a periodic concern of management. However, they also know that if they wait long enough, the focus of management will vary over time and the given performance area will no longer be a significant concern of management. In essence, staff adopt an attitude that if they "stay below the radar" or simply "lie low", management's immediate concerns will pass and their performance of a specific duty will not receive attention for very long.

The latter view develops among staff because they become aware that management does not consistently follow through on various issues of concern. Lack of management follow through represents an ineffective approach to supervision and should not occur. Nonetheless, many staff are likely to have experienced this situation in the past. A supervisor can negate such a view at least in part by simply informing staff that the performance of concern will be monitored again (and, of course, actually conducting subsequent monitoring and feedback sessions). Following up in this manner helps indicate that the performance is important and will be attended to by the supervisor on a regular basis. The end result of informing staff about continued monitoring and feedback is increased motivation among some staff to perform their duties proficiently.

STEP 7: END FEEDBACK SESSION WITH A POSITIVE OR EMPATHETIC STATEMENT

The last step of the evidence-based feedback protocol is to end the feedback session in a pleasant manner. This can be accomplished as with initiating the session by providing a generally positive or empathetic statement. The positive statement can reiterate the performance aspects performed correctly accompanied by clear expressions of approval (e.g., "Your teaching is looking real good; your prompting is giving the client increased assistance as needed, and your reinforcement is occurring each time the client performs an independent response. This will really help the client learn."). Alternatively, the statement can be more empathetic in nature (e.g., "I know this is a tough assignment and I really appreciate your efforts in getting it done.").

The primary purpose of this step is to enhance staff acceptance of the feedback. The simple act of ending a feedback session in a positive manner can have a significant effect on the staff person's acceptance of the supervisor's feedback. It can also make the staff person's anticipation of future feedback sessions more pleasant.

SPECIAL CONSIDERATIONS WHEN USING THE EVIDENCE-BASED FEEDBACK PROTOCOL

The evidence-based feedback protocol represents a very valuable tool for supervisors. It is a readily available means of effectively supporting proficient staff performance and improving nonproficient performance. When each of the steps are followed during respective feedback sessions, this method of providing feedback usually is also well received by staff. However, there are some special considerations warranting a supervisor's attention to use the feedback protocol most effectively and in a way most acceptable to staff.

FEEDBACK AS A UNIQUE SKILL

Providing feedback in a way that affects staff work performance in the desired manner and is well received by staff is a unique supervisory skill. There is a common misconception in the human services that if a supervisor knows how to perform a work task that staff are expected to perform, then the supervisor will be able to provide effective feedback regarding how staff perform the task. A supervisor being skilled in performing the job task that staff are expected to perform is a prerequisite to providing effective feedback. However, such skills are not sufficient. A supervisor must also be skilled specifically in providing feedback, such as in using the steps of the evidence-based protocol.

Research has clearly shown that just because a supervisor is skilled in performing a respective job task, the supervisor will not necessarily be skilled in giving feedback to staff about their completion of the task. That is, the supervisor may not be effective in providing feedback in a manner that supports proficient staff performance or improves nonproficient performance regarding the task. Failure to recognize this fact is one of the reasons that some staff who are very skilled in working in a direct support position are not very effective supervisors when promoted to a supervisory position.

Supervision of direct support staff requires a number of unique skills beyond being able to provide direct support to individuals with disabilities, including providing effective feedback. Unless staff promoted to supervisory positions receive training specifically related to use of effective supervisory strategies, they are not likely to succeed very well in their new roles. Of particular concern here, supervisors must exert the time and effort to become thoroughly competent in providing feedback as a means to support quality staff performance and correct inadequate performance.

Giving feedback using the evidence-based protocol is a *performance* skill. Like any other area of performance, supervisors can improve their skill in providing feedback with practice. Hence, the more a supervisor uses the feedback protocol, generally the better the supervisor will be at giving feedback to staff. When initially using the protocol, it is helpful if a supervisor reviews each of the steps of the protocol before meeting with a staff person for a formal feedback session. It can also be helpful at first if a supervisor has a brief, written summary of the steps to refer to when actually meeting with a staff person for feedback purposes. Over time, the supervisor will no longer need the summary, as following the steps will essentially become routine for the supervisor.

> **For supervisor feedback to be effective, supervisors must be skilled in performing the staff work task for which feedback will be provided *and* skilled in the process of providing feedback.**

Providing Feedback in Difficult Situations with Staff

There are several situations in which providing formal feedback to staff can be particularly difficult for supervisors. One situation is when a supervisor is giving feedback to a staff member who is considerably older and has much more work experience than the supervisor. In this situation, many supervisors feel uncomfortable evaluating the staff person's work performance and providing formal feedback. Supervisors nonetheless must still be able to provide feedback effectively in this situation to perform their jobs successfully.

The feedback protocol has several inherent aspects that can help inexperienced and young supervisors overcome their uneasy feelings when giving feedback to older and more experienced staff. First, as just noted, simply using the feedback protocol over time will help supervisors become more comfortable providing feedback. Again, giving effective feedback is a performance skill and supervisors will get more proficient and fluent using the protocol with practice.

Another aspect of the protocol that can be especially helpful for new supervisors pertains to the second feedback step. When supervisors are very specific in describing what work behaviors a staff person performed proficiently, there are several benefits beyond those already noted. In particular, the act of describing specifically what a staff person performed proficiently makes the staff person aware that the supervisor is knowledgeable about the work performance of concern. It also makes the staff person aware that the supervisor is very knowledgeable about how well the staff person performed the given duty. Such awareness helps the staff person gain respect for the supervisor, regardless of the supervisor's age or inexperience. The staff person's respect for the supervisor in this regard is usually reflected in the person's demeanor during the feedback session. In turn, the staff person's respectful response during the session can help make the supervisor feel more confident in interacting with the staff person and providing feedback.

Another situation that can be difficult for a supervisor is when a staff person becomes defensive or argumentative during a feedback session. This typically occurs when the supervisor indicates how the staff person's observed performance was not correct and what needs to be done differently to improve the performance. One means to help a supervisor manage this situation is to focus on following each step of the protocol, despite what the staff person may object to or question. The supervisor simply listens to the staff person's concerns and then proceeds with the steps of the protocol. The supervisor does not need to engage in arguing with or contradicting the staff person, but just politely acknowledges what the staff person has to say and then provide information relevant to each step of the protocol.

FEEDBACK MUST BE SINCERE

For a supervisor's feedback to be effective, it must be sincere. The supervisor must be sincerely concerned about the quality of a staff person's work behavior and want to help the staff person perform proficiently. If the supervisor is not sincerely concerned in this respect, the lack of sincerity will usually become apparent to the staff person and multiple problems result. Most notably, the staff person will lose respect for the supervisor and not attend to the feedback provided. This type of situation occurs, for example, when a supervisor is required to provide formal feedback on a regular basis by agency executives but the supervisor either does not want to provide feedback or sees no utility in providing feedback.

Being sincerely concerned about the quality of staff work performance is not something with which this or any other text can be of much help. If supervisors are not sincere in their concern, it is highly unlikely they will be successful in their supervisory roles. Sincerity can not be taught, though it can develop over time in some cases. The primary point here is that if a supervisor is not sincere in wanting to promote quality work among staff, or help staff enjoy their work, no supervisory strategy will be very successful. The only suggested action in such situations is for the supervisor to seek employment in another job that does not involve supervising direct support staff.

There is another important issue regarding sincerity and a supervisor's likelihood of providing effective feedback. Not only does a supervisor have to be sincere, the supervisor's feedback has to appear sincere to the staff recipient of the feedback. In some cases, such as with young or inexperienced supervisors as referred to earlier, supervisors are very sincere about working with staff but have difficulty providing feedback in a way that comes across as sincere to the staff person. This is usually due to the supervisor being uncomfortable in providing feedback as also illustrated earlier.

If a supervisor is sincere, providing feedback in a way that appears sincere to staff is something that can be learned by the supervisor. Again, providing feedback is a performance skill and supervisors can improve how they provide feedback with practice. Using steps of the protocol repeatedly as discussed previously will usually help supervisors begin to provide feedback in a way that comes across sincerely.

It can also be helpful for a supervisor to learn to provide feedback that comes across sincerely if the supervisor carefully attends to how a staff person responds to the feedback. A supervisor should observe whether a staff person appears accepting of how specific information is presented, or not very accepting. The supervisor can then alter how information is presented, such as how the feedback session is initiated or terminated, for example, based on the staff person's response. If the response seems to be accepting of what the supervisor said, then that approach can be continued in future feedback sessions. If the response appears to indicate lack of acceptance or even apathy or discontent by the staff person, then the supervisor should present information in a somewhat different manner in subsequent feedback sessions.

An illustration of the type of situation just referred to is with staff who appear uncomfortable when the supervisor explicitly commends an aspect of their performance. Many staff are not used to a supervisor complimenting their work and are not sure how to react. Upon noticing that a staff person appears uncomfortable with receiving positive feedback, a supervisor could alter how such information is provided. For example, the supervisor could limit the amount of complimentary information provided to the most important aspects of the performance (e.g., so that the staff person is not seemingly overwhelmed when presented with multiple compliments about observed performance). As the staff person becomes more accustomed to receiving positive feedback, then the supervisor can be more elaborative in complimenting additional features of the individual's performance. Staff discomfort with certain aspects of feedback is another reason a supervisor's feedback has to be sincere and come across sincerely to the staff person. If a staff person questions the sincerity of a supervisor's positive feedback, then the staff person will not become more comfortable with the feedback over time.

> **Supervisors must be sincerely concerned about quality staff performance when giving feedback and provide feedback in a manner that comes across as sincere to staff.**

MAINTAINING PRIVACY WITH FEEDBACK

When providing formal feedback, supervisors should take special care to respect the privacy of individual staff members. A general rule is that feedback using the evidence-based protocol should be provided to a staff person in a *private* manner that cannot be heard by other staff. Many staff seriously dislike a supervisor providing feedback to them in front of other staff, or what is referred to as *public feedback*. This is especially the case when feedback includes information about what a staff person did not perform appropriately. Hence, supervisors should make sure to meet with a staff person for a feedback session in an area that is not within earshot of other staff, or in a separate room altogether.

Some supervisors recognize the importance of providing feedback in a private manner when the feedback involves informing what a staff person performed incorrectly, but believe it is acceptable to provide positive feedback in a public manner. The rationale is that a staff person is not likely to mind, and might even enjoy, being complimented for good performance by a supervisor in front of other staff. There are certain situations in which presenting positive feedback publicly has important benefits as will be discussed later. However, even with positive feedback, a supervisor should carefully consider whether it would be acceptable to a staff person to receive such feedback in front of other staff. Some staff do not like to be singled out in front of their peers—which happens when feedback is presented to them in a public manner—even if they are being complimented for their good performance.

> **Formal feedback should generally be provided *privately* to staff members, and especially feedback that includes information about what a staff person performed incorrectly.**

DIFFERENT WAYS OF PROVIDING FEEDBACK

Providing feedback to support proficient staff performance has been discussed to this point in regard to formal feedback presentations by a supervisor. A supervisor meets individually with a staff person for the explicit purpose of providing feedback concerning previously observed work performance. There are also several other ways for a supervisor to provide feedback to staff. These include, for example, informal feedback presentations and written forms of feedback.

As with formal feedback sessions that a supervisor conducts with a staff person, other ways of providing feedback are based on the evidence-based feedback protocol. However, some steps of the protocol are not always necessary with certain ways of providing feedback. There are also special considerations associated with each distinct way of providing feedback.

Before describing different ways to provide feedback and the associated considerations, it should be emphasized that **Step 2** of the protocol should always be included as part of any feedback presentation. All feedback should include a description of the specific work behavior that a staff person performed in a proficient or quality manner. This is the step that is most useful for helping staff continue performing their work appropriately and feel good about their work performance.

Informal Feedback

As discussed in **Chapter 5**, an ongoing responsibility of supervisors is to monitor staff performance on an informal basis. As also stressed, a primary reason for supervisors to informally monitor staff performance is to be able to provide frequent positive feedback for work performed appropriately. When positive feedback is presented after informally monitoring staff work, it is usually of an informal nature.

Informal feedback involves a supervisor simply telling a staff person about one or more aspects involved in completing a task that were performed proficiently. In essence, informal feedback involves carrying out **Step 2** of the evidence-based feedback protocol as just noted for at least one specific area of staff performance. Again, frequently informing staff about work behavior they have performed proficiently is the most readily available and effective means for a supervisor to support proficient work and enhance staff enjoyment with their work.

Supervisors should be continuously looking for good work performance of staff for which they can provide positive feedback on an impromptu or informal basis. Supervisors should strive to inform staff about the good aspects of their work behavior essentially every day. Frequent provision of informal feedback in this manner is a key characteristic of successful supervision. Many direct support staff also report that they respect and enjoy working for supervisors who frequently recognize and acknowledge their good work.

Many experienced supervisors are well aware of the importance of providing frequent feedback regarding proficient staff performance. However, because supervisors are often very busy, many supervisors also encounter difficulties in providing positive feedback to staff as frequently as they would like. Consequently, it is helpful if supervisors take specific steps to ensure they provide positive feedback to staff on a routine basis.

There are a variety of steps supervisors can take to ensure they routinely provide positive feedback to staff. One way is to always follow informal monitoring of staff performance with at least some positive feedback as discussed in the previous chapter. Another way is for supervisors to identify something like "provide feedback" on their daily or weekly to-do lists, along with other supervisory tasks that need to be completed. In this manner, providing feedback tends to be viewed more readily as a regular job responsibility of supervisors in contrast to a task that is considered separate from their more traditionally expected duties.

Considering provision of feedback as a routine supervisory duty is important because supervisors are not always held accountable by their superiors for providing feedback relative to completing other duties. Supervisors are often held accountable by management for duties such as completing various documentation and other paperwork tasks on time, maintaining schedules regarding when different staff are assigned to work, and attending designated agency meetings. There is a natural tendency for supervisors to prioritize those duties for which they are held accountable by management (e.g., the supervisors are likely to receive negative consequences from management if the duties are not completed in a timely fashion). Other important duties—such as giving staff positive feedback—receive less attention by supervisors and are not completed as often as they should be relative to completing the former types of duties. Hence, again, supervisors must take special steps to ensure they find the time to provide frequent positive feedback to staff.

Making sure positive feedback is presented frequently to staff can be particularly difficult for supervisors who work with large numbers of staff or with staff in different workplaces. In these cases, supervisors should attempt to include informal feedback within interactions they have with staff for other purposes. For example, when interacting with a staff person to provide a duty assignment or related information, the supervisor can take an extra minute or two and express commendation for an aspect of the staff member's recently observed performance. It can also be helpful in some cases for supervisors to maintain a table or chart on which they record when positive feedback has been provided to respective staff. Supervisors can review their recordings on a weekly basis to ensure each staff person has been provided with at least some feedback. If supervisors notice that they did not provide feedback to certain staff during the week, they can then make special attempts to interact with those staff as soon as reasonable for the purpose of providing feedback.

Supervisors should be continuously looking for quality staff performance that they can informally commend or praise.

WRITTEN FEEDBACK

Throughout the previous discussion on feedback, provided on both a formal and informal basis, the focus has been on supervisors speaking to staff about their work performance. Feedback can also be provided using a variety of *written* formats. Some ways to provide written feedback are quite formal, such as with a form specifically prepared to provide information on the quality of a designated area of staff performance. To illustrate, a form may be prepared that lists each expected behavior of a staff member's assigned teaching task with a client. The supervisor then writes in information or scores check boxes regarding how well, for example, the staff member provided prompts in the designated manner, and reinforced client responses. The form that summarizes how well the staff person performed each teaching behavior is then given to the staff person. Other ways to provide written feedback are more informal, such as with a brief note or short e-mail correspondence about one particular work behavior that was performed commendably by a staff person.

Written feedback can also vary in its comprehensiveness. Some feedback forms may be quite comprehensive in terms of providing information pertaining to each step of the evidence-based protocol (with the exception of soliciting questions from the staff person). Other formats may simply describe one aspect of performance that was performed particularly proficiently as just indicated. Regardless of the degree of formality or comprehensiveness though, each format for providing written feedback should always include a specific description of some aspect of performance that was performed well (i.e., again, **Step 2** of the feedback protocol).

Advantages and Disadvantages of Written Feedback. There are several advantages of providing feedback to staff in written form. The most notable advantage is that it provides a permanent product of the evaluation of a staff person's performance. In turn, having a written copy of a supervisor's positive feedback can enhance the importance of the feedback for a staff person. Many staff maintain their copies of feedback and periodically review the positive information about their work that the supervisor took the time to prepare. The increased importance associated with written feedback can enhance a staff person's acceptance of the feedback, and help the staff person feel good about the recognized work performance.

The permanent product inherent in written feedback can also be useful for supervisors in several ways. In particular, copies of the feedback provide information that a supervisor can review periodically to maintain an up-to-date, objective view of a staff person's overall work performance. Relatedly, when a supervisor is having difficulty helping a staff person improve aspects of work performance, copies of the written feedback represent documentation of the supervisor's attempts to help the staff person. As will be discussed in **Chapter 8** on corrective management, such documentation can be important if more serious action is later needed to bring about improvement in work performance.

Another advantage of written feedback pertains to supervisor time and effort involved in providing feedback, and especially for supervisors who work with many staff in different locations. Supervisors can prepare written feedback for several staff persons and then send the information through interagency mail or e-mail to each individual. This process is much quicker relative to supervisors going to each staff person's workplace to speak with staff individually to present the feedback.

In contrast to the advantages of written feedback, there is one primary disadvantage: written feedback does not involve face-to-face interactions between a supervisor and a staff person as does feedback provided vocally. As noted earlier, face-to-face interactions are important for evaluating how a staff person responds to a supervisor's feedback. Providing feedback in written form also does not allow a supervisor an immediate opportunity to solicit information from the staff person about the feedback that was provided, or for the staff person to seek clarification if necessary.

Because of the noted disadvantage of written feedback, it is recommended that supervisors not rely solely or even predominantly on this means of providing feedback to staff. Written feedback should be a periodic supplement to feedback presented vocally to staff in face-to-face interactions. Vocal feedback, and particularly informally presented vocal feedback, should be the primary means for supervisors to provide information to staff about their work quality and to support proficient performance overall.

One way to capitalize on the advantages of both vocal and written feedback is to provide feedback both ways for a given aspect of staff performance. This means of providing feedback pertains primarily to more formal feedback presentations. The supervisor meets with a staff person, provides vocal feedback in accordance with the feedback protocol, and then gives the staff person a written summary of what was just described. The inclusion of the written summary in this manner often makes the feedback more appreciated by the staff person relative to just listening to the supervisor's presentation of the feedback.

The only drawback to combining vocal and written feedback is the extra time and effort required of supervisors relative to presenting the feedback in just one of the two ways. Hence, supervisors will need to be somewhat judicious in their use of combined vocal and written feedback. A helpful guideline for when to provide feedback in both spoken and written formats is to reserve this approach for the most important aspects of staff performance and those aspects that have been observed to be especially commendable.

As with presenting vocal feedback, supervisors typically need to take special steps to ensure that providing written feedback becomes a regular part of the supervisors' work routine. One means of facilitating provision of written feedback is to develop prepared forms for providing feedback. In this manner, supervisors maintain a supply of the forms and on a planned schedule fill out the information on one of the forms for a given staff member's noteworthy performance. The feedback is then sent to the staff member. More detailed information on this approach to providing written feedback is provided in **Chapter 7** on **Supporting Staff Performance: Special Recognition Procedures**. The point of concern here is that the availability of such forms facilitates the supervisor's provision of feedback because all a supervisor has to do is complete a form and send it to a deserving staff member. The availability of prepared forms can also serve as a prompt or reminder for supervisors to provide written feedback on a regular basis.

> **Supervisors should routinely acknowledge quality work of staff in face-to-face interactions, supplemented with periodic written commendation.**

Special Considerations with Providing Written Feedback. For written feedback to serve its intended purpose of supporting proficient performance and enhancing work enjoyment of staff, several considerations warrant attention. A primary consideration is the same as that described earlier with spoken feedback in terms of sincerity: written feedback must be sincere on the part of the supervisor and be presented in a manner that comes across sincerely to the staff person. The main concern with written feedback in this regard—assuming that the supervisor is sincere in appreciating quality staff performance—is how the information is written.

Care must be taken by supervisors to ensure written feedback is provided *accurately.* Accuracy is important in two respects. First, the information must accurately describe some aspect of a staff person's work that was performed proficiently such that it warrants commendation. Hence, the information must be based on a staff person's work that the supervisor has observed first hand to be performed proficiently. Second, the written information must be accurate in regard to identifying the staff recipient. The supportive effect of written feedback will be diminished significantly or entirely eroded if, for example, the supervisor misspells the staff person's name.

Noting the importance of correctly identifying the staff recipient of written feedback may appear to be stating the obvious. However, problems have arisen in a number of cases when a supervisor or agency executive has actually misspelled a staff person's name when providing written feedback. This situation has occurred when supervisors or executives have become rushed and simply want to get the feedback notice sent out quickly. The situation also occurs when a supervisor is not sincerely concerned about staff performance but is required to provide periodic feedback by agency policy or management. The supervisor does not take the time to ensure that a staff person's name is correctly spelled, or delegates preparation of the written feedback to a secretary or assistant who in turn does not check the accuracy of what is written. The end result is the staff recipient is given the impression that the supervisor was not seriously interested in the staff person's performance. Receipt of the misinformation actually hinders rather than supports the staff person's work motivation, as well as respect for the supervisor.

Another consideration with using written feedback is the frequency with which the feedback is provided. In a number of agencies, written feedback is provided very infrequently to staff. A common example is when the only written feedback a staff person receives is through an annual evaluation of the staff person's performance that a supervisor prepares. If written feedback is to effectively support proficient performance and work enjoyment, it must be provided frequently. Written feedback also must be provided soon after a staff person performs the work duty for which feedback is provided. Annual evaluations are far too infrequent to meet these two criteria.

When written feedback is limited to annual evaluations, the following type of scenario often occurs. The supervisor begins preparing a staff member's evaluation in accordance with agency policy requiring an annual review. The supervisor tries to recall the staff person's work activities during the preceding year to decide what to address in the evaluation. Because the supervisor has not frequently evaluated the performance during the year and provided written feedback, the resulting evaluation is usually incomplete and not representative of the individual's overall performance; the supervisor simply cannot remember all aspects of how the staff person has performed.

In contrast to the scenario just described, if a supervisor has provided written feedback frequently during the year, then the supervisor will be in a much better position to provide an accurate annual evaluation. The supervisor can review copies of the written feedback and use that information to provide a detailed summary of the performance covering the entire year. In this manner, frequent written feedback serves two important functions. First, it can support the staff person's performance and work enjoyment when it is provided. Second, the availability of the written information facilitates the supervisor's job of providing an accurate annual evaluation.

Individual Versus Group Feedback

To this point, the discussion on spoken and written feedback has centered on a supervisor presenting feedback to an individual staff person regarding that individual's work performance. Another way to provide feedback is to present information to a *group* of staff. For example, during a staff meeting a supervisor may commend an aspect of the group's previous work performance (e.g., "Everybody completed their client progress notes on time this month. Nice work...and thanks!"). Alternatively, a supervisor might enter the workplace of a group of staff such as a classroom and commend an aspect of what the group of staff have accomplished (e.g., "You folks have really maintained your classroom in a well-organized and attractive manner.").

Providing feedback to a group of staff has several benefits. In particular, it is an efficient way for a supervisor to support staff performance. The supervisor only has to provide the feedback once to the entire group relative to providing feedback multiple times for each staff person. Additionally, commending the performance of a group of staff can facilitate an atmosphere of cooperation among staff and promote their support of each other's work performance. As with presenting positive feedback to individual staff, group feedback can also help staff feel good about their work performance and enhance their work enjoyment.

Group feedback also has its disadvantages from a supervisory perspective. Most noticeably, providing feedback to a group of staff runs the risk of presenting information about work performance that may be partially inaccurate. The most common example is a supervisor commending the work performance of a group of staff even though all staff in the group did not proficiently perform the duty of concern.

When a supervisor provides positive feedback to a group of staff but the performance of one or more staff members does not warrant commendation, there are multiple problems. In particular, for the staff persons who did not perform the respective duty proficiently, their nonproficient performance is in essence being supported by the supervisor. Consequently, such staff may continue performing the given duty in a less than acceptable manner.

Commending the work of all staff when some staff did not perform proficiently also has deleterious effects on the staff who did complete the duty appropriately. The latter staff are usually aware that some of their peers did not perform the work as diligently or proficiently as it should have been performed. The staff whose performance was commendable can resent their peers receiving commendation when the work of their peers was not so deserving. Such staff also tend to lose respect for the supervisor. Specifically, it becomes apparent that the supervisor is not sufficiently aware of which staff are performing proficiently versus nonproficiently. Each of these features can reduce the overall supportive effects of feedback presented in a group format.

Because of the issues just summarized, supervisors must be careful when providing feedback to a group of staff. Group feedback should not be provided unless supervisors are sure that the performance of *each staff member in the group* is sufficiently proficient to warrant positive feedback. It is only when supervisors are assured that each member of the group performed the duty of concern appropriately that group feedback can be effective in supporting quality staff performance.

Supervisors should present positive feedback to a group of staff only when the supervisor is sure the performance of each staff member in the group warrants commendation.

Publicly Posted Feedback

One means of providing feedback that is used in some agencies is through *public posting*. Public posting involves providing written feedback regarding staff performance in a location where all staff in a given workplace can view the feedback. For example, a form may be posted outside a supervisor's office or on a bulletin board in a hallway on which information about staff performance is presented. Publicly posted feedback has been used regarding the performance of individual staff as well as groups of staff.

The intent behind publicly posted feedback is several-fold. The primary intent is to commend some aspect of staff performance so that other staff in the workplace become aware of the commendation. It is expected that when other staff see the positive comments, they will provide additional positive feedback to the staff whose performance was publicly recognized. In this manner, the staff for whom the supervisor is providing feedback actually receive multiple commendations (i.e., from the supervisor as well as from other staff who view the feedback and then provide positive comments).

Another intent of publicly posting feedback is to enhance the supportive impact of the supervisor's positive feedback for staff. The fact that the positive feedback is made public can enhance its importance for the receiving staff. Staff often feel especially good about their performance when the commendable aspects of their work are made apparent to other agency personnel.

Providing feedback in a publicly posted manner may seem contradictory when considering the concerns noted earlier about respecting the privacy of staff when providing feedback. Posting feedback in a public place obviously does not maintain privacy of the staff receiving the feedback. Public posting nonetheless is noted here as a means of providing feedback because it has been used effectively in some situations.

Due to the enhanced importance of publicly posted feedback for staff as just noted, it can be a useful means for supervisors to support proficient staff performance. However, because of the issue regarding privacy of staff receiving the feedback, publicly posted feedback must be used wisely and carefully by supervisors. In particular, public posting should only involve presentation of *positive* feedback. As discussed earlier, there are problems associated with providing corrective feedback to staff in a way that makes other staff aware of the feedback. Hence, information about staff performance that was problematic or otherwise not proficient generally should not be publicly posted.

Even when publicly posting commendation for staff performance with positive feedback, special care should be taken. Reasons for concerns with positive feedback presented vocally in a nonprivate manner as discussed earlier are also relevant with public posting. A related concern pertains to one of the advantages of publicly posted feedback—that of other staff seeing the positive comments about the performance of certain staff and then offering their own commendation to the latter staff.

The concern with positive feedback that is publicly posted is a supervisor has no control over what other staff say to the staff whose performance is addressed with public posting. Although the intent is for other staff to provide additional commendation, such staff may provide negative comments to the staff whose performance was addressed with public posting. The negative nature of the comments is due to features also discussed previously with presentation of feedback in a nonprivate manner (e.g., the staff may be jealous of the staff whose performance was publicly commended or believe that the latter staff have been trying to gain special favor with the supervisor in inappropriate ways).

> **If publicly posted feedback is provided by a supervisor, it should be used only after careful consideration and should only present positive feedback about staff performance.**

In consideration of the advantages and disadvantages of publicly posted feedback, it is generally recommended that this means of providing feedback be used by supervisors only occasionally if used at all. Again, when publicly posted feedback is used it should only provide positive feedback on quality performance. Additionally, publicly posted feedback should only be used when a supervisor is confident that staff have a good working relationship with each other. If a supervisor has observed staff behavior that suggests a working relationship may be problematic because for example, certain staff criticize other staff, staff tend to bicker with each other, or various staff complain to the supervisor about other staff, then public posting would not be recommended.

IMMEDIATE VERSUS DELAYED FEEDBACK

The power of positive feedback for supporting proficient staff performance is usually maximized when the feedback is presented *immediately* after the performance is observed. As discussed in the previous chapter on performance monitoring, providing feedback immediately to staff after observing their work also is usually appreciated by staff and enhances their acceptance of the monitoring. However, supervisors are not always able to provide feedback to staff immediately after staff performance is observed. Sometimes supervisors do not want to interrupt ongoing work performance of staff to provide feedback as also discussed in the previous chapter. At other times supervisors cannot take the time to give comprehensive feedback to staff immediately after observing staff performance due to other, competing responsibilities of the supervisors.

When supervisors cannot provide immediate feedback upon observing staff work activities, feedback should still be provided later in a *delayed* manner. Generally, delayed feedback is usually not as helpful for supporting staff performance and work enjoyment as immediate feedback. However, delayed feedback is certainly better than not providing any feedback.

There is also an advantage to periodically providing delayed feedback. When a supervisor returns to the staff workplace for the sole purpose of providing feedback to staff regarding work behavior that was previously observed, many staff are appreciative of the supervisor's efforts. Also, due to the fact that the supervisor made a special visit or arranged a specific meeting with staff to provide feedback about something that occurred previously, the importance of the targeted work duty can become heightened for staff. Staff tend to reason that the duty must be important if it warrants a special visit or meeting with the supervisor to discuss how they performed the duty. These features can increase the overall supportive effect of the supervisor's feedback for the specific area of concern.

Supervisors should strive to provide feedback immediately after observing staff performance; on occasion when it is not feasible to provide immediate feedback, supervisors should still provide feedback at a later time.

Outcome-Based Feedback

To this point discussion has focused on providing feedback based on observed staff performance. Feedback can also be presented based on the *outcome* of staff work activities. Instead of using the evidence-based protocol to deliver feedback about how staff have performed a given work task, the feedback is provided regarding the outcome or effect of performing the task.

Outcome-based feedback is generally used with two types of staff work responsibilities. One type pertains to staff duties that result in an observable change in some aspect of consumer welfare. The other type involves staff performance that results in a change in the physical environment of the workplace or completion of an observable product.

A common example of providing feedback based on improvement in consumer welfare that results from proficient staff performance relates to consumer skill development. Staff may be assigned, for example, to teach certain types of daily living skills to consumers with severe intellectual disabilities, such as how to set the table for supper. After designated staff have been carrying out the teaching program for setting the table for a week or so, a supervisor may observe that a consumer is now setting the table independently at supper time. The supervisor could then provide feedback to staff about how well the consumer is setting the table. In this situation all feedback steps usually would not be necessary, just a variation of **Step 2** in which the appropriate table-setting activities of the consumer are described for the responsible staff accompanied by commendation for their success in teaching the consumer.

There are numerous other examples of staff work activities that directly affect consumer welfare for which outcome-based feedback could be provided to staff. Some of the most common include reductions in a consumer's challenging behavior following staff implementation of the consumer's behavior support plan, apparent increases in a consumer's happiness or enjoyment accompanying staff provision of certain leisure activities, and productive work performance of a consumer following increases in staff prompting and reinforcing of the consumer's work behavior.

There are also a number of staff work duties that are expected to result in a change in the physical work environment for which supervisors can provide outcome-based feedback. To illustrate, supervisors could offer positive feedback to staff based on the cleanliness or attractiveness of a part of the workplace (e.g., the front porch of a group home, a classroom, the agency van) for which staff are responsible for the physical upkeep. Relatedly, many work duties of staff result in a physical product, such as monthly progress notes about consumer functioning or completion of data sheets regarding the occurrence of challenging behavior. Supervisors could use outcome-based feedback to support the quality and timeliness of the preparation of these work products by staff. Alternatively, if there are some problems with the designated work products, outcome-based feedback could be used to correct how the products are completed (i.e., carrying out **Steps 2** and **3** of the feedback protocol, as well as the other steps as appropriate).

Outcome-based feedback is somewhat indirect relative to feedback provided based specifically on what staff have been observed to be doing. That is, the feedback is indirectly based on what they have been doing by relating to the accomplishment of their work activities. However, because the accomplishment is a clear result of what staff have done in the workplace, it is still a highly useful means of supporting quality work as well as work enjoyment of staff.

There are a number of advantages of providing feedback to staff based on the outcome of their work. One advantage is a practical one for supervisors. Often it is easier for a supervisor to observe the outcome of staff work to evaluate its quality and then provide feedback relative to observing staff actually performing a task. In the former situation, the supervisor does not have to be present at the exact time staff are performing the task of concern. The supervisor simply checks the outcome of staff work at a time that is convenient for the supervisor. Hence, somewhat more flexibility is afforded the supervisor regarding when feedback is provided to staff.

Another advantage of outcome-based feedback is that it is sometimes easier for supervisors to provide feedback about work accomplishments in a manner that comes across sincerely to staff. This is especially the case when supervisors may be uncomfortable providing feedback to some staff as described previously. When the feedback is based on the outcome of staff work, such as commending specific features of the staff workplace that appear especially attractive, it is typically rather straightforward—the outcome is usually readily apparent to both the supervisor and the responsible staff. As such, staff who may be somewhat uncomfortable receiving commendation for their work behavior per se are usually not as uncomfortable when a supervisor commends what they accomplished. In turn, the process of providing the feedback to staff becomes more comfortable for the supervisor because of a more positive reaction by staff when the feedback is presented.

A third advantage of outcome-based feedback is that at times, the feedback has heightened supportive effects on staff performance and work enjoyment. By specifically commending certain features of something that resulted from staff work efforts, the supervisor makes those features stand out for staff. The commendation highlights that staff work performance is having an important outcome. Such feedback can impress upon staff that their work is really fulfilling an important purpose, and that the benefits of what they have accomplished are clearly appreciated.

ADVANTAGES OF OUTCOME-BASED FEEDBACK

Provides more supervisor flexibility for providing feedback to staff.

Makes it more comfortable for supervisors to provide feedback to some staff.

Increases the supportive effect of feedback on staff work proficiency and enjoyment in some cases.

The only drawback to outcome-based feedback is that there are limitations to how many staff responsibilities can be addressed with this type of feedback. There are some staff duties that do not result in readily apparent or quick outcomes. For example, a desired job expectation may be for staff to interact with adult consumers in ways that are appropriate and dignified for adults (see previous discussion in **Chapter 3** about the importance of staff interacting in certain ways with adult consumers who have disabilities). Often, there is no clear outcome of staff interacting in dignified ways with adult consumers that supervisors could observe at a later time in order to provide outcome-based feedback. Nonetheless, there are many performance responsibilities of staff that do result in clear outcomes and for those, outcome-based feedback can be an advantageous way for supervisors to support quality staff performance and work enjoyment.

PROVIDE FEEDBACK IN MULTIPLE WAYS

Each of the various ways of providing feedback has its respective advantages and disadvantages. The advantages and disadvantages should be considered by supervisors in determining how and how often to provide each type of feedback. Generally though, supervisors should provide informal, vocal feedback to staff every day. More formal vocal feedback should be provided on an as-needed basis following the guidelines previously presented. Supervisors should also supplement their vocal feedback with the other ways of providing feedback on a less frequent basis, including providing feedback in written form, on a group and individual basis, in a delayed fashion when necessary, and perhaps occasionally in a publicly posted manner.

Supervisors who are very successful in supporting proficient work performance of staff as well as staff enjoyment with their work usually provide feedback in multiple ways. Again, most of the feedback is presented to staff informally in a face-to-face manner. However, supplementing the usual vocal feedback with other ways of presenting feedback as just noted has some special benefits. One noted benefit is that as feedback is provided to staff in different ways, the supportive effect of the feedback tends to be enhanced. Because the feedback is presented in a different way than usual, it tends to evoke increased attention among staff—due in large part to its relative novelty. Additionally, providing feedback in multiple ways can facilitate the supervisor's job of presenting feedback in a manner that comes across sincerely to staff relative to always providing feedback in the same way. Each way of providing feedback requires different actions on the part of the supervisor and reduces the likelihood that the supervisor's feedback will appear rote or repetitive.

CHAPTER SUMMARY: KEY POINTS

1. *A critical component of successful supervision is supervisors routinely taking active steps to support proficient work performance of staff.*

2. *Providing positive feedback to staff is the most readily available, effective means for a supervisor to support proficient staff performance and enhance staff enjoyment with their work.*

3. *A basic, evidence-based protocol for providing feedback involves: (1) beginning the feedback session with a positive or empathetic statement, (2) specifying what staff performed correctly, (3) specifying what staff performed incorrectly, if applicable, (4) specifying what staff need to do to correct the performance noted in step 3, (5) soliciting questions from staff about the information provided, (6) informing staff about subsequent supervisory actions regarding the target staff performance and, (7) ending the feedback session with a positive or empathetic statement.*

4. *For supervisor feedback to be effective, supervisors must be skilled in the staff work duty for which feedback is provided, and skilled in the process of providing feedback.*

5. *Feedback can be provided by supervisors in multiple ways, including vocally in both a formal and informal manner, in written form, in a group and individual format, publicly posted, in an immediate and delayed manner, and based on the outcome of staff performance. Supervisors should be familiar with the advantages and disadvantages of each type of feedback and use each type accordingly.*

6. *Generally, supervisors should provide informal positive feedback in face-to-face interactions with individual staff as their primary means of supporting staff performance, supplemented with other types of feedback on a periodic basis.*

CHAPTER 7

SUPPORTING PROFICIENT WORK PERFORMANCE: SPECIAL RECOGNITION PROCEDURES

As stressed in the previous chapter, providing positive feedback is the most effective means for supervisors to routinely support both quality performance and work enjoyment among staff. Supervisors should provide positive feedback to at least some staff in informal, face-to-face interactions every day. More formal feedback using the evidence-based protocol should also be provided in face-to-face interactions on a regular basis, though not as frequently as informal feedback. These two ways of providing feedback should be periodically supplemented with positive feedback provided in written form. Other types of feedback, such as in a group format (versus individually presented), in a delayed manner, and through public posting can be provided on occasion as well.

Another means for supervisors to supplement routinely provided, informal feedback is through *special recognition procedures*. Special recognition procedures include both formal and informal ways to support quality performance and work enjoyment. Formal ways generally involve *special recognition awards* that represent public recognition for quality work performance. Informal ways involve *special recognition actions* taken by a supervisor in a private manner with individual staff.

Many agencies have various types of special recognition awards. These are represented, for example, by presenting selected staff with an "Employee of the Year Award", an "Outstanding Client-Instructor Award", or "Perfect Attendance Award". Presentation of the respective awards often occurs with a special ceremony to honor the award recipient. In contrast, special recognition actions are much less ceremonious, involving a supervisor doing something special to privately recognize commendable performance of a staff member. To illustrate, a supervisor may unexpectedly request a staff person to report to the supervisor's office. When the staff person arrives at the office, the supervisor then explains that the sole reason for the meeting is to express appreciation and commendation for an aspect of the person's work performance.

Before describing ways supervisors can provide special recognition for staff accomplishments, two critical considerations warrant mention to ensure the procedures are used effectively. The first consideration is that the procedures must be used as a periodic *supplement* to more routine supportive actions. In particular, special recognition procedures should be used in a manner that periodically supplements frequent presentation of informal feedback in face-to-face interactions with staff.

Most special recognition procedures by their nature occur infrequently (e.g., an "Employee of the Year Award" is only going to occur once per year). The infrequency of the procedures means that they are likely to have minimal effect on routine, day-to-day staff performance. As indicated in the last chapter, supportive actions taken by a supervisor need to occur immediately or soon after the performance that the supervisor is intending to support. Additionally, such actions must occur frequently if the actions are to motivate staff to continue performing in a proficient manner.

Another feature of most special recognition procedures that minimizes their effectiveness for supporting daily staff performance is the limited number of staff whose performance is specially recognized. That is, the procedures usually are provided for only one or a small number of staff at a time (e.g., generally only a very small number of staff will be recognized as employees of the year for a given year). Hence, the work performance and enjoyment of staff who do not receive the special recognition will be essentially unaffected.

> **Special recognition procedures should not be the primary means for supervisors to support staff work performance or enjoyment; special recognition should periodically supplement routine provision of informal, positive feedback.**

The second consideration regarding special recognition procedures pertains to the effects that the procedures *do have* on staff performance and work enjoyment. Although the procedures usually have limited impact on everyday work behavior, they can have a significant impact on staff behavior immediately after the procedures are implemented. When staff work accomplishments are specially recognized, either formally with an award or more informally by a supervisor, staff motivation can be enhanced significantly. Most noticeably, staff typically are very appreciative when they receive special recognition for their performance. Although this effect is usually short-lived, it nevertheless helps staff feel good about their work at least for a while. Because feeling good about one's work can enhance work motivation, special recognition procedures represent one thing a supervisor can occasionally do to support staff performance and work enjoyment.

The two considerations just noted will be discussed in more detail as various ways to provide special recognition are presented. The point of concern here is that special recognition procedures can be effective ways for supervisors to occasionally support work performance and enjoyment when used on a supplemental basis as just described. In some agencies, special recognition procedures and particularly special awards are viewed as the primary means of supporting staff performance. Agency executives tout the procedures as indication that they strongly support the performance of front-line staff. The latter view, though well intended, is misconceived and generally will do little to ensure quality staff performance on a day-to-day basis.

SPECIAL RECOGNITION AWARDS

Special recognition awards can be provided on an agency-wide basis or just for a supervisor's own staff contingent. Initially, a decision must be made by agency executives or supervisors regarding the type of performance to be recognized with an award. A useful guideline for making such decisions is to focus the awards on performance areas that relate most directly to consumer attainment of desired outcomes. For example, in educationally related agencies such as schools and adult education programs, desired consumer outcomes typically involve acquisition of functional skills. Hence, an area of staff performance that would be appropriate to recognize with a special award is success in teaching designated skills to one or more consumers (e.g., "Instructor of the Month Award").

Another initial decision necessary for implementing special recognition awards is how often the awards will be presented. Usually, the awards should be provided on a preplanned schedule, such as monthly, quarterly, or annually. Occasionally, the awards also can be provided on an impromptu or unscheduled basis when a staff person has done a particularly commendable job with the performance addressed by a special award (e.g., a staff person has successfully taught an important skill to a consumer who historically has had difficulty learning new skills).

To ensure that awards for quality performance have a truly special meaning for staff, they usually should involve presentation of a certificate or plaque that formally recognizes the target performance. Presentation of certificates or plaques also can be accompanied by monetary awards or special gifts. However, the latter components require increased financial investment that can be difficult to maintain over long periods of time. If it is expected that monetary awards and gifts cannot be provided with the special awards on a consistent and long-term basis, then generally they should not be used. When a component of special awards has to be discontinued due to financial or related considerations, the impact of the awards for staff recipients can be diminished relative to when the extra components previously accompanied the awards for other staff.

For special recognition awards to be a useful supplement to routine provision of feedback for supporting staff performance and work enjoyment, two key steps must be taken. The first step is to ensure that presentation of an award is clearly based on specified performance of the staff recipient. Supervisors must have accurate information that the recipient clearly has performed respective duties in a quality manner. If special recognition awards are not clearly based on quality performance, they will not have a supportive effect on desired work behavior and may actually support nonproficient performance.

The second step a supervisor must take is to ensure the performance basis of the awards is made apparent to all staff in an agency. Otherwise, staff may develop inaccurate views regarding why a given staff person received an award. To illustrate, if staff are not aware of the work accomplishments of their peer who received an award, they may believe that the peer has a special relationship with a supervisor that has nothing to do with quality performance (e.g., the award recipient has a social or familial relationship with the supervisor). When the latter situation occurs, presentation of the award can have deleterious effects on staff whose performance seems more deserving relative to the work accomplishments of the award recipient. The former staff tend to view the supervisor's actions as representing concern for the supervisor's relationship with the award recipient and not for quality work behavior of staff. The end result is presentation of the award can actually diminish staff motivation to perform their duties proficiently.

> **Special recognition awards should be made based on *performance accomplishments* of staff and the *performance basis* of the awards should be made apparent to all of an agency's staff.**

PEER AWARDS

One type of special recognition award that warrants additional consideration by supervisors to ensure a supportive effect on staff performance is *peer awards*. Peer awards involve a group of staff determining, usually through a voting process, which of their peers should receive a special performance award. When a staff person receives a special award based on the opinion of the person's peers, the supportive effect of the award can be particularly powerful for the staff person. Many people are especially appreciative of being recognized by their peers for work accomplishments.

The specific consideration warranting attention by supervisors with peer awards is that supervisors cannot control what influences the peer basis of the award. That is, although the intent is for staff to recognize a peer for work accomplishments, staff may base their recommendation on other factors such as social popularity. Hence, supervisors must take care in setting up the award process to require staff to nominate a peer for a special award with a clear indication of why the peer's *work accomplishments* are deserving of the award.

FORMAL STAFF APPRECIATION EVENTS

Many agencies recognize staff performance through *formal staff appreciation events*. Common examples include holding a "Staff Appreciation Day", providing a "Staff Appreciation Luncheon", or having a "Staff Appreciation Party". Sometimes the appreciation events include presentation of special recognition awards as described in the previous section. In other cases, the event itself is considered to represent an award for staff accomplishments.

Generally, staff appreciation events have the same benefits as special recognition awards. However, one benefit tends to stand out with formal appreciation events: a considerable amount of staff enjoyment is often generated within the workplace. Although the enjoyment is usually limited in time to the actual occurrence of the event, and perhaps for a few days in anticipation of the event, the enjoyment is nonetheless significant.

Staff appreciation events also share the same limitation as special recognition awards. That is, they rarely impact staff work proficiency and enjoyment on a day-to-day basis due to their infrequency. Because the events are conducted with groups of staff, either on an agency-wide scale or for a supervisor's contingent of staff, the events also share the same risks as presenting positive feedback in a group manner. Specifically, appreciation may be provided to some staff within the group whose performance has not been worthy of recognition.

In some cases the risk of expressing appreciation for staff whose performance is not deserving of commendation is considered irrelevant by supervisors who sponsor the appreciation events. The reasoning is that staff should be shown appreciation because they are part of an agency and their participation in providing the agency's services should be recognized (regardless of potential concerns with the specific work performance of some staff). Such reasoning is risky, as it can provide the impression that staff work activities are appreciated regardless of whether or not work performance is of an acceptable quality.

Despite the risks associated with formal appreciation events for staff, such events can be a useful means of *occasionally* enhancing staff enjoyment with their work situation. The events can also increase staff appreciation for the supervisors who sponsor or help sponsor the events. Formal appreciation events can be especially useful in this respect when it is clear that all staff have contributed something worthwhile to a particular service component within an agency.

Formal appreciation events for staff should be considered in light of their benefits and potential detriments for supporting staff performance and enjoyment. An additional consideration pertains to the amount of time and effort (and potential financial cost) for supervisors to sponsor the events. Typically, a significant amount of supervisor time and effort, as well as that of other agency personnel, is necessary to sponsor an event for which staff are truly appreciative. This is another reason formal appreciation events should be a supplement to more routine means of supporting staff performance and work enjoyment, and should be provided only occasionally.

> **Formal staff appreciation events generally increase staff enjoyment with their work for a limited period of time, but do little to impact everyday work proficiency.**

PERFORMANCE LOTTERIES

A rather unique way to provide special recognition awards is through *performance lotteries.* A performance lottery involves the following basic process. A criterion of acceptable performance initially is established in regard to completing a respective work task. Next, staff performance of the task is formally monitored on a regular basis. On a set schedule, such as monthly, the monitoring results are then reviewed and a determination is made regarding the staff whose performance met the established criterion. The names of the latter staff subsequently are placed into the lottery and one or more names are randomly drawn to represent the lottery winners. Finally, the lottery winners are provided with a preferred item, activity, or privilege. To illustrate, various agencies have provided winners of performance lotteries with gift certificates for local stores or restaurants, opportunities to be relieved of a chosen work task for a period of time (usually to be performed by the supervisor for the staff person), and desired work schedules or preferred parking places for a specified time period.

An example of how a performance lottery can be used pertains to staff completion of client teaching duties. The rationale for the lottery may be that client teaching is considered highly important given the mission of the agency, but a number of staff are not completing as many client teaching sessions as desired on a monthly basis. A criterion would be established to determine the goal for number of teaching sessions to complete each month. Next, staff teaching performance would be monitored on a regular basis to determine how many of the desired teaching sessions are completed for a given month. The names of all staff who completed the criterion number of sessions would go into the lottery at the end of the month and a small sample of the names would be randomly drawn. The lottery winners would then receive designated awards for their performance.

There is a relatively substantial body of evidence supporting the effects of performance lotteries on increasing designated areas of staff work proficiency. Performance lotteries have received attention in this respect for two reasons. One reason is that the process establishes desirable consequences for specific areas of proficient performance (i.e., the items, activities, or privileges provided to lottery winners). In turn, the chance to receive desired consequences can help motivate staff to perform the respective duties in a proficient manner.

The second reason for attention given to performance lotteries is that they can be an efficient and cost effective means of supporting quality performance. The desired consequences do not have to be provided to all staff whose performance meets the quality criterion, only to the lottery winners. This can be especially advantageous when the consequences involve a significant financial cost to provide. Additionally, there may be a limited number of designated consequences, such as preferred parking places, such that the consequences could not be provided to all or many staff.

As with all special recognition awards, there are also some notable disadvantages with performance lotteries. One disadvantage is that only a small proportion of staff actually receive the desired consequences even if many staff meet the performance criterion. Over time, performance quality of staff who do not win the lottery may diminish as the staff lose motivation for trying to win the lottery based on their work efforts.

Another disadvantage is that performance lotteries have sometimes been viewed as somewhat artificial or condescending by staff. Some staff tend to view lotteries as more of a gimmick by supervisors relative to true concern for supporting quality work. Operating performance lotteries on a regular basis also can require considerable time and effort on the part of supervisors.

Again as with all recognition awards, use of performance lotteries to support staff performance and work enjoyment should be considered in light of their advantages and disadvantages. In considering a performance lottery in this regard, one other advantage warrants attention. When used as a supplement to more frequent, informal ways of supporting staff performance, lotteries can have a rather special effect on workplace enjoyment. Because of the somewhat novel nature of lotteries within a work setting, they can generate some enthusiasm and excitement among staff. If upon trying a performance lottery a supervisor observes such a reaction among staff, then there would be support for continuing the lottery procedure. If such a positive reaction is not observed, or if a more negative reaction is apparent in terms of staff opinions of the lottery as just illustrated, then it would probably be wise to discontinue the lottery.

> **Various types of special recognition awards should be considered in light of the respective advantages and disadvantages associated with their use.**

Special Recognition Actions

As indicated earlier, special recognition actions refer to ways supervisors can interact privately with a staff person to provide particularly noteworthy commendation for quality performance.

These ways of specially recognizing staff work accomplishments are much more informal than use of special recognition awards. In essence, they represent means of providing feedback that generally have heightened significance for staff relative to more routine ways of providing positive feedback.

Special recognition actions generally have the same advantages and disadvantages as special awards for supporting proficient performance and helping staff feel good about their work. However, informal actions taken by supervisors to specially recognize staff performance usually have more of an impact on supporting routine work behavior than special awards. The greater impact of special recognition actions occurs because they can be provided more often than special awards and they can be provided more quickly in response to commendable performance.

This chapter section describes a number of supervisory actions for providing special recognition for proficient staff performance. The ways to be described are by no means exhaustive. Successful supervisors usually are effective in creating their own means of specially recognizing commendable performance. Supervisors should decide how to specially recognize staff performance based on what they are comfortable with and how staff respond to various recognition procedures. The following special recognition actions are meant only as a guide for supervisors. They are presented here because a number of experienced supervisors have found the respective ways to be particularly effective for supporting staff proficiency and helping staff feel good about their work.

Special Recognition Meetings

Earlier it was noted that one way a supervisor can provide positive feedback in a special manner is to unexpectedly request a staff person to report to the supervisor's office. When the staff person arrives at the office, the supervisor then informs the staff person that the sole reason for the meeting is to commend a particular aspect of the person's performance. This means of providing positive feedback is referred to as a *special recognition meeting.* Arranging a meeting with a staff person for the exclusive purpose of recognizing the individual's work accomplishment tends to heighten the importance of the recognition. It usually becomes apparent to the staff person that the supervisor sincerely appreciates the performance accomplishment because the supervisor took the time to arrange the meeting just to commend the individual's performance.

Special recognition meetings can also be especially appreciated by staff because the purpose of such meetings stands in stark contrast to why supervisors call impromptu meetings with staff in many agencies. Often when staff are notified that their supervisor wants to meet with them, the initial reaction of staff is one of apprehension—staff expect that the supervisor has concerns about some aspect of their work. This typically occurs in those agencies characterized by a negative management style.

As indicated previously, when agencies are operated in a predominantly negative manner, management attention usually focuses on problematic staff performance and good performance receives minimal recognition. Hence, when informed that a supervisor needs to meet with staff, the staff suspect that something is wrong and criticism is forthcoming. When staff subsequently become aware that the purpose of the meeting is not to discuss problematic issues but to acknowledge good performance though, two beneficial effects result. First, staff are relieved that their work is not being criticized. Second, staff tend to feel good about their performance that is commended, and appreciate their supervisor's expression of commendation.

An alternative and more efficient way to conduct a special recognition meeting is for the meeting to take place in conjunction with a regularly scheduled meeting that occurs for another purpose. For example, a supervisor may hold a meeting to inform staff of an upcoming agency event and at the end of the meeting, request a staff person to meet a few extra minutes with the supervisor. The supervisor then indicates that the purpose of meeting privately with the staff person is to express appreciation or commendation for some aspect of the person's performance. Positive feedback is then presented that specifies precisely what the staff person has done that warrants special commendation.

Taking Home the Goods

One effect of special recognition meetings as just described is that they can change traditionally negative events for staff into positive events. Specifically, what staff initially expect to be an unpleasant meeting with a supervisor (i.e., to discuss something problematic with their work) actually becomes a pleasant meeting (a supervisor's expression of commendation for a job well done). Turning traditionally negative events in the staff workplace into positive events represents a particularly effective means of supporting work performance and enjoyment.

As suggested previously, one means of enhancing the amount of enjoyment staff experience with their jobs is for supervisors to actively strive to increase the good aspects of staffs' work situation and decrease the bad aspects. In essence, the more positive events a supervisor can make happen for staff in lieu of negative events, the more enjoyable the work environment becomes for staff. Additionally, when positive events provided by a supervisor occur in response to good work performance, the supervisor's actions can support staff in continuing to perform their work duties in a proficient manner.

A means of turning negative aspects of the staff work routine into positive events in addition to special recognition meetings involves what is referred to as *taking home the goods*. There is a rather common view in the human services that staff should not take work home with them. This actually means that staff should not let negative or unpleasant events at work impede their quality of life when not at work—staff should not take home the bad aspects of a job. A typical example is when staff have an unpleasant experience at work and then tend to focus on the bad work experience while at home. Staff may worry about what happened at work, or experience frustration or anger about something that happened. The more staff think about the negative job experience, the worse it makes them feel.

Thinking about the bad aspects of work while at home, or "taking home the bad" as referred to here, is usually not a pleasant situation for staff. Supervisors can turn the situation around by helping staff take home the good aspects of a job. Specifically, an opportune time for a supervisor to meet with a staff person to provide positive feedback about work performance is immediately before the staff person leaves work for the day. When the last thing that happens for a staff person before leaving work is that the supervisor sought out the staff person for the sole purpose of commending the person's work performance, the person's workday ends on an upbeat or pleasant note.

In the situation just described, if a staff person does think about work when at home, it is likely the staff person will focus at least in part on the last event that happened at work—the positive things the supervisor made a special effort to say about the individual's work. This process can help the staff person feel good about the job. Again, it represents a means of turning a potentially negative experience of being discontented about work while at home into a pleasant experience associated with thinking about the supervisor's positive feedback.

> **An opportune time for supervisors to provide positive feedback and help staff feel good about their work is immediately before staff leave the job site at the end of the work day.**

RECEIVING THE GOODS AT HOME

Another way to turn something that is often negative for staff into something positive is referred to as *receiving the goods at home*. A number of jobs in the human services require supervisors to occasionally call staff at home regarding a work issue. A common example is in residential settings in which a supervisor has to call a staff member at home to request the person come to work on an unscheduled basis. Typically this situation occurs when another staff member has not reported to work as scheduled and the supervisor needs a replacement staff person to maintain adequate coverage for client services. Receiving such a call at home is often a negative or unpleasant experience for a staff person. The individual's home or personal routine is unexpectedly altered when the staff person is informed about needing to report to work on an unplanned basis.

Many supervisors know first-hand the negative reaction that can result from receiving work calls at home. A number of supervisors, and particularly those in residential settings, often receive calls at home due to a problematic situation at work for which the supervisor's assistance is needed to resolve. Responding to such calls, and especially if the supervisor has to report to the work site to resolve the problem, disrupts the supervisor's home life and is frequently an unpleasant event. Again, a similar reaction occurs among staff when a supervisor calls them at home.

Supervisors can turn the negative reaction staff often experience when receiving a call from work at home into a more positive reaction. Specifically, supervisors can call a staff person at home for the sole purpose of expressing commendation for something the staff person performed at work. Relatedly, the supervisor may call the staff person when there is good news for the staff person such as, for example, a staff member's special request for a desired vacation has been approved.

When staff receive a call from work that provides good news or is otherwise positive in nature, the call usually represents an unexpectedly pleasant event for staff that is associated with their job. Receiving good news in this manner is often appreciated by staff. Staff are also frequently appreciative of the supervisor's actions in this regard, which can help staff feel good about working for the supervisor and about the job in general.

Calling staff at home to commend performance or present good news of some type should be done carefully and on an infrequent basis. Although the call usually represents an unexpectedly pleasant event for staff, it can still disrupt the home or personal routine of staff, albeit only briefly. This process should generally be done only when there is particularly good news to present. It can also be beneficial in situations when a supervisor desired to provide special commendation for noteworthy performance that the supervisor observed, but did not have time to meet with the staff person before the individual left work. The supervisor can apologize for calling at home but indicate that the person's actions at work were sincerely appreciated and the supervisor did not want to let the actions go unrecognized.

SAYING GOOD THINGS BEHIND THE BACK

Still another way for supervisors to turn traditionally negative experiences at work into positive experiences for staff is *saying good things about a staff person's performance behind the back.* The world of work is in some ways like many other social situations in which a group of people interact with each other. One relatively common occurrence in social situations is that some people tend to say negative things about a person when the latter individual is not present; they essentially engage in negative gossip by saying bad things behind the person's back. Supervisors can turn this type of situation around by saying good things about a staff person's work accomplishments when the staff person is not present. That is, the supervisor says good things behind the person's back.

When a supervisor commends a staff person's performance when the person is not present, two beneficial outcomes often result. First, the supervisor is describing a specific type of work behavior that the supervisor values. When the staff who are present hear the supervisor's description of valued performance, it can serve to prompt those staff to perform the respective duty in the described manner. Second, usually the staff person whose performance was commended eventually becomes aware of the supervisor's positive comments.

It is well known in many human service organizations that the informal communication processes among staff are more effective for disseminating information than formal communication channels between management and staff. When a staff person hears from other staff the good things a supervisor said to those staff about the person's work, the person usually feels good about the work accomplishments. Relatedly, hearing about the supervisor's positive comments can have a supportive effect on the staff person's likelihood of continuing to perform the commended duties in a proficient manner.

A related means of specially recognizing a staff person's work accomplishments is by saying good things about the person's performance to executive personnel when the person is not present. Describing a staff person's quality work to executives can help establish a good reputation for the staff person among executive and management personnel. Additionally, in a number of cases, executives themselves will then relay to the staff person the commendation that the supervisor expressed. The end result is the staff person receives positive feedback from people who are considered especially influential and important in the agency. Receiving feedback in this manner can have supportive effects on promoting the staff person's continued performance and helping the staff person feel good about the performance.

In considering saying good things about a staff person's performance when the staff person is not present, it should be noted that the process essentially involves providing feedback in a public manner. Hence, all of the cautions noted in the previous chapter about providing feedback publicly warrant attention by supervisors before commending a staff person's performance to other staff or agency executives. Nonetheless, when presented in a thoughtful manner by supervisors, this means of providing positive feedback can have special importance for many staff.

> **Supervisors can promote work enjoyment among staff by actively striving to decrease bad events in the staff workplace and increase good events.**

STAND UP SUPERVISION

A means of supporting proficient performance that is related to saying good things about a staff person's work to executives when the staff person is not present is *stand up supervision*. In many agencies executive personnel receive negative information about a staff member's work that is inaccurate. The information may be inaccurate due to any number of reasons. To illustrate, the information may be exchanged through several individuals before reaching an executive and in the process become distorted. Additionally, someone may not be knowledgeable about what a staff person is doing and inaccurately judge the activity to be problematic. In other cases, someone may simply have malicious intent due to personal differences with the staff person and want to present the person in an unfavorable light to upper management.

When a supervisor becomes aware that an executive has received inaccurate information and formed a negative impression of a staff person's performance, the supervisor must act to correct the impression. Supervisors can act to correct an executive's inaccurate perception of a staff member's work proficiency by "standing up" for the staff person. Supervisors should clearly express to the executive that the impression is inaccurate or not representative of the staff person's typical work behavior. The intent is to prevent the executive from giving inaccurate, negative feedback to the staff person or otherwise imposing negative sanctions that are unwarranted.

By standing up for a staff person's work performance, the supervisor can prevent a negative event from occurring with the staff person—the supervisor prevents the person from unwarranted negative actions that the executive may initiate. This process does not directly support the staff person's proficient performance in terms of promoting continuation of the performance, but it does prevent action that could diminish proficient work. When staff receive negative feedback or related sanctions for work that is proficient, the ultimate effect is to diminish their overall motivation to work proficiently. It does not matter if the staff person is unaware of the supervisor standing up for the staff person's performance and preventing the negative sanctions. What matters is that the staff person's good work performance is not erroneously criticized by management.

Stand up supervision as just described is an important responsibility of supervisors. However, it can be a difficult responsibility for supervisors to fulfill in some situations. Some executives are not pleased to be informed by a supervisor that their views are not accurate (in this case their views regarding a particular staff person's work proficiency or lack thereof). Nonetheless, because of the detrimental effect of staff receiving inaccurate, negative sanctions when their work does not deserve such, supervisors must stand up for good work performance of staff.

When standing up for staff performance, it is critical that supervisors have direct knowledge of how well respective staff are performing their duties. This represents another reason for frequent monitoring of staff performance as discussed in previous chapters—monitoring is the best way to maintain up-to-date knowledge regarding the quality of staff work. Supervisors should only stand up for performance of their staff that warrants support. If supervisors stand up for performance just to support their staff in general regardless of the proficiency of staff performance, over time executive personnel will devalue the supervisors' opinions. Executives will become aware that no matter how poorly certain staff perform, for example, a supervisor will likely support the staff in interactions with the executives. In contrast, when supervisors only stand up for good work performance, executives will become aware of the appropriateness of the supervisor's representation of staff work quality and tend to listen more carefully to the supervisors' opinions.

Ways Supervisors Can Turn Negative Workplace Events for Staff into Positive Events

1. Limit specially called meetings for discussing problems with staff performance; periodically hold unexpected meetings solely to provide positive feedback to staff about work performance.

2. Strive to help staff avoid taking home bad aspects of work; help staff take home the good aspects by providing positive feedback about work performance immediately prior to staff leaving work at the end of the work shift.

3. Refrain as much as possible from calling staff at home to discuss problematic work issues; occasionally call staff at home to provide good news about their work.

4. Avoid discussing problematic issues about a staff person's work behind the individual's back; periodically commend the person's performance to other agency personnel when the person is not present.

5. Do not let agency executives form inaccurate, negative impressions about a staff person's work behavior; stand up for the individual's appropriate performance by attempting to correct the inaccurate impressions of executives.

RELIEF OF DUTY

One of the nicest ways supervisors can take action to specially recognize noteworthy staff performance is through *relief of duty*. This process involves a supervisor providing a staff person with temporary relief from performing an especially demanding task that the staff person has persisted in performing proficiently. The supervisor acknowledges the staff person's efforts and indicates that because of the special efforts, the supervisor has found a way for the task to be completed by someone else to give the staff person a temporary break.

An illustration of how relief of duty can occur pertains to when a staff person is working with a client who is having a noticeably difficult time. The client may be engaging in a high rate of disruptive behavior, for example, that requires considerable effort by the staff person to remediate. The supervisor, upon becoming aware of the staff person's extra work effort, indicates that such effort is seriously appreciated and the staff person deserves a break from the routine. The supervisor then provides relief by assigning another staff person to work with the client, or the supervisor works with the client for a period of time while the staff person works on a less demanding task.

Providing relief of duty in a manner as just indicated obviously requires some planning and time on the part of the supervisor, and is not always possible. Hence, this means of providing special recognition for staff work accomplishments usually cannot occur very frequently. When a supervisor can provide temporary relief following particularly effortful work though, it is typically well appreciated by staff. It also tends to indicate that the supervisor is aware of staff work efforts and is sincerely concerned about their work. Such effects can help promote continued diligence and help staff feel good about their work efforts.

USING MONEY FOR SPECIAL RECOGNITION

There is a common view in human service agencies that the most effective way to promote work performance and enjoyment among staff is to reward quality performance with pay raises and other monetary compensation. Money is of course important and it certainly can affect staff motivation. However, the effects, though important, are usually circumscribed. The amount of pay staff receive typically affects whether they initially accept a job in a human service agency, and whether they leave the job for other employment. In contrast, salary levels and other financial compensation often have little effect on day-to-day staff performance or work enjoyment.

The lack of effect of monetary compensation on staff work activities is due to one primary reason: pay levels rarely change sufficiently frequently to impact routine performance. Relatedly, supervisors of direct support staff usually do not have the capability of providing frequent pay raises to staff. As stressed previously, to effectively impact day-to-day work behavior, supportive actions of supervisors must occur frequently and in close proximity to the staff performance that warrants support. In most agencies, supervisors usually cannot provide special monetary compensation in this manner.

Monetary compensation usually affects whether staff accept jobs in human service agencies and whether they leave current jobs for other employment; amount of compensation rarely impacts daily work performance or enjoyment.

Frequently, the only time supervisors have any control over pay raises for staff is on an annual basis as part of formal performance reviews. In these cases, supervisors may be able to provide pay raises to deserving staff or at least recommend to agency executives who should receive the raises. Even the availability of annual pay raises are not very consistent in many agencies though, due to factors beyond supervisor control such as the agency's current financial status. In short, supervisors generally should not count on the availability of monetary compensation to provide special recognition for proficient staff performance on a regular basis.

In those relatively infrequent cases when supervisors have access to providing extra compensation for staff, then all of the guidelines for providing special recognition awards as described earlier should be followed. Most importantly, supervisors should have good records of the quality of each staff person's work performance based on frequent monitoring of the performance. The extra compensation should then be provided based exclusively on quality performance that has been objectively observed and documented.

CHAPTER SUMMARY: KEY POINTS

1. *Special recognition procedures including formal awards and informal actions taken by supervisors can be an effective, periodic supplement to more routine provision of feedback for supporting staff performance and workplace enjoyment.*

2. *Special recognition awards should always be based on well-documented performance accomplishments of staff and the performance basis of the awards should be made apparent to all agency staff.*

3. *Some special recognition awards such as peer awards and staff appreciation events can support staff work proficiency and enjoyment for a period of time but generally do little to impact routine, day-to-day work activities of staff.*

4. *Different types of special recognition awards should be considered in light of their respective advantages and disadvantages for supporting staff work proficiency and enjoyment.*

5. *Supervisors should take special actions to occasionally support quality work performance and staff enjoyment on an informal basis, such as with impromptu recognition meetings, helping staff "take home the good aspects of the job", providing good news for staff while away from work, "saying good things about staff performance behind their backs", standing up for good staff performance with executive personnel, and providing temporary relief from performing especially demanding tasks.*

6. Supervisors should strive to promote work enjoyment among staff by decreasing bad events in the staff work routine and increasing good events.

7. Due to typically infrequent opportunities to follow commendable staff performance with monetary compensation, supervisors should not count on use of money as a means of motivating staff work proficiency or enjoyment.

CHAPTER 8

CORRECTING NONPROFICIENT WORK PERFORMANCE

Every supervisor in the human services faces issues with problematic staff performance at times. Problems with work performance may be extremely serious and require immediate action to resolve, such as repeated failures of staff to report to work or abuse of clients. Other problems are less extreme, such as inconsistent teaching of clients or incomplete recordkeeping, though still warranting corrective action to ensure clients receive quality supports and services. Consequently, supervisors must be thoroughly skilled in how to quickly correct nonproficient and otherwise unacceptable staff performance.

Correcting nonproficient performance represents the sixth step in evidence-based supervision. This chapter describes how supervisors can correct nonproficient performance, or *corrective supervision* procedures. Before describing what constitutes corrective supervision, however, some prerequisites warrant attention that need to be in place prior to implementing corrective actions.

PREREQUISITES FOR CORRECTIVE SUPERVISION

To effectively correct nonproficient staff performance in an efficient manner, the steps of evidence-based supervision described in preceding chapters should be routinely practiced. As noted previously, there are a number of reasons staff do not perform various duties satisfactorily. Successfully correcting problems with staff performance must be based on the reasons for the problems. Each step of the supervisory protocol discussed to this point has a distinct relationship to one or more of the most common reasons for problematic staff performance. Hence, when the steps are followed by supervisors, the reasons for problematic performance frequently are prevented or quickly resolved.

In contrast, when the steps of evidence-based supervision are not consistently implemented by supervisors, problematic staff performance is much more prevalent. To illustrate, if staff performance expectations are not clearly specified, staff may not perform certain duties because they are unaware of what they should do in respective situations. Staff also may not complete various duties proficiently because they are not sure precisely how to perform the (poorly specified) duties. Additionally, if supervisors do not routinely monitor staff performance, they will have difficulty determining the precise reasons for problematic performance. Supervisors will subsequently have difficulty responding to problematic performance in a manner to effectively resolve the problems.

The training step of evidence-based supervision is likewise important when considering nonproficient performance. If staff are not effectively trained how to do what is expected, fulfilling daily job responsibilities is almost always problematic. Finally, if quality staff performance is not actively supported by supervisors, then that performance will likely deteriorate and nonproficient work will result.

> **Problematic performance is most likely to be prevented or quickly corrected if job responsibilities have been clearly specified, staff have been well trained to perform their duties, work activities have been routinely monitored, and proficient work activity has been actively supported.**

A Serious Misconception About How to Correct Nonproficient Performance

When considering the prerequisites for corrective supervision, actively supporting quality work warrants special attention. Routinely supporting proficient staff performance enhances the effectiveness of supervisory actions needed to correct nonproficient performance that may occur. When supervisors regularly support proficient performance, corrective action that is taken by supervisors appears in clear contrast to their usual supportive actions. The corrective action tends to stand out for staff and evokes serious staff attention directed to improving the designated performance.

The importance of routinely supporting quality work on supervisor success in correcting nonproficient performance when necessary cannot be overemphasized. Such importance is highlighted when considering a serious misconception about supervision in general. Specifically, good supervision is often equated with persistent punishment of inappropriate or nonproficient staff work. There is a rather common view that strong supervisors are known for their frequent and harsh response to inadequate staff performance; the supervisors have a reputation for frequently imposing seriously negative sanctions for problematic performance.

There are of course times when supervisors should impose negative sanctions for staff performance. However, *such actions should be the exception and not the rule.* When the steps of evidence-based supervision are routinely practiced, negative sanctions represent exceptions to a supervisor's regular actions with staff. The sanctions also usually do not have to be severe to be effective. In contrast, when a supervisor routinely takes negative actions with staff, the actions almost always have to become progressively more severe to improve staff performance.

The detrimental effects of supervising with a predominantly negative focus have been discussed previously. To review briefly, there are three most serious effects. First, staff tend to decrease their work motivation and do only what is necessary to avoid the wrath of the supervisor. Staff do little beyond what is minimally necessary because in essence, they realize the more they do the more likely it is the supervisor will find something wrong with what they are doing. Second, because there is little recognition for quality performance, staff motivation to perform in a quality manner is diminished. Third, frequent negative sanctions by a supervisor seriously decrease staff enjoyment with their work and further reduce motivation to work diligently and proficiently.

There is also a more global effect of a predominantly negative supervisory style. When staff receive frequent criticism and other negative sanctions from their supervisor, *workplace withdrawal* increases. Workplace withdrawal refers to staff avoiding their jobs. The most specific and serious examples are frequent absenteeism among staff and high rates of staff turnover.

The research underlying evidence-based supervision was initiated in large part due to recognition of problems with supervisory styles that focus on punishing unacceptable performance. The research has resulted in effective strategies for supervisors to correct nonproficient performance *without* the serious problems associated with predominantly negative supervisory approaches. Again, the first consideration in this regard is to ensure the other steps of evidence-based supervision are routinely practiced.

> **Routinely practicing the steps of evidence-based supervision reduces a supervisor's need to take severely punitive actions to resolve problems with staff performance.**

Common Reasons for Nonproficient Staff Performance and Supervisor Corrective Actions

Reasons for nonproficient and otherwise problematic staff performance vary widely across agencies and staff. Supervisors have to be astute in assessing the various reasons in order to determine appropriate corrective action. However, there are also four reasons for problems with staff performance that are most prevalent. These include lack of skills to perform respective duties, insufficient resources or time, incapability of performing certain duties, and lack of motivation to complete work tasks in a quality manner.

Lack of Skills to Perform Job Duties

One relatively common reason for nonproficient performance is staff do not have the skills to perform certain job tasks. This typically occurs because staff have not been trained in the skills to perform the tasks, or the training they received was not effective. In other cases, staff may have been effectively trained in designated work skills but over time have forgotten how to perform the duty of concern. The latter situation typically occurs with duties that staff perform infrequently such as monthly or every few months.

When nonproficient performance is due to lack of skills on the part of staff, the appropriate supervisor action is to provide effective training. As discussed in detail in **Chapter 4**, effective training involves performance- and competency-based training strategies. If staff have not received previous training, then usually the entire protocol of evidence-based training should be implemented by supervisors in a formal training session. Supervisors should hold a meeting with staff and describe the skills to complete the respective work duty, provide a written summary of the skills, demonstrate the skills, and have staff practice the skills either on the job or in role plays. Feedback from the supervisor should then follow staff practice of the work skills until they demonstrate competence.

If staff received previous training but the training was not totally effective or they have forgotten how to perform various aspects of a task, then often the training only needs to be directed to specific aspects (versus all the skills necessary to perform the duty). Typically this type of training can be conducted informally within the staff workplace. The supervisor summarizes what needs to be done differently, demonstrates the target skills, and then observes as staff perform the task. Feedback is then provided and the process continued if need be until staff are observed to perform the task proficiently.

Lack of Resources to Perform Job Duties

Another relatively common reason for nonproficient staff performance is that staff lack the resources to complete a job task appropriately. For example, a common duty expected of staff in residential centers for adults with severe disabilities is to promote age-appropriate leisure activities during the evening. To successfully involve consumers in desired leisure activities, an adequate supply of leisure materials is usually necessary. That is, the consumers must have something with which to engage in an activity. A resource problem that occurs in many of these settings is that there is an insufficient supply of leisure materials. It is also rather common that the materials that are available are intended for use by children and not adults, so it is difficult to promote age-appropriate leisure activities.

The apparent corrective action for supervisors in the situation just illustrated is to ensure an adequate supply of age-appropriate materials. It should also be noted though that providing sufficient materials can be difficult for supervisors at times. Often supervisors have inadequate budgets for securing necessary materials or have no control over the funds for procuring materials. In these cases, the problem of insufficiently promoting leisure activity among consumers should not be viewed as a staff performance issue—it is a resource issue. Staff cannot be expected to perform their duties in a quality manner if they lack materials necessary to complete job tasks. Supervisors must persist in securing the needed resources or change job expectations of staff.

Sometimes the issue concerning lack of resources to perform a duty proficiently pertains not to materials but to staff time; there is insufficient time for staff to complete a given duty in the appropriate manner. To illustrate, a job expectation of staff may be to embed teaching within early morning routines associated with assisting consumers prior to leaving a group home to go to a day program site. However, because there is often a limited time period to get ready to leave the home in the early morning, staff must do tasks for consumers in order to get everything accomplished on time—it generally takes more time initially to teach consumers how to perform certain activities relative to doing the tasks for them. In such a case, there realistically is not enough time allotted in the early morning to allow staff to embed teaching within the preparatory routine.

When lack of desired staff performance is due to insufficient time to perform a duty appropriately, supervisors must reconsider the scheduled routine to adjust time allotments for the duty to be performed. This can be a difficult consideration at times for supervisors. The difficulty is due to adequately knowing if there is truly insufficient time versus staff reporting there is not enough time when the allotted time is actually sufficient. Some staff will report they cannot complete certain duties appropriately due to lack of time when the real reason is those staff do not want to exert the effort to complete the duties (see later chapter section on **Lack of Staff Motivation**).

Having an awareness of when duties are not performed due to a reported lack of time versus insufficient staff motivation is another reason supervisors should carefully specify work duties and routinely monitor their fulfillment. When supervisors have specified how to perform a given job task and routinely monitored staff performance associated with the task, they will usually know whether sufficient time exists to complete the task. Such awareness can then facilitate correction of the problem by either adjusting the work activity schedule or acting to better motivate staff, respectively.

> **Lack of proficient staff work due to insufficient materials or time to complete a task satisfactorily is not a staff performance problem; it is a resource or scheduling problem that a supervisor needs to resolve.**

INCAPABILITY OF PERFORMING DUTIES

The jobs of direct support staff in some agencies can be rather physical in nature. To illustrate, staff may have to lift and transfer clients who are nonambulatory, engage in strenuous physical interactions with clients to prevent injury due to highly aggressive or self-injurious behavior, or be required to be on their feet for long periods of time. In certain cases, some staff may not be physically able to perform these types of tasks appropriately due to health-related conditions (e.g., weight issues, previous injuries).

Physical incapability to perform certain duties represents another reason for lack of proficient staff performance. This reason is not as prevalent as lack of staff skills or resources to perform duties proficiently, but nevertheless represents a situation supervisors are likely to encounter from time to time. When a supervisor becomes aware that certain staff cannot physically perform aspects of their job duties, there are usually two corrective actions a supervisor can implement. The most apparent action is to change the job of respective staff to reduce or eliminate the physical demands that the staff cannot perform through various workplace accommodations. In some cases, staff have to be reassigned to another job within the agency, such as one that involves working with clients who do not require the types of physical demands that the staff cannot perform.

The second corrective action is to remove the staff person from the agency's work force, which usually requires the involvement of upper management. Such action is typically the only recourse when there are no jobs in an agency to which a staff person could be reassigned that do not involve the physical demands that pose problems for the individual. Removing a staff person from the work force can be difficult for supervisors because it means they must discontinue an individual's employment. Nonetheless it is a task supervisors must be willing to perform.

In some cases, supervisors avoid actions that result in discontinuing a staff person's employment in an agency because of their concern for the individual's welfare. However, there are serious detriments of not taking necessary action in this regard. In particular, if a staff person cannot physically perform aspects of the job then those aspects will be unfulfilled and client services will not be provided appropriately. Maintaining the staff person also can place the individual at risk of personal harm and potentially place clients at risk as well (e.g., when a staff person cannot safely lift or transfer a nonambulatory client). Hence, all reasonable attempts should be made to alter the job demands or make other accommodations to overcome the physical challenges, or find another job for the staff person within the agency. When such attempts fail though, a supervisor is left with no choice but to act to terminate the individual's employment in accordance with relevant agency policies.

Incapability to perform a job can also be due to more mental issues than physical limitations. For example, some staff may not be able to read proficiently to perform some tasks. Other staff may not be able to acquire certain job skills despite repeated training efforts of supervisors. Ideally, these limitations of staff would become apparent during the initial screening process when they apply for a direct support position such that they would not be hired within the agency. However, experienced supervisors are usually aware that the initial screening process does not always function in this manner.

When it becomes apparent that staff lack certain skills that are critical to the job (e.g., reading skills in some cases), or fail to acquire necessary skills despite repeated training sessions, a supervisor must implement the same corrective actions as just described with physical incapability of performing job duties. The corrective actions can be difficult for supervisors for the same reasons as the difficulty faced with physical limitations to performing a job. Nonetheless, actions must still be implemented—again for the same reasons why corrective action is needed due to physical limitations.

> **Corrective action due to staff incapability to perform a job can be especially difficult and unpleasant for a supervisor, but nevertheless must be carried out for the welfare of all staff and agency consumers.**

Lack of Motivation

The reasons for nonproficient staff performance discussed to this point are relevant in almost every human service agency from time to time. However, by far the most common reason for problematic performance is due to one primary factor: lack of sufficient staff motivation to exert the time and effort to perform their work proficiently. That is, staff have the necessary work skills as well as the time, resources, and capability to engage in quality work but are essentially unmotivated to do so on a consistent basis. Every supervisor will likely face periodic problems with lack of work motivation among some staff.

A considerable amount of attention has been devoted to reasons for insufficient work motivation among staff within the professional literature and human service agencies. Lack of appropriate motivation has been considered, for example, as a result of a poor labor pool in some situations for finding motivated workers to employ, lack of an acceptable work ethic among some staff, and the working conditions within respective agencies. Sometimes these explanations are relevant and accurate and sometimes they are not. Regardless of the relative appropriateness of the explanations, it is still a supervisor's job to find ways to motivate staff to perform their job duties appropriately.

As with all aspects of a supervisor's job, taking action to overcome insufficient work motivation among staff is most likely to be effective if the action is evidence-based. An evidence-based approach to overcoming lack of work motivation is essentially a two-step process, with each step involving multiple components. The first step is to provide *performance feedback*. The second step, which is necessary when the first step is not effective, is to initiate *disciplinary action*.

Providing Feedback to Overcome Insufficient Work Motivation. An evidence-based means of providing feedback was discussed in-depth in **Chapter 6**. Although the focus was on using feedback to support proficient performance, the same protocol for providing feedback is relevant for correcting nonproficient performance due to lack of staff motivation. The steps constituting the protocol are presented below.

EVIDENCE-BASED FEEDBACK PROTOCOL

Step 1. **Begin feedback with a positive or empathetic statement.**

Step 2. **Specify what staff performed correctly.**

Step 3. **Specify what staff performed incorrectly if applicable.**

Step 4. **Specify what staff need to do to correct the work behavior identified in Step 3.**

Step 5. **Solicit questions from staff about the information provided.**

Step 6. **Inform staff about subsequent supervisory actions regarding the target work behavior.**

Step 7. **End feedback with a positive or empathetic statement.**

For correcting nonproficient or otherwise unacceptable staff performance, the key steps of the feedback protocol are **Steps 3** and **4**. These steps specify for the staff person what aspect of a work task was not performed correctly and how the aspect should be performed. To illustrate, in a sheltered workshop a supervisor may observe that a staff person is sitting at a work table with several consumers and periodically instructing consumers at other tables to do their work. The desired performance that has been previously specified in this case is for the staff person to walk around all work tables and provide instructions to consumers privately in close physical proximity to each consumer. The supervisor could pull the staff person aside and indicate that the staff person should not be sitting at a table and instructing consumers at other tables (**Step 3**). The supervisor could further instruct the staff person to walk around each table and talk to consumers by approaching them individually to provide necessary instructions (**Step 4**).

When correcting staff performance with feedback, it is important to use all the steps of the feedback protocol and not just **Steps 3** and **4** that pertain specifically to incorrect work behavior. This is especially the case with **Step 2** that specifies what the staff person performed correctly. In the illustration just referred to, this may involve an initial statement such as "You were doing a nice job observing the consumers' work and providing instruction when needed to promote their continued work; that is important to do.".

Informing staff about some aspect of their performance that they performed well when correcting other aspects of performance is important for several reasons (again see **Chapter 6** for more detailed discussion). One reason is that if the feedback focuses only on the incorrect performance of staff, the feedback is entirely negative in nature. Staff may inaccurately consider that the supervisor is being overly critical or perhaps "picking on" them unfairly. In contrast, by including explicit information about related work behavior that staff performed well, the feedback will usually not be seen as overly critical and unfairly presented.

Another reason for specifically commending some aspect of staff work performance is that the overall feedback session is generally viewed as more pleasant by staff (which is further enhanced by **Steps 1** and **7** of the feedback protocol that involve beginning and ending the feedback session on a positive note). Commending work performed appropriately also has the added benefit of supporting staff in continuing to perform those aspects of a task in a proficient manner.

A third reason for providing positive feedback on proficient performance when correcting nonproficient performance relates to future actions a supervisor may need to take to improve work activities. Sometimes feedback alone will not be sufficient to overcome lack of motivation among some staff to perform their work appropriately. As indicated in the next section, more serious steps subsequently may be needed to bring about improvement in staff behavior through formal disciplinary action. When disciplinary action is taken, many staff respond quite defensively or in an otherwise negative manner.

Sometimes the negative effect of disciplinary action causes staff to retaliate toward the supervisor. Some staff may complain, for example, that the supervisor is harassing them. However, if the supervisor has consistently commended good performance when providing corrective feedback about unacceptable performance, complaints of harassment can be quickly dismissed. It can be pointed out that the supervisor has not been interacting in an overly critical or negative manner with staff; the supervisor has been pointing out both the good and bad aspects of staff work. This process shows that it is not staff per se who are the focus of the negative feedback (i.e., staff are not being harassed) but that the supervisor is simply engaging in the appropriate supervisory activity of letting staff know what is being performed acceptably and unacceptably.

> **When attempting to correct problematic staff performance by providing feedback, supervisors should not only specify what is not being performed appropriately but also what performance aspects have been performed correctly.**

Again, providing feedback is the first step a supervisor should take to improve nonproficient performance due to lack of staff motivation. In many if not most cases, staff performance will improve if feedback is provided in the manner described—although it may take repeated presentations of feedback across several days. If, however, the performance of concern does not improve after three or four feedback sessions, then a supervisor must take more significant steps to improve the performance. Such steps usually involve *disciplinary action.*

Taking Disciplinary Action to Improve Nonproficient Staff Performance Due to Lack of Motivation. Disciplinary action represents one of the most unpleasant duties of a supervisor. It involves imposing punitive sanctions with staff and as such, usually has a negative effect on their quality of work life. Nevertheless, if unacceptable staff performance exists despite repeated feedback sessions (as well as implementation of the other components of evidence-based supervision), it is a supervisor's responsibility to take more severe action to solve the performance problems.

Essentially every human service agency has a policy regarding when and how to use disciplinary action. Usually the policies follow a less-to-more severe continuum. Disciplinary action is first implemented because of a staff person's problematic performance with a relatively mild punitive sanction, such as a formal counseling session that is documented in the staff member's personnel file. If the problematic work behavior does not improve, then more severe action is taken with, for example, a written warning. This process continues if necessary with the final, most severe action of terminating the staff person's employment with the agency.

Most disciplinary action policies also have a provision for taking punitive action with staff on a one- or two-time basis. This process occurs for highly unacceptable work behavior such as sleeping on the job, client abuse, use of illegal drugs or alcohol on the job, or stealing agency property. In these cases, disciplinary action involves an immediate suspension from employment, followed by job termination if the behavior occurs again, or immediate job termination.

Supervisors typically must be prepared to use disciplinary action in the less-to-more severe nature and the one- or two-step manner. The primary concern here is with the former process, as that is what is usually required with performance problems due to lack of sufficient motivation among staff. However, the issues to be discussed for effectively using disciplinary action generally apply to both ways of invoking such action.

The importance of using disciplinary action to suspend or fire a staff person for highly unacceptable behavior in the workplace is generally well acknowledged within human service agencies. In contrast, using disciplinary action to improve nonproficient performance of a less severe nature is not so well acknowledged or practiced. There is a common misconception that staff can only be fired for the most egregious forms of work behavior, such as client abuse and other major work infractions. This view is particularly prevalent in government agencies such as state-operated residential facilities.

In many government agencies, nonproficient performance that is not as severe as that warranting immediate suspension or termination is viewed as something supervisors should strive to improve but unlikely to result in staff being fired. In these settings, staff are rarely terminated due, for example, to consistently poor teaching of clients or inconsistent implementation of behavior support plans of clients. However, these types of nonproficient performance can have highly detrimental effects on consumer welfare and should not be tolerated by supervisors.

A multitude of reasons are offered across various agencies why different types of nonproficient work behavior are unlikely to result in job termination. Many of the reasons involve inaccurate interpretation of government-based regulations regarding workplace behavior that warrants job termination. Most disciplinary action policies, including those in government agencies, *do* allow for firing of staff because of generally poor performance, as well as more egregious behavior. The real reason the former performance problems usually do not result in job termination is supervisors and agency executives do not want to exert the time and effort required to follow through with disciplinary action. Relatedly, supervisors and executives do not want to experience the unpleasantness usually associated with terminating a staff person's job.

The time, effort, and unpleasantness involved in proceeding through the less-to-more severe disciplinary action process to eventually fire a staff person are a real phenomenon. Again though, this process is necessary at times and supervisors must be willing to terminate a staff person's job if all other attempts to improve performance have failed. The focus should not be on the difficulties associated with using disciplinary action to fire a staff person for nonproficient performance of a recurring nature; the focus should be on ensuring that the process is used appropriately and effectively—in this case to remove the staff person from the agency.

There are several key considerations for effectively using disciplinary action when staff repeatedly perform work duties nonproficiently due to lack of motivation. The first consideration is the same as when using corrective supervision procedures in general: the previously discussed steps of evidence-based supervision are necessary prerequisites for effective use of disciplinary action. Formal disciplinary action should not be implemented if performance expectations have not been clearly specified for staff, staff have not been effectively trained in their work duties, staff performance has not been routinely monitored, or active support has not been provided for proficient work behavior. When these supervisory procedures have been followed though, if disciplinary action is necessary it can usually be carried out effectively and at least relatively efficiently.

> **Formal disciplinary action should not be considered for nonproficient performance due to lack of staff motivation unless the other components of evidence-based supervision have been practiced by a supervisor.**

The second consideration for effectively using disciplinary action pertains to agency policies regarding how such action should be implemented. Supervisors must become astutely aware of what the policies involve regarding when and how disciplinary action should be applied. Likewise, supervisors must then adhere to all policy requirements.

When repeated, nonproficient performance occurs due to lack of staff motivation, the goal of using disciplinary action is two-fold. The first goal is to improve the performance of concern. The second goal is to remove the staff person from the agency's employment if the first goal is not met. If agency policies for using disciplinary action are not followed, then it is likely neither of these goals will be met.

The most detrimental effect of not following relevant agency policies on supervisor success in meeting the goals of disciplinary action is that whatever action supervisors take will be overturned or dismissed. Receiving disciplinary action is an unpleasant experience for staff. Many staff will retaliate toward the action because they believe it is unfair or inappropriate, or simply because they do not want the action recorded in their personnel file (even if they are aware that their work performance has been lacking). If supervisors have not followed appropriate disciplinary action policies, it is likely staff will be able to have the action negated or removed by agency executives or personnel officers. The end result is that any potential effect on improving the performance of concern will be negated. Similarly, if a staff person's employment has been terminated and the person challenges the action, it is likely the individual will be reinstated in the agency if appropriate polices were not followed in the termination process.

The effect of a supervisor's disciplinary action being overturned by executives or otherwise negated not only defeats the purpose of disciplinary action, it impedes the supervisor's future use of disciplinary action. Staff will become aware that even though receiving disciplinary action is not pleasant, it will likely be negated if they challenge it. Hence, when the supervisor implements disciplinary action at a future time, staff realize it is only a temporary inconvenience and they continue their (nonproficient) work as usual.

Supervisors must be knowledgeable about, and adhere to, agency policies regarding use of disciplinary action for nonproficient staff performance.

A third consideration when using disciplinary action to resolve problems with staff performance is that supervisors should inform agency executives *prior to* taking such action. Informing executives about forthcoming disciplinary action, and the documented reasons why such action is needed, helps to obtain management support for the action. Most importantly, it reduces the likelihood that upper management may overturn or negate the action.

If supervisors do not inform their superiors before taking disciplinary action, often the superiors become aware of the action when disgruntled staff complain to the superiors. In turn, the executives may form inaccurate perceptions regarding the appropriateness of the disciplinary action taken by supervisors and act to have it negated. This situation does not represent appropriate management response, because executives have not taken the time to obtain all relevant information. That is, the executives only consider information presented by staff recipients of the action, and not the performance problems observed by supervisors regarding why disciplinary action is needed. Nevertheless, the situation occurs in many agencies and all the problems with disciplinary action being overturned as discussed previously are likely to result.

> **Supervisors should inform agency executives *prior to* taking disciplinary action with problematic staff performance.**

The fourth consideration pertains to two common effects of disciplinary action. Supervisors should be aware of, and prepared for, both short- and long-term effects. The short-term effects can be rather troublesome for supervisors. Whenever serious disciplinary action is taken, such as suspension or job termination, there is a common reaction among a supervisor's staff contingent. Staff often will have empathy for the staff recipient of the punitive action, and believe the supervisor acted too harshly in taking the action with the staff person.

A result of staff reacting in the manner just described is that they view the responsible supervisor in a negative light. The supervisor will be the focus of staff complaints and related negative comments. This situation can add a significant degree of unpleasantness to the supervisor's job. Fortunately however, such a reaction can be temporary.

The negative reaction of staff to having one of their colleagues receive serious disciplinary action is almost always short-lived if the action stands in clear contrast to usual supervisory action as described previously. It will usually be readily apparent to staff that the punitive action represents unusual activity on the part of the supervisor. It will likewise be apparent that the reason for the disciplinary action is failure of the respective staff person to respond to more typical, supportive supervisor actions. In this regard, staff are typically well aware when one of their peers is not performing appropriately on the job.

Over time staff tend to develop respect for supervisors who will take significant action to improve recurring performance problems of a given staff person and if need be, remove the staff person from the agency's employment. The respect staff develop represents the long-term effect of appropriate use of disciplinary action by a supervisor. Such respect occurs in part because when a staff person is not performing job duties appropriately, it makes the job of the remaining staff more difficult. The latter staff essentially have to work extra to perform the work that their peer is not completing. Hence, many staff actually want supervisors to take action with a staff member who is repeatedly performing inappropriately. Most staff also understand that it is a supervisor's job to remediate problematic performance issues and expect supervisors to fulfill this supervisory responsibility.

In contrast, when supervisors do not act to improve recurrent performance problems of a given staff person, other staff have to continue working more diligently due to incomplete or unsatisfactory work of their peer. In addition, staff hold supervisors responsible for their extra work efforts. Staff are aware that supervisors are not doing their jobs in terms of correcting inappropriate work activities. The end result in such a situation is staff lose respect for their supervisor.

The essential point is supervisors should be aware that many staff may be displeased when disciplinary action is initially taken. Supervisors should likewise be aware that such displeasure will be short-lived if they routinely support proficient work and use disciplinary action only when all other actions have failed to resolve recurring performance problems. Using disciplinary action in this manner can enhance staff respect for supervisors.

The final consideration for using disciplinary action to resolve recurring performance problems due to lack of staff motivation has been referred to with the previously noted considerations: disciplinary action should be considered a *default* supervisory strategy. Disciplinary action is considered as a default strategy because it is relied on only when all other, evidence-based supervisory procedures have failed to correct the performance problems. It is the last thing a supervisor should do to resolve problematic performance.

As a default supervisory strategy, disciplinary action should not be a routine activity of supervisors. If supervisors are using disciplinary action frequently, then something is wrong with their overall supervisory approach. Usually this means that one or more of the other component strategies of evidence-based supervision are not being practiced sufficiently frequently or effectively by supervisors. Frequent use of disciplinary action results in all of the problems previously discussed with predominantly punitive supervisory styles. Such use also means that ongoing supervision is not being successful and serious changes are warranted in how supervisors are attempting to fulfill their performance responsibilities.

> **Use of disciplinary action with recurring performance problems due to insufficient staff motivation should be the *default* supervisory strategy; it should only be used when the other steps of evidence-based supervision have been consistently practiced but have failed to resolve the performance problems.**

PERFORMANCE PROBLEMS DUE TO REASONS OUTSIDE OF THE WORKPLACE

To this point, the discussion on correcting nonproficient work activities among staff has focused on reasons for problematic performance within the workplace. There are also reasons some staff have difficulty meeting their performance expectations that are due to factors outside of the job. There are many factors that can exist independent of the job that negatively affect performance on the job. For example, many direct support staff work one or more jobs in addition to their job within a supervisor's agency. Working several jobs can result in staff fatigue that affects their job performance. Staff also may have difficult marital or familial issues that frequently require their presence at home or elsewhere such that they have significant job absenteeism.

When nonproficient job performance is due to reasons beyond the immediate workplace, supervisors are faced with a difficult issue. In particular, supervisors are likely to have no control over the reasons for the problematic performance. Additionally, it can be inappropriate for supervisors to become involved in the personal activities of staff that occur outside of the workplace, which would be necessary to help resolve the issues.

Personal issues of staff outside of the workplace that affect job performance can also be difficult for supervisors because they have empathy for affected staff. Supervisors may be aware, for example, that certain staff want to do their jobs well but the personal issues present challenges that make it exceedingly difficult to perform their work appropriately. Nevertheless, supervisors are responsible for ensuring proficient staff performance on the job so that consumers receive the quality supports and services they deserve; supervisors must still act to improve nonproficient work performance.

When performance problems appear to be due to staff issues beyond the workplace, the generally recommended supervisory action is to focus on what happens on the job. Supervisors should use the steps of evidence-based supervision, including disciplinary action if needed, to correct whatever problems occur *on the job*. Issues that staff face separate from the job basically are beyond the responsibility of the supervisor to address. This can be a difficult approach for supervisors who have sincere concern about the welfare of their staff, but is typically the most advisable course of action. Supervisors can acknowledge their concerns with staff about personal issues affecting work performance, but should also acknowledge that they have the primary responsibility to ensure the job gets done and agency clients are well served.

Chapter Summary: Key Points

1. *A basic prerequisite for effectively correcting recurring problems with staff performance is a supervisor's routine implementation of all the component steps of evidence-based supervision.*

2. Routinely practicing the steps of evidence-based supervision, and especially supportive supervisory strategies, reduces a supervisor's need to take severely punitive actions to resolve problems with staff performance.

3. Common reasons for nonproficient staff performance and corrective supervisory actions include: (1) lack of skills to perform job duties—provide performance- and competency-based training, (2) lack of resources to perform duties—secure resources or alter job expectations, (3) physical or mental inability to perform duties—staff job reassignment or termination, (4) lack of motivation—provide feedback and if needed, disciplinary action.

4. The most pervasive reason for recurring performance problems among staff is lack of sufficient work motivation.

5. Effective use of disciplinary action requires: (1) consistent implementation of all steps of evidence-based supervision, (2) adherence to agency policies, (3) informing agency executives prior to implementing disciplinary action, (4) supervisor awareness of the short- and long-term effects of severe disciplinary action, and (5) reliance on disciplinary action as the default supervisory procedure.

CHAPTER 9

PROMOTING STAFF ENJOYMENT: MAKING DISLIKED WORK TASKS MORE ENJOYABLE TO PERFORM

Throughout preceding chapters a number of ways supervisors can promote staff enjoyment with their work have been described. Routine provision of positive feedback has been particularly emphasized as a readily available, effective means to help staff feel good about their work and enhance work enjoyment. Interacting with staff in pleasant and socially courteous ways has likewise been stressed, along with periodically providing special recognition for commendable performance. More specific ways to promote work enjoyment also have been presented in regard to implementation of each step of the evidence-based supervisory protocol.

Another way supervisors can increase staff enjoyment with their work pertains more specifically to certain work tasks that staff are expected to perform. Direct support jobs, like any jobs, typically include some work tasks that are not very enjoyable to do—or at least are less preferred relative to other job duties. In many cases supervisors can enhance staff work enjoyment by actively striving to make the most disliked job tasks more desirable to perform.

It has also been discussed in preceding chapters that from an overall perspective, workplace enjoyment can be enhanced by increasing the good things associated with staffs' work situation and decreasing the bad things. When supervisors can make highly disliked tasks more pleasant to perform, they are in essence turning a bad thing into a good thing for staff (or at least reducing the negative features of a bad thing). The purpose of this chapter is to describe a step-wise process for supervisors to make undesired work tasks more enjoyable for staff.

The process to be described is the *Task Enjoyment Motivation Protocol*, or *TEMP*. The *TEMP* process, like other procedures discussed throughout this text, has been evaluated through research in the human services to demonstrate its effectiveness—in this case for enhancing workplace enjoyment among staff. Before describing specific procedures constituting the *TEMP* process though, several general considerations warrant attention for making job tasks more enjoyable for staff.

GENERAL CONSIDERATIONS FOR MAKING WORK TASKS MORE ENJOYABLE FOR STAFF TO PERFORM

A primary consideration for making work tasks more enjoyable for staff pertains to a main premise underlying successful supervision: enhancing staff enjoyment should be addressed in conjunction with promoting quality work performance of staff. Again, successful supervision involves supervisors working actively to ensure staff work diligently and proficiently *and* to help staff enjoy their work. Working to increase staff work enjoyment without promoting quality work does not represent effective supervision.

The *TEMP* process for making highly disliked work tasks more enjoyable for staff was developed in situations in which staff were performing specific job tasks proficiently. However, it was apparent that staff were not particularly enjoying their work associated with the tasks. When supervisors implemented steps of the *TEMP* process, staff continued to perform the designated duties in a proficient manner. Evidence likewise indicated staff enjoyed performing those tasks more after the *TEMP* process was carried out. In this manner, the *TEMP* approach fulfilled the essence of supervision in terms of enhancing work enjoyment *and* promoting quality work.

> **Making disliked work tasks more enjoyable for staff to perform should be undertaken by supervisors with the intent of also ensuring the tasks are performed in a quality manner.**

Another general consideration for making work tasks more enjoyable to perform pertains to the training part of evidence-based supervision. In some cases staff do not like a given work task because they do not feel competent performing the task; they have not been effectively trained how to perform that aspect of their job. Because staff are not sure how to complete the task in the correct manner, they tend to be uncomfortable when expected to perform the task.

Staff dislike of a work task due to being unsure of their competence in performing the task is most common in two situations. The first situation is with newly employed staff who are assigned certain duties before they have had opportunities to be trained in the skills to perform the duties. This situation occurs frequently in residential settings because direct support staff usually are needed quickly in the workplace once hired to maintain necessary staff-to-consumer ratios. Hence, new staff are expected to work with consumers before completing necessary training programs. Because new staff usually have no experience working with people who have disabilities, the staff are often anxious regarding how to provide various supports and services. Being unsure how to perform certain duties increases their anxiety and makes performing the tasks particularly unpleasant.

The second situation in which staff frequently dislike work tasks due to concerns over their competence is when they are expected to perform certain duties that potentially place consumers at risk of harm. A common example is when a staff person is initially assigned to feed a consumer with multiple disabilities who cannot eat independently and has physical challenges that result in frequent choking. Feeding someone with such challenges can be very anxiety arousing for staff because they witness the choking as they feed the individual and are afraid they might harm the person.

The best way to prevent staff anxiety and unpleasantness when being expected to perform duties for which they feel unprepared is to ensure they are very well trained in the performance skills of concern. In this regard, it is critical that the training includes the on-the-job component discussed in **Chapter 4**. The on-the-job component is needed not only to ensure the training is effective as discussed previously, but also to allow the staff trainer (e.g., supervisor) to respond to concerns that staff may have as they begin performing the target duty. If such concerns are not addressed, and particularly if the concerns relate to issues associated with immediate consumer welfare such as with the feeding example just illustrated, staff will experience an unnecessary amount of anxiety and unpleasantness with the task.

Ensuring staff are well trained to perform duties in which consumers may be at risk of harm, and provided with close supervision once they initially perform the duties, cannot be overemphasized. As just indicated such training and supervision are critical for ensuring staff are well versed in the necessary work skills and do not feel anxious performing them, and consumers are adequately protected from harm. Additionally, evidence has indicated that one of the key reasons some staff resign from human service agencies is that they never overcome the anxiety and concern with performing these types of duties. Consequently, one means of reducing at least some of the turnover among direct support staff that occurs in many agencies is to ensure new staff are especially well trained and supervised in these particular duties.

> **When staff have not been well trained to perform a job task they often feel uncomfortable or anxious when expected to complete the task, which results in their dislike of the task.**

A third consideration for generally making work tasks more enjoyable to perform is somewhat indirect in nature. Specifically, sometimes supervisors can determine that certain tasks staff dislike are not really necessary to perform. The unpleasantness associated with completing the task can be eliminated simply by discontinuing the task requirements. This is often the case with various types of documentation duties expected of staff.

Sometimes staff are required to provide various types of written documentation that over time are no longer used (or needed) within an agency. However, the paper work assignments of staff continue to exist. As noted previously with documentation duties expected of supervisors, if various types of documentation required of staff are not routinely used for clearly apparent purposes within an agency, such requirements should be discontinued.

Supervisors should periodically review various recordkeeping requirements of staff and determine if the resulting information is still needed. If not, staff should be informed that the duties associated with the recordkeeping are no longer necessary. Staff are often very appreciative of supervisors who stay knowledgeable about their job duties and relieve them of respective duties that become unnecessary. This situation is particularly relevant when staff are aware that nobody is really attending to their documentation and their recordkeeping appears to be serving no functional purpose in terms of agency supports and services.

A fourth and related consideration for making work tasks more enjoyable to perform pertains to the time and effort required of staff to complete certain job duties. Sometimes supervisors can make work tasks more desirable for staff by reducing the time and effort involved in performing the tasks, yet maintaining the proficiency with which the duties are completed. It is general human nature to dislike tasks that are more effortful to complete relative to tasks that are less effortful.

A relatively common example of work tasks that can be altered to reduce staff time and effort also involves recordkeeping or documentation duties. Again, direct support staff frequently have to complete various types of paper work, such as collecting data on challenging behavior of consumers, describing events surrounding consumer accidents or unusual incidents, and summarizing progress on teaching programs. For every documentation duty required of staff, supervisors should review how the documentation is expected to be completed. Such review should focus on how the documentation can be streamlined for staff such that the amount of actual writing required is as minimal as possible, while still providing the necessary information.

The most apparent way to minimize staff time and effort to provide a necessary type of documentation is to use prepared forms that involve staff checking specified boxes or spaces on the forms to provide answers to questions. Providing areas on the forms to answer questions by simply providing a checkmark should be used in lieu of requiring staff to write out narrative responses to the questions whenever possible. For example, instead of a general question pertaining to an unusual incident such as "What time and place did the incident occur?", the form could have prepared times and places such that the staff person only has to check or mark the time and place. The latter process takes less time for the staff person than the former.

The same general process for streamlining completion of various documentation requirements can often be accomplished through computer-based processes. Instead of filling out a paper form by answering questions in a narrative fashion, staff can provide the necessary information by responding to menu-driven questions on the computer screen. Of course this process requires development of a computer format for securing the necessary information (and staff having ready access to a computer). The time to develop the computer format is usually worthwhile in the long run though when considering the subsequent savings in staff time required to complete the necessary documentation.

> **Supervisors should review all documentation required of staff and devise forms or computer formats that minimize the amount of writing required of staff to provide the documentation.**

A final consideration for generally making disliked tasks more desirable for staff relates to an issue also noted previously: staff should be well aware of the *reason* they are required to perform the tasks. Again using the example of documentation requirements, sometimes staff are instructed to complete various types of recordkeeping but are not given a good explanation as to why the documentation is necessary. When staff are required to perform certain duties but they are unaware or unclear as to what purpose the duties serve, it almost always results in staff disliking those duties. Supervisors should always provide an honest and explicit reason why staff are required to complete a given paperwork duty, or any duty.

An Evidence-Based Approach for Making Disliked Work Tasks More Enjoyable to Perform: TEMP

In order for supervisors to make disliked work tasks more enjoyable for staff to perform, the supervisors must know what specific job duties are highly disliked by staff. If supervisors are routinely monitoring staff work performance, and particularly on an informal basis as described in **Chapter 5**, they will usually be well informed regarding specific job duties staff find particularly undesirable. Such information results from the direct observation of staff work activities and the interactions with staff that occur as supervisors provide feedback to staff following the monitoring.

Supervisors can also obtain information regarding job duties that staff find especially unpleasant in a more formal manner. Most notably, supervisors can periodically conduct a scheduled meeting with staff to question what aspects of their duties they find more and less enjoyable to perform. Alternatively, supervisors can periodically develop preference assessment forms and request staff to rate or rank specific job tasks regarding the relative preferences or enjoyment associated with performing each task.

The processes for assessing staff preferences for different work tasks also have a benefit beyond obtaining information about highly disliked work tasks. Specifically, the process often conveys to staff that the supervisor is sincerely concerned about their quality of work life—provided of course that the supervisor follows up the meeting by acting to improve something staff report they do not like. As noted repeatedly already, when staff are aware that their supervisor is truly concerned about their welfare, they tend to respect the supervisor and their enjoyment associated with working for the supervisor is enhanced.

Once supervisors have obtained information from staff regarding identification of a highly disliked work task, the *TEMP* process can be initiated to make the task more enjoyable to perform. The process can be conducted with just one individual staff person who experiences significant displeasure in performing a given task. However, it is usually more efficient from a supervisory perspective if the process is undertaken with a certain job duty that several staff seriously dislike. Regardless of whether the process is implemented with one staff person or a group of staff, it should be conducted in a step-wise fashion. A summary of the basic steps of the process is presented in the following illustration.

SUPERVISORY STEPS CONSTITUTING THE TASK ENJOYMENT MOTIVATION PROTOCOL: TEMP

Step 1: Meet with staff and solicit their opinions about the specific aspects of the job task that make it undesirable to perform.

Step 2: In conjunction with Step 1, solicit and discuss ideas about what can be reasonably changed to make the task more enjoyable to perform.

Step 3: Make as many of the changes identified in Step 2 as realistic, supplemented where possible with the supervisor's ideas for making the task more enjoyable.

Step 4: Meet again with staff to solicit their opinions about how well the changes are working, and obtain additional ideas if necessary about other changes that may be needed.

TEMP STEP 1: IDENTIFY REASONS STAFF DISLIKE PERFORMING A WORK TASK

The first step of the *TEMP* process is to meet with staff for the explicit purpose of obtaining their opinions regarding why performing a certain job task is so disliked. Often, staff will be quite forthcoming and readily offer explanations as to why they dislike performing the task. In other cases, supervisors will need to question staff and otherwise prompt discussion about why they dislike the task.

When supervisors find that they need to prompt staff to discuss what they do not like about the task, a useful approach is to ask questions regarding the most common reasons job duties are often disliked as referred to in preceding sections. For example, supervisors could question whether staff do not feel totally competent in performing the work task, or if the task seems especially effortful or time consuming to complete. Supervisors could also ask if staff do not agree with, or understand, the reason why the task needs to be completed. Usually posing such questions to staff will result in a useful discussion regarding the unpleasantness of the job duty of concern.

TEMP STEP 2: IDENTIFY POTENTIAL WAYS TO ALTER THE WORK TASK

The second step of the *TEMP* process is to solicit staff ideas about how the task can be changed to make it more desirable to perform. As with the first step, often staff are quite forthcoming in expressing ideas about how to change the task. However, supervisors should also be prepared to question and prompt staff to express their ideas. Supervisors should also be prepared to offer their ideas regarding how to make performing the task more enjoyable. Hence, supervisors should prepare for the meeting with staff by thinking about some possible ways to alter the task that can be shared with staff.

Generally, ways to change a work task that is disliked by staff will need to be based on the reason for the dislike. To illustrate, if completing the task is reported to be overly time consuming relative to other, competing duties expected of staff, then ways to streamline performing the task could be considered. In some cases though, neither the staff nor supervisors will have an immediate idea about how to change the task. In the latter cases, supervisors can indicate to staff that they will talk with other supervisors or executive personnel to obtain possibilities for how the task could be altered. Subsequently, supervisors will need to meet with staff again to discuss whatever ideas are generated.

In some situations it can be rather challenging for supervisors to come up with ideas about how to make a job task more desirable to perform, and particularly if staff themselves are not sure how the task can be modified. Supervisors will be best equipped to provide useful ideas in this regard if they are very familiar with the task of concern. Supervisors will usually have the necessary familiarity if they have been actively involved in training relevant work skills to staff and monitoring their performance of the tasks in the manner described in **Chapters 4** and **5**, respectively.

There will also likely be situations from time to time for which there are no reasonable ways to alter a job task to make it more desirable to perform. Supervisors should readily acknowledge when such is the case, but only after they have consulted with other agency personnel about ways to alter the task as noted previously. Although in these situations the ultimate goal of making the task more enjoyable to perform will not be met, the overall *TEMP* process can still be beneficial. In particular, often staff will be appreciative of a supervisor who acknowledges that a given work duty is unpleasant to perform and has actively worked with them to try to reduce the unpleasantness. It can also be beneficial if, upon acknowledging that there is no apparent way to make the task more desirable to perform, the supervisor then initiates the *TEMP* process with another task that staff dislike performing. Hopefully, there will be more success in making the latter task more enjoyable to perform.

TEMP STEP 3: MAKE AS MANY IDENTIFIED TASK CHANGES AS POSSIBLE

Following the meeting with staff, the next step of *TEMP* is for supervisors to make as many of the specified changes with the work task as reasonably possible. Again, usually the changes will need to be based on the identified reasons regarding why performing the task is disliked. In some cases re-training of staff how to perform the task proficiently may be needed because staff feel unprepared to complete the task. In other cases, supervisors may need to find ways to make performing the task less time consuming or effortful. This may involve, for example, preparing forms or computer formats for streamlining completion of documentation duties as discussed earlier. Reducing the time and effort to complete a task also frequently involves rearranging the physical environment, such as by making necessary materials for completing the task more readily accessible to staff so they do not have to spend extra time retrieving the materials.

TEMP STEP 4: MEET AGAIN WITH STAFF TO REVIEW ACTIONS AND DETERMINE ADDITIONAL ACTIONS

After the task changes have been made, the final step of the *TEMP* process is to meet again with staff. The purpose of this meeting is two-fold. The first purpose is to review the changes that have been made with staff and solicit their feedback regarding whether the changes have been successful in making the task more desirable to perform. The second purpose is to solicit staff ideas regarding additional changes that may be needed, based on the feedback staff provide.

Earlier it was noted that in some situations there may be undesired work tasks for which there are no reasonable ways to alter the task that would make it significantly less unpleasant to perform. It was likewise noted that when this situation occurs, it should be discussed with staff. Meeting with staff when it is apparent that it has not been possible to effectively alter an undesired work task also serves two purposes. First, it provides staff with a rationale regarding why the task cannot be changed. In this manner, staff are not left with the impression that their concerns were ignored. Second, as also referred to earlier, it makes staff aware that the supervisor has listened to them and at least tried to resolve their concerns with the particular work task. Although not as successful as actually making the work task nicer to perform, fulfilling these two purposes can have a beneficial impact on staff work enjoyment.

AN EXAMPLE OF HOW TEMP HAS BEEN USED TO MAKE A DISLIKED WORK TASK MORE ENJOYABLE TO PERFORM

An illustration of how the *TEMP* process has been used to make a highly disliked work task more enjoyable pertains to the task of writing monthly progress notes. Most human service agencies require designated staff to complete some type of written summary regarding client progress on various programs, such as those for teaching adaptive skills or reducing challenging behavior. This task was selected because a supervisor had surveyed staff in one unit of a residential facility regarding liked and disliked work tasks, and writing progress notes was reported to be very disliked. The example to be presented involved applying the *TEMP* process with one staff person. However, the same process subsequently was used with other staff in the facility with similar results.

When the supervisor met with the staff person to discuss why writing monthly progress notes was so disliked (**Step 1** of *TEMP*), the staff person indicated that the task required more time to complete than seemed reasonable. Upon further questioning by the supervisor, the staff person indicated that the excessive amount of time was due to frequent interruptions when she was working on the notes each month. The interruptions were due primarily to other staff interacting with her while she was working on the notes in her routine work station.

During the initial meeting, the supervisor and staff person also discussed various ways to reduce the amount of time to complete the progress notes (**Step 2**). It was determined that if the staff person had another place to work on the notes each month that was separate from her usual work station and other staff, the interruptions would likely be avoided. Hence, it was decided that an office space would be provided one day per month for the sole purpose of the staff person completing the progress notes.

The next step of *TEMP* (**Step 3**) involved the supervisor scheduling an office for use solely by the staff person one day per month when progress notes were assigned to be completed. The supervisor located an office that was jointly used by other personnel at different times, and arranged with the latter individuals to free up the office for the designated day. The staff person then began writing her progress notes in the assigned office.

After several months, the supervisor met again with the staff person to review how the new office arrangement was working (**Step 4**). The staff person indicated that interruptions were eliminated and significantly less time was required to complete the progress notes each month relative to the previous arrangement. The staff person also reported that completing the progress notes was no longer her most disliked task, and was even more liked than a number of her other routine duties.

The example just illustrated indicates how the *TEMP* process has been used to have a significant, albeit somewhat circumscribed, effect on one aspect of a staff member's work enjoyment: the staff member's enjoyment with completing one routine work duty was enhanced. In considering the example, it should not be interpreted that the same exact procedures should be used to make progress note writing more desirable for staff in general (nor that writing progress notes is necessarily a highly disliked work task for all staff). However, the same *process* for making a specific work task more desirable to perform can be used with other job duties that are highly disliked by direct support staff. In this regard, one of the beneficial features of the *TEMP* approach is that by its nature, it is individualized across staff and work tasks.

SPECIAL CONSIDERATIONS FOR ADDRESSING HIGHLY DISLIKED WORK TASKS

By addressing common reasons why some work tasks are disliked in general as discussed previously and using the *TEMP* approach with specific work tasks, supervisors can usually reduce the unpleasantness of performing certain duties. There are also some special considerations related to staff dislike of respective work tasks that warrant attention. These include tasks that are disliked due to characteristics of respective clients, supervisor time and effort to use the *TEMP* approach, and disliked tasks that cannot be altered.

WORK-TASK DISLIKE DUE TO CHARACTERISTICS OF INDIVIDUAL CLIENTS

Sometimes the dislike staff experience with certain work tasks pertains to a particular client with whom the tasks are associated. A relatively common example is when staff are working with a client who displays seriously challenging behavior such as aggression. The dislike associated with working with the client often exists because staff have been injured by the client, or are worried about being hurt by the client's aggressive behavior. Staff apprehension, and in the most serious cases actual fear, about working with a given client is not always officially recognized in human service agencies; it is essentially expected that part of the job of direct support staff is to work with clients who have problem behavior. However, staff concerns in this type of situation must be addressed by supervisors because otherwise, staff quality of work life and overall well being on the job can be seriously compromised.

Staff dislike of working with certain clients who engage in harmful behavior should be addressed by supervisors on a case-by-case basis because each situation is usually different. In many cases though, the best action involves ensuring there is an effective treatment plan to prevent or reduce the challenging behavior, and staff have the skills and resources to carry out the plan. It is beyond the scope of this text to describe what constitutes appropriate treatment plans for challenging behavior. Generally however, it is the supervisor's responsibility to be aware of staff concerns about being hurt by a client and to take action to secure an effective treatment intervention by the appropriate clinician. It is also the supervisor's responsibility to inform agency executives about the situation, as resolving the issue usually requires the support of upper management (e.g., to obtain additional staff resources, secure more clinician involvement with a client's treatment plan).

> **If staff have concerns about being harmed when working with certain clients, supervisors *must* work actively to make changes in the workplace to resolve those concerns.**

Focus on *Most Disliked* Work Tasks

To this point, discussion regarding the *TEMP* process has centered on how it can be used to effectively alter disliked work tasks. There is also a practical issue regarding *TEMP* that warrants attention: it often involves relatively considerable time on the part of a supervisor to be successful. The time investment is due in part to having to meet several times with staff. More noticeably however is the time that is frequently required to make designated changes with a given work task. Making specified changes (rearranging the work environment of staff, securing additional materials, developing alternative recordkeeping processes that are more streamlined, etc.) is often rather time consuming for a supervisor.

Because of the amount of supervisor time that is frequently required to implement all steps of the *TEMP* process, it is usually unrealistic for a supervisor to address very many work tasks that staff dislike at a given point in time. This is especially the case when considering that the process should only be used in conjunction with all other evidence-based supervisory procedures necessary to promote quality work. Hence, it is recommended that a supervisor focus use of the *TEMP* approach on a work task that is *most disliked* by several staff. As time permits, the process can later be applied with other work tasks that are less seriously disliked, or disliked by only one staff member.

> **Generally, use of the *TEMP* process should focus on a work task that is the *most disliked* by a group of staff.**

DISLIKED WORK TASKS THAT CANNOT BE CHANGED

In any job situation, there are likely to be some tasks that staff find especially undesirable that cannot be realistically altered without negatively affecting the proficiency with which the tasks are completed. As indicated previously, when the initial steps of the *TEMP* process are undertaken and it becomes apparent that a particularly disliked task cannot be significantly altered, this situation should be directly acknowledged by a supervisor with staff. However, staff work enjoyment may still be enhanced not by changing the actual task itself but by altering staff assignments related to completing the task.

Sometimes a task that is highly disliked by several staff can be assigned in a manner that requires no single staff person to have to complete the task on a frequent basis. For example, a work task that can be disliked by a number of staff pertains to cleaning wheelchairs of clients who are nonambulatory and do not have the physical capacity to clean their wheelchairs themselves. Often with this type of task, staff are expected to do a rather cursory cleaning on a daily basis and a more involved cleaning once or twice per week. The more involved cleaning, which typically represents the most disliked aspect of the task, could be rotated among all staff such that no individual staff person would have to conduct the detailed cleaning every week.

When considering rotating certain disliked tasks among different staff, it is most helpful if a participative management process is used as discussed in **Chapter 3**. Upon acknowledging that a given work task must be completed as it currently exists (i.e., wheelchairs must be cleaned), a supervisor could meet with staff and discuss whether it would be more desirable if the task assignment was rotated across staff at different times. As just indicated, with the wheelchair cleaning task it is likely that staff do not mind performing a light cleaning on a daily basis relative to having to conduct the more intensive cleaning once or twice per week. The latter task could be rotated among staff such that, for example, each staff person had to perform it only once per month even if it meant that they would have to do the intensive cleaning on more wheelchairs on a monthly basis (i.e., to intensively clean wheelchairs that otherwise would have been cleaned by other staff during the given week). As discussed previously, involving staff in decisions affecting their job assignments not only takes advantage of their knowledge about performing respective duties, the participative process itself is usually appreciated by staff.

CHAPTER SUMMARY: KEY POINTS

1. *General considerations for making work tasks more enjoyable for staff to perform include: (1) ensuring quality work is still promoted while making the tasks more enjoyable for staff, (2) ensuring staff are well trained to perform the tasks and feel confident performing them, (3) discontinuing disliked tasks required of staff if the tasks are not really necessary to complete, (4) streamlining tasks where possible to make them less time consuming and effortful to perform and, (5) ensuring staff know the reason each task needs to be performed.*

2. *Steps of the Task Enjoyment Motivation Protocol (TEMP) for making highly disliked work tasks more enjoyable to perform involve: (1) meeting with staff to solicit their opinions about why the task is disliked, (2) obtaining staff ideas about how to change the task, (3) making as many of the specified changes as reasonably possible and, (4) meeting again with staff to solicit their*

feedback about the changes that were made and obtain ideas about additional changes if needed.

3. When staff dislike a task because they are worried about being harmed by a consumer while performing the task, supervisors must be especially active in working to make changes to resolve the concerns.

4. Due to the time and effort often required of a supervisor to use the TEMP approach to make a disliked task more enjoyable for staff to perform, the process should primarily be used with a task that is most disliked by several staff.

5. Sometimes the displeasure associated with performing certain tasks can be reduced by rotating assignments for completing the tasks across different staff.

SECTION III

RESOLVING COMMON PERFORMANCE PROBLEMS

CHAPTER 10

Resolving Common Performance Problems: Overview

Consistent adherence to evidence-based supervisory practices usually results in successful supervision. Evidence-based supervision represents the most tried and tested means of promoting diligent and proficient work performance among direct support staff. Implementing steps of the evidence-based supervisory protocol in ways discussed in preceding chapters also represents an effective means of helping staff enjoy their work.

Evidence-Based Supervisory Protocol: A Review

Step 1: Identify desired consumer outcomes.

Step 2: Specify what staff must do to assist consumers in attaining desired outcomes.

Step 3: Train staff in the performance skills specified in Step 2.

Step 4: Monitor staff performance.

Step 5: Support proficient staff performance.

Step 6: Correct nonproficient staff performance.

Step 7: Continuously evaluate staff performance and consumer outcome attainment.

In essence, the evidence-based supervisory protocol provides a template for how supervisors should go about working with staff. However, this does not mean that effective supervision can be provided in a cookbook fashion. What a supervisor does to affect staff work behavior must take into consideration each respective situation related to a performance area of concern. Component steps of the supervisory protocol should be used as a guide for determining supervisory actions that are relevant in each situation.

The importance of addressing specific situations related to a performance area of concern is most apparent in regard to resolving recurrent problems with staff performance. As emphasized in **Chapter 8**, resolving recurrent problems with staff work behavior must address the *reasons* for the problems. There are also certain types of performance problems that have rather special or idiosyncratic considerations that supervisors must take into account.

It is beyond the scope of this text to discuss all of the special considerations necessary for resolving each performance problem that supervisors may encounter. However, there are certain types of problematic performance that tend to be most common in human service agencies. The following chapters discuss three of the most common performance problems, and specific considerations that warrant supervisor attention to resolve the problems. Respective chapters also illustrate that even though different performance problems involve special considerations, the evidence-based supervisory protocol is still a highly valuable guide for determining how to effectively address the issues of concern.

The three performance problems to be discussed include high absenteeism among support staff (**Chapter 11**), inadequate provision of client-teaching and related therapeutic services (**Chapter 12**), and frequent occurrence of staff nonwork behavior that interferes with completion of job duties (**Chapter 13**). These performance problems were selected because again, they are among the most common types of problematic performance within human service agencies. As will be discussed in the following chapters, each type also has especially serious implications for the quality of supports and services provided to agency consumers.

Before addressing the three common performance problems supervisors are likely to encounter, a basic premise underlying successful supervision in regard to resolving recurrent performance problems warrants highlighting. The premise pertains to *accountability* associated with the job of a human service supervisor.

THE BASIC PREMISE OF SUPERVISOR ACCOUNTABILITY

In most human service agencies, direct support staff are considered accountable for the quality of consumer services they provide and the degree to which consumers attain associated outcomes. If consumers are not learning skills addressed by teaching programs carried out by support staff, for example, then the proficiency with which staff are implementing the programs is usually a concern. Similarly, when consumers do not make progress overcoming challenging behavior, then staff proficiency in carrying out the consumers' behavior support plans is often a relevant issue. Of course, in these situations other factors also must be considered such as the quality of the programs that staff are expected to carry out. Nonetheless, when consumer services are not provided appropriately on a day-to-day basis, the performance of direct support staff almost always warrants increased supervisory attention.

Holding direct support staff accountable for the services they provide is a necessary requirement for ensuring quality services. As indicated in the introductory comments to this text, the most significant determinant of the quality of an agency's supports and services is the proficiency with which support staff fulfill their job responsibilities. However, accountability in this regard should not be limited to the performance of support staff; supervisors must also be accountable.

Supervisor accountability means *supervisors must view the quality of staff performance as a direct reflection of the effectiveness of their supervision.* This premise of supervisor accountability stems directly from the essence of supervision: actively working to improve staff performance that is not adequate and actively working to support performance that is adequate. When staff performance is frequently inadequate, then supervisors are not being effective in improving staff performance. When quality staff performance does not maintain over time, then supervisors are not effectively supporting desired performance.

If supervisors are to have success in working with staff, they must accept the premise that they are accountable for the quality with which staff perform their duties. Supervision can only be considered successful when staff are consistently performing their duties in a proficient manner. When staff do perform proficiently on a consistent basis, which usually means staff also enjoy their work, then supervisors can feel good about their own work accomplishments. If supervisors do not accept responsibility for the quality of work that their staff perform, then they are not likely to be successful. In short, the bottom line indicator of a supervisor's effectiveness is that staff are providing supports and services in a quality manner—and consumers are attaining desired outcomes.

Many supervisors accept the premise of accountability for the performance of staff they supervise. However, many supervisors also view the premise as unfair in some respects. The unfairness is usually based on the view that reasons for problematic staff performance can be outside the supervisors' control. A somewhat common illustration is when, due to agency budget problems, supervisors are unable to hire new staff to fill vacant positions when certain staff leave the agency. As a result, there are not enough direct support staff to adequately fulfill all work duties. This situation frequently results in staff who are present working harder to complete expected duties. Over time the latter staff become frustrated and lose their motivation to work diligently.

As noted in **Chapter 8**, supervisors will encounter situations in which factors beyond their control tend to affect the quality of staff performance. Nonetheless, supervisors still have the responsibility of working actively to promote diligent and proficient staff performance. Supervisors must make sure performance expectations of staff are clearly specified, staff have the skills to perform expected duties, staff performance is regularly monitored, proficient performance is actively supported, and necessary actions are taken to improve performance that is not acceptable. Supervisors should focus on fulfilling these critical responsibilities and not focus on other factors over which they have no control. If supervisors do not consistently perform these basic supervisory actions regardless of other factors affecting staff performance, then in essence they *will not be supervising.*

> **Supervisors must accept responsibility for the quality of work performed by the staff they supervise.**

Avoid the Cop-Out Attitude of Supervision

Sometimes supervisors dismiss the premise of accountability for staff performance by taking a *cop-out* attitude of supervision. The cop-out attitude refers to situations in which supervisors are aware that staff are not performing certain duties appropriately and view the problematic performance as a staff problem. To illustrate, a common scenario is when supervisors report that some staff know what to do on the job but will not do it, or will not do it unless the supervisor is present. The supervisors further report that their staff have no work ethic or are otherwise unmotivated, and there is nothing they can do with those staff.

Some staff frequently do avoid performing assigned duties, and represent significant challenges for supervisors. However, when supervisors respond to these situations by blaming the lack of work performance on the staff themselves, the supervisors are copping out—they are not assuming responsibility for the performance of their staff. Such an attitude leads to ineffective supervision, persistently poor performance of staff, and inadequate supports and services for agency consumers.

Supervisors must avoid adopting the cop-out attitude, even in situations involving very difficult staff. As discussed repeatedly, there are effective, evidence-based ways to motivate and otherwise promote quality staff performance. There are also appropriate ways to remove staff from an agency when their problematic performance does not respond to repeated supervisory actions. As emphasized in **Chapter 8**, removing staff from an agency due to recurrent performance problems represents the last-step, or default, supervisory action.

When supervisors truly accept the basic premise of supervisor accountability, then the poor performance of staff is seen as an indication that the supervisors need to do something differently in their work with staff. Such supervisors do not consider the inadequate performance to be inherent among staff. Rather, they realize that the work environment is not conducive to promoting quality performance. The supervisors then work actively to improve the work situation by addressing the problems for poor work performance.

> **Successful supervisors avoid a cop-out attitude of blaming staff for problematic performance; problems with staff performance are considered a result of ineffective supervision or other issues with the work environment.**

Accepting the premise of supervisor accountability and avoiding a cop-out attitude is a key characteristic of successful supervisors. However, it is also important for supervisors to be aware of certain situations in which consistently promoting quality staff performance is likely to be quite difficult. Awareness of these situations can help supervisors be prepared to persist in their efforts to promote diligent and proficient staff performance.

SUPERVISING IN DIFFICULT SITUATIONS

Several situations supervisors are likely to face that make effective supervision especially difficult are relatively common in a number of agencies. One situation is when executive personnel who have positions of authority over a supervisor engage in practices that interfere with the supervisor's work with staff. For example, some executives may give directives to a supervisor's staff that conflict with the supervisor's instructions or make decisions about staff work schedules without the supervisor's input. In other cases, an executive may repeatedly provide special recognition for certain staff whose performance does not warrant such recognition. An example of the latter situation is when an executive shows special favoritism to a staff member based not on good work performance, but because of a particular social or familial relationship with the staff person.

Another situation supervisors are likely to face at times that makes their job challenging involves agencies in which the executive management style is predominantly negative. Deleterious effects of a negative management style have been discussed repeatedly in previous chapters. Of particular concern here is a typical response of executive personnel in these agencies whenever there is a perceived problem with staff performance. Management essentially demands that the supervisor take formal disciplinary action to punish the involved staff. Relatedly, a supervisor may be directed to impose disciplinary action with staff because an executive wants to make an example of the consequences of their problematic performance as a deterrent to other staff. Disciplinary action is mandated even if the supervisor knows the problematic performance is not due to staff intentionally avoiding their responsibilities (e.g., the staff try to perform appropriately but lack the necessary resources or time to complete various duties proficiently).

When supervisors are working in an agency with a predominantly negative management style they are likely to face frequent problems with effectively supporting and maintaining quality staff performance. As noted previously, a major effect of such a management approach is a reduction in staff work effort—staff tend to do only what is necessary to avoid negative sanctions from management. Promoting staff work enjoyment is likewise difficult for supervisors when the overall management style in an agency is predominantly negative.

An additional situation that arises in some agencies that makes it difficult for supervisors to effectively promote quality performance, and especially work enjoyment, is when events external to an agency negatively affect staff motivation. This situation is illustrated in agencies that have experienced extremely negative press in the local media or have been targeted by law suits. The negative press or litigation is usually due to an undesirable incident involving a consumer, such as a serious accident. In other cases an undesirable incident resulting in negative press or litigation involves inappropriate staff activities, such as distribution of illegal substances at work. Still in other cases, there is no undesirable incident but someone causes negative attention to be directed to an agency due to personal reasons, such as by a disgruntled individual who was fired from the agency.

When negative attention is publicly directed to an agency as just illustrated the work environment of staff tends to become increasingly negative in nature. Management demands on staff performance expectations are usually increased, often to the point of being unrealistic, and executive personnel become increasingly critical of staff performance. Correspondingly, complaining among staff themselves is likely to increase. Staff may also encounter critical comments about the agency and their work in the agency from friends and neighbors who become aware of negative publicity about the agency. The end result is the increased negativity makes it difficult for staff to maintain their motivation to work diligently and proficiently.

There is no specific way for supervisors to handle the various types of situations just noted and maintain effective supervision of staff. However, there are several general strategies supervisors can take across all of the situations to enhance their likelihood of maintaining supervisory effectiveness. These include ensuring frequent communication with staff, staying focused on specific supervisory responsibilities, and actively promoting their own work motivation.

MAINTAIN FREQUENT COMMUNICATION WITH STAFF

Negativity resulting from the types of situations just illustrated is often exacerbated due to poor communication between upper management and staff. Staff are readily aware of negative events in the agency, but are not sufficiently aware of why various events are occurring. Staff likewise receive, through informal communication channels, inaccurate information about what is going on within an agency. Lack of accurate information about agency events that are generally negative in nature almost always increases staff discontent with their work situation.

When difficult or otherwise unpleasant situations arise within an agency, supervisors must make special efforts to ensure staff are accurately informed about what is occurring. This usually means supervisors must conduct frequent meetings with staff for information sharing. Supervisors should also have more frequent interactions than usual with individual staff to provide information and respond to staff questions or inaccurate perceptions. Supervisors should strive to frequently let staff know what is happening and the reasons behind each particular situation.

In some cases supervisors feel unprepared to adequately share with staff why certain agency events occur. The supervisors may not be privy to relevant information, or are unable to share all necessary information because of confidentiality concerns. Nevertheless, supervisors should provide as much information to staff as possible. Supervisors should also acknowledge that the information they are providing may be limited, but it represents as much information as they possess or that they are allowed to share. Although staff may not receive all the relevant information they would like about undesirable events within the agency, they are usually appreciative of supervisors who take the time to share as much information as they can. Such appreciation helps maintain staff enjoyment associated with working for the supervisor.

> **When especially unpleasant events occur within an agency, supervisors should provide staff with as much information as possible about what is occurring and the reasons for the events.**

STAY FOCUSED ON ACTIVELY SUPERVISING STAFF PERFORMANCE

One advantageous way for supervisors to maintain supervisory effectiveness during difficult times in an agency is to adopt a *piece-of-the-pie attitude* to help stay focused on their supervisory responsibilities. The agency represents the entire pie and a supervisor's staff contingent represents the piece of the pie. Supervisors should accept that unpleasant events can occur within the agency as a whole over which they have no control. However, supervisors can still affect what goes on with their staff and focus on making those things go as well as possible. The intent is to maintain an attitude that no matter how negative the agency work environment is overall, the supervisors' own area of responsibility—their piece of the pie—is going to function as effectively and pleasantly as possible.

Staying focused on promoting quality performance and work enjoyment among a supervisor's group of staff is especially important during those times when negative press or legal issues affect an agency's general operation. Among all the negativity in the agency, the supervisor's staff can still function proficiently and at least somewhat enjoyably relative to the rest of the agency if the supervisor persists in implementing sound supervisory procedures. Again, the supervisor focuses on the piece of the pie that represents the supervisor's area of responsibility, and tries not to worry about what is happening in the rest of the agency.

There is another benefit of supervisors staying focused on promoting quality work and enjoyment among their specific staff contingent. When supervisors persist with effective supervisory strategies, staff are usually aware that their work situation is better or more enjoyable relative to that of staff in other parts of the agency. Consequently, the supervisors' staff are usually appreciative of the supervisors' efforts and their enjoyment associated with working for their particular supervisor is enhanced.

Staff enjoyment associated with working for a given supervisor during difficult times is especially enhanced if the supervisor makes special efforts to keep staff informed about agency events as summarized earlier. Difficult situations within an agency also represent times when supervisors need to be especially visible and available to staff (refer back to **Chapter 4** on the importance of supervisor visibility). Most importantly, these are times that supervisors need to be particularly vigilant about supporting appropriate work performance of staff and providing frequent positive feedback. Increasing support for staff work activities helps staff overcome the existing negativity in the agency as a whole by in essence, counteracting the "bad things" happening within the agency with more "good things" (**Chapter 6**).

> **Supervisors should increase their support for good staff performance, and especially with positive feedback, during particularly difficult or unpleasant times in an agency.**

Supervisor Self-Motivation

The importance of supervisors working actively to motivate staff to perform their jobs proficiently and enjoy their work has been stressed repeatedly. To be consistently successful in fulfilling this critical supervisory function, supervisors themselves must be well motivated. Supervisor self-motivation is especially important when difficult situations arise within an agency. If supervisors are not able to maintain their own motivation during these times, their supervisory effectiveness will be limited and the quality of staff performance will likely deteriorate.

What a supervisor does to maintain self-motivation will vary across supervisors and particular work situations. However, there is one strategy that can be helpful for maintaining supervisor self-motivation in general, regardless of ongoing events in an agency. The strategy involves a three-step process: (1) establishing a supervisory work goal, (2) performing necessary duties to achieve the goal and, (3) reinforcing the work accomplishment.

Establish a Work Goal. The first step of supervisor self-motivation is for supervisors to regularly *establish goals* to attain on the job. The goals should pertain directly to carrying out specific actions designed to promote quality staff performance or work enjoyment. For example, a supervisor could set a goal to provide face-to-face, positive feedback to every staff person regarding some aspect of each individual's job performance at least once during a given week. Another goal may be to implement a special recognition procedure for deserving staff members by the end of the week. Still another goal may be to meet with every staff person during the week to begin the process of making a highly disliked work task more enjoyable for staff to perform (refer to **Chapter 9**).

Goals that supervisors establish to help maintain their motivation to carry out supervisory duties should be short-term in nature. Generally, the goals should relate to something a supervisor desires to achieve on a daily or weekly basis, though on occasion a supervisory goal may involve a monthly time frame. Selecting goals that can be met relatively quickly (i.e., versus long-term goals involving several months or a year to achieve) can help supervisors stay focused on what should be done each day to meet the goal.

Achieve the Goal. The second step of self-motivation is for supervisors to do whatever is necessary to actually *achieve the goal*. Once a goal is established, specific action steps must be clearly specified. The action steps are usually straightforward when the goal pertains to actively working to promote quality staff performance or work enjoyment. The supervisor simply follows through with the designated work activities, such as giving positive feedback to each individual staff person.

Reinforce the Accomplishment. The third step is for supervisors to *reinforce their goal achievement*; supervisors should do something they enjoy to recognize their work accomplishment. It is usually most helpful if the way a supervisor will reinforce a work accomplishment is determined when the goal is initially set. Upon completing the action steps necessary to achieve the goal, the supervisor should then engage in the desired activities.

What a supervisor does to reinforce work accomplishments will be highly individualized across supervisors, as everyone has their own preferences. Some supervisors do something outside of work following a job accomplishment, such as treating themselves to a favorite meal or buying a desired item. Other supervisors do something enjoyable at work as a means of reinforcing their goal achievement, such as working on a task that is more desired relative to other tasks.

Supervisors can promote their own work motivation by: (1) establishing a work goal, (2) completing supervisory duties necessary to achieve the goal and, (3) doing something enjoyable to reinforce their work accomplishment.

Some supervisors view the self-motivation strategy, and especially the self-reinforcement step, as being artificial or otherwise unlikely to truly motivate them to fulfill their supervisory responsibilities. However, there is a good evidence base that demonstrates the strategy is often an effective approach to self-motivation. By its nature, the process ensures supervisors will experience enjoyable events associated with work—whenever they achieve a goal, they do something enjoyable for themselves. Because the process requires supervisors to complete the supervisory duties necessary to achieve the goal, they will also be performing important duties for promoting quality staff performance or staff enjoyment with their work.

There is also a less apparent but valuable benefit of supervisors using the self-motivation strategy. The process puts supervisors in control of their motivation relative to relying on someone else to motivate them. In this regard, sometimes executive personnel such as a supervisor's supervisor will be a source of motivation. However, this is not always the case. Successful supervisors do not rely on someone else to consistently motivate them on the job; they take charge of their own motivation to ensure they work diligently and experience enjoyment with their work. If other people also provide work motivation for supervisors, the supervisors should be appreciative but again, not rely solely on someone else to be responsible for their own work effort and enjoyment.

Chapter Summary: Key Points

1. *Supervisors must accept the basic premise of supervisor accountability: they are responsible for the quality with which staff perform their work.*

2. *Supervisors must avoid the cop-out attitude of supervision; when problematic performance is frequent it is not a staff problem but a problem with the supervision being provided or other factors in the work environment.*

3. *When negative events occurring within an agency impede staff work motivation, supervisors must have frequent communication with staff, stay focused on fulfilling supervisory responsibilities with their staff, and actively work to maintain their own work motivation.*

4. *A useful self-motivation strategy for supervisors to maintain their work effort and enjoyment involves: (1) establishing a supervisory work goal, (2) completing duties necessary to achieve the goal and, (3) reinforcing their work accomplishment.*

CHAPTER 11

REDUCING ABSENTEEISM

In the most basic sense, absenteeism refers to staff not being present at work when they are scheduled to be working. Because of its pervasive effects on consumer services, frequent absenteeism among direct support staff is arguably the most serious performance problem in human service agencies. Problems with absenteeism are most prevalent in residential agencies, including public and private residential centers as well as community living arrangements of a congregate nature. A number of day support programs also experience problems with absenteeism, though generally not to the same degree as residential settings.

The most apparent effect of staff absenteeism is a reduction in the quantity of services provided to agency consumers. When the number of staff who are at work is below the number scheduled to be working, the amount of consumer services provided is almost always less than what is intended to be provided. For every staff person unexpectedly absent on a given day, reductions in consumer services become more significant.

Frequent absenteeism likewise reduces the *quality* of consumer services. When there are inconsistent numbers of staff at work due to unexpected absences, services tend to become inconsistent in their delivery. Duties usually performed by staff who are absent typically have to be assigned to other staff who are present. The latter staff are likely to perform the duties somewhat differently than the former staff. Relatedly, staff who are re-assigned to perform consumer-related duties that otherwise would be performed by absent staff typically are at least somewhat unfamiliar with such duties, as well as the consumers themselves. The relative unfamiliarity with certain duties, such as carrying out a given consumer's teaching programs, often results in the duties being completed less proficiently than usual.

Frequent absenteeism also has detrimental effects on direct support staff. Staff who report to work usually have to work harder when other staff are absent; the former staff have to perform their duties plus duties left unattended by the absent staff. Additionally, it is quite common for staff to dislike having to be re-assigned duties with which they are less familiar, which occurs when they have to perform duties usually completed by other staff. This is particularly the case when staff have to work in a different setting within the agency relative to where they usually work (e.g., staff are "pulled" to work in the setting in which the absent staff usually work).

When the situations just noted occur frequently because of high absenteeism, staff motivation tends to erode. Problems with motivation are also likely to be intensified because frequent absenteeism often occurs among a circumscribed number of staff. Hence, staff who do routinely report to work repeatedly experience the negative effects of persistent absenteeism among a group of their staff peers.

Another effect of high levels of staff absenteeism pertains to supervisors. When staff do not report to work as scheduled, supervisors have to spend extra time finding replacement staff and rearranging work schedules. A number of supervisors find that compensating for frequent absenteeism in this manner represents their most time consuming duty, which detracts from available time to fulfill other supervisory responsibilities. Many supervisors likewise experience unpleasant effects of absenteeism on their home or nonwork time. Supervisors receive calls at home due to staff failing to report to work and have to spend nonwork time to resolve problems associated with the staff absences.

Still another effect of frequent absenteeism is increased financial cost for an agency. The most common increase is with overtime pay. Overtime is required in many cases to secure staff to work extra shifts to cover for absent staff. Alternatively, staff may be provided with compensatory time to work extra hours to cover for absent staff. Providing compensatory time for staff then results in them being absent from work at a later time to take off the accumulated, extra work time (i.e., to prevent them from working more than the allotted amount during a work week or pay period). In the latter case, overtime may be needed to cover for staff who are absent due to taking off their extra work time.

> **Frequent absenteeism is arguably the most serious performance problem in human service agencies; it has negative effects on consumers, staff, and supervisors as well as the cost of agency operations.**

Reasons for Frequent Absenteeism

Staff absenteeism historically has been much more frequent in human service agencies, and especially residential settings, relative to other work situations such as jobs in business and industry. Why frequent absenteeism is more prevalent in the human services is unclear, though a number of explanations have been offered. One common explanation centers on the relatively low wages provided for direct support staff. It is assumed that the low pay level reduces staff motivation to report to work. It is likewise assumed that the low pay makes it difficult to consistently recruit applicants for direct support jobs who have good work histories, which results in employment of certain staff who are likely prone to frequent absenteeism.

It is not clear whether the relatively low pay of direct support staff is a true cause of problematic absenteeism. Despite the rather common view associating low pay with high absenteeism, several factors suggest that pay levels should not be considered a primary cause of frequent absenteeism. One factor is that many if not most direct support staff do not exhibit frequent absenteeism, despite being paid commensurate with staff who are frequently absent from work. Another factor is that there are many jobs outside of the human service area for which staff receive less pay than direct support staff yet absenteeism in those jobs is much less than that in the human services.

Another common explanation for frequent absenteeism in the human services pertains to other characteristics of the direct support work force. Most direct support staff are women and at least historically, often have not been considered the primary wage earner for their family. Consequently, when a child or other family member is sick or otherwise requires someone to be at home, the direct support person is expected to be at home to care for the individual instead of the primary wage earner.

Again, the degree to which common reasons offered for high levels of absenteeism among direct support staff are accurate is unclear. In this respect, certainly many direct support staff do have good work histories prior to being employed in a direct support capacity, and many are the primary wage earner for their families. Even if purported reasons for frequent absenteeism are accurate in some cases, supervisors of direct support staff have essentially no control over these potential causes of absenteeism. As with other areas of staff performance problems, supervisors should focus their efforts on what they can control to prevent and reduce high levels of absenteeism.

One factor affecting frequent absenteeism over which supervisors can have control pertains to prevailing attitudes in some agencies regarding acceptable absenteeism. As will be discussed later, agencies typically have established policies regarding use of sick leave and other absent time. Often these policies allow for more frequent absent time, and particularly in publicly operated agencies such as state residential centers, relative to nonhuman service jobs. There is an underlying attitude in many agencies, though not always officially acknowledged, that staff should be allowed to take as much sick time as a policy allows over a designated time period whether they are sick or not. Such an attitude can actually promote absenteeism.

Supervisors should not espouse an attitude that staff should be allowed to use as many sick days as a policy grants whether they are sick or not. Sick leave is intended for use only when a staff person is truly sick (or a family member is sick that requires staff time away from work if agency policy provides for sick time to care for a family member). Supervisors should actively support appropriate use of absent time and correct inappropriate use. To successfully function in this manner, supervisors first have to clearly delineate what constitutes acceptable versus unacceptable absenteeism.

Supervisors must clearly specify for staff what constitutes acceptable versus unacceptable absenteeism.

Specifying Acceptable and Unacceptable Absenteeism

As indicated previously, absenteeism in its basic sense is defined as staff not being present at work when they are scheduled to work. Hence, defining absenteeism would seem rather straightforward. However, specifying what constitutes *acceptable* versus *unacceptable* absenteeism is much more complex.

The complexity in determining what constitutes acceptable levels of absenteeism is due to the fact that some absences are expected and even desirable to a degree. There are times when people should be absent from work because, for example, they are ill and it would be undesirable for them to report to work and potentially infect other staff or consumers. Hence, a zero level of absenteeism usually is not an appropriate criterion for specifying acceptable rates of staff absences.

Most agencies have at least an implicit criterion for what constitutes acceptable levels of absenteeism. The criterion is reflected in policies regarding use of unscheduled leave time, or sick time. A common example is an agency policy that provides for a certain amount of unscheduled leave time, such as granting one sick day per month on average, or 12 sick days per year. It is at least implicitly assumed that if a given staff member is not absent on an unscheduled basis more than 12 days per year, then that staff member has an acceptable level of absenteeism.

Relying on an agency policy regarding appropriate use of absent time as just illustrated should be only a general guide for determining acceptable and unacceptable levels of absenteeism. There are a number of factors affecting whether certain absences should be considered acceptable or not beyond the total number of times a staff person is absent during a given period. The most relevant factors pertain to the pattern of absences, or what is considered different types of absenteeism. There are three common types of absenteeism: *high frequency absenteeism, predictable absenteeism,* and *extended duration absen-*

teeism. Specifying acceptable versus unacceptable absenteeism usually must address certain considerations associated with the respective type of absenteeism that is posing a problem.

High Frequency Absenteeism

The most common type of absenteeism problem in many agencies is *high frequency absenteeism.* This type of absenteeism refers to a staff person being absent from work much more frequently relative to the average level of absences among an agency's entire work force. The staff person also is usually absent on more days than the number of days allotted by agency policy. The staff person typically uses the allotted number of paid sick days within a given time period and then continues to be absent despite not being paid for the absent days. High frequency absenteeism is further characterized by a staff person not being absent for extended time periods but rather, being absent for a day or two every few weeks or several times per month.

Predictable Absenteeism

In contrast to high frequency absenteeism, *predictable absenteeism* often does not involve a staff person being absent from work on more days than what is allotted by agency policy. In many cases, staff fail to report to work for the exact number of days that a policy allots over a given period of time (e.g., for use of sick time). However, the fact that absences are predictable usually means the absenteeism should be considered unacceptable.

Predictable absenteeism means that the likelihood of a staff person being absent from work on a given day is significantly greater than what would be expected by chance. The most common example involves a staff person who frequently fails to report to work on the day immediately preceding or following scheduled days off, such as just before or after a weekend or holiday. Other examples of predictable absenteeism supervisors have experienced with certain staff include increased absenteeism the day after pay day, on days when local public schools are not in session, and during summer months.

Predictable absenteeism usually warrants a supervisor's attention for reduction, even when staff are not using more sick time than allotted by agency policy. Again, legitimate use of sick time for absences means a staff person (or designated family member) is sick. Sickness usually does not occur on a predicable basis, such as immediately before or after a holiday. Hence, when a staff person is predictably absent, it typically means the individual is abusing use of sick time. Because any unscheduled absence has the deleterious effects of absenteeism noted earlier, predictable absences should be prevented or reduced by supervisors.

EXTENDED DURATION ABSENTEEISM

The third primary type of staff absences is *extended duration absenteeism*. This type of absenteeism involves a staff person being absent from work for a number of consecutive days, usually involving at least one week. Extended duration absenteeism is typically due to an injury at work or elsewhere, surgery or other major medical procedure, or a serious illness.

Extended duration absenteeism generally does not warrant as much attention to reduce compared to high frequency and predictable absenteeism. The reasons for extended absences as just exemplified are usually well out of a supervisor's control, and often the control of the involved staff. Hence, there is typically little a supervisor can do to affect this type of absenteeism.

Extended duration absenteeism also does not warrant supervisory action to reduce because in part, it often represents *planned* absences. In a number of situations, staff know in advance and inform a supervisor that they must be absent for an extended time period such as when they are scheduled for surgery. Also, when an injury occurs that prohibits a staff person from reporting to work for a likely extended period, at that time the continued absence can be considered as being planned. Planned absences, though still deleterious for an agency, are not as problematic as *unplanned* absences. With planned absences, a supervisor has more time to prepare for a staff person's absence and potentially reduce the negative effects of the absence by altering various work schedules or securing temporary assistance.

> **Absenteeism problems warranting a supervisor's attention usually involve a high frequency of staff absences across work periods or a predictable pattern of absences.**

ABSENTEE-REDUCTION STRATEGIES

Overall, strategies for reducing absenteeism should be based on the steps constituting evidence-based supervision. The first step is specifying what constitutes acceptable and unacceptable absences along the lines just described. Again, agency policies regarding allotted absent time can be used as a general guide for what constitutes acceptable absenteeism. Subsequently, if absenteeism occurs on a high-frequency or predictable basis, then such absenteeism should usually be considered unacceptable and actions should be taken to reduce the absences.

The second step of evidence-based supervision, that of performance- and competency-based staff training, is usually not much of an issue when addressing unacceptable absenteeism. When staff repeatedly fail to report to work, the problem is not one of staff lacking appropriate work skills per se. The only staff training requirement that is usually necessary involves ensuring staff are thoroughly aware of what constitutes acceptable versus unacceptable levels of absenteeism.

Ensuring staff awareness of acceptable versus unacceptable absenteeism typically involves three key steps. First, staff must be adequately informed about relevant agency policies in general regarding absent time. Second, staff should be informed about specific criteria related to acceptable versus unacceptable absences whenever new strategies are implemented to reduce absenteeism. The information usually should be based on the type of absenteeism being addressed. Third, the consequences for acceptable and unacceptable absenteeism should be made particularly clear to staff (see subsequent sections relating to implementing absentee-reduction strategies).

Monitoring staff absences is also a part of evidence-based supervision that usually does not require much extra time by supervisors when addressing absenteeism problems. Agencies typically have established systems for maintaining records of staff absences. The only special consideration for monitoring in regard to absenteeism is to ensure supervisors frequently review the absentee records and respond accordingly. Appropriate responding in this regard means acting to support appropriate levels of work attendance and to correct unacceptable levels of absenteeism in accordance with whatever absentee-reduction strategy is implemented.

SUPPORTING ACCEPTABLE WORK ATTENDANCE AND CORRECTING UNACCEPTABLE ABSENTEEISM

Applied research has developed a number of strategies for reducing high levels of absenteeism among direct support staff. The strategies share common procedures but also have respective components that are somewhat unique based on the type of absenteeism being addressed. Overall however, the best strategy is to *prevent* unacceptable absences from developing into a significant problem within an agency.

Preventing Absentee Problems: Promoting Work Enjoyment as Part of Supervision. As indicated previously, the causes of frequent absenteeism are not totally clear despite some commonly offered reasons. However, on a most basic level, an underlying cause is that it is more desirable for staff to stay away from work than to be at work. This is especially the case when staff abuse their leave time but stay within the allotted amount of absent time reflected in agency policy. In this case, staff are in essence being paid for not reporting to work (e.g., when a staff person is paid for a day of sick leave when the individual is not at work but is not sick).

Considering the underlying cause of absenteeism as just referred to, it logically follows that the more staff enjoy their jobs the less they will be absent from work in an unacceptable manner. This is one key reason supervisors should actively promote staff enjoyment with their work. The more supervisors effectively enhance work enjoyment among staff along with diligent and proficient work performance, problems with absenteeism will be less likely to occur.

Throughout this text various ways supervisors can promote work enjoyment as part of their routine supervisory duties have been highlighted. Supervisors should be constantly attending to how their actions affect work enjoyment among staff, and strive to promote as much work enjoyment as reasonably possible. No single action to enhance work enjoyment will likely affect how often staff report to work but cumulatively, consistent supervisory actions to promote work enjoyment can have long-term effects on preventing high levels of absenteeism.

> **Supervisors who consistently act to promote staff enjoyment with their work tend to reduce problems with unacceptable absenteeism.**

The importance of supportive supervisory practices that promote quality performance and staff enjoyment on preventing problems with absenteeism cannot be overemphasized. However, as with other types of performance problems, supervisors should be prepared to take corrective action with unacceptable absenteeism if and when it occurs. As discussed in previous chapters, corrective action is based on frequent delivery of feedback and if repeated problems continue, appropriate use of disciplinary action. Essentially every evidence-based approach to resolving problems with absenteeism involves both supportive and corrective actions by supervisors. Specifically how supervisors can support good attendance and correct unacceptable absenteeism depends in large part on the type of absenteeism addressed and the absentee-reduction strategy employed.

Group-Contingency Strategies. One evidence-based way to reduce unacceptable absenteeism is through *group contingencies*. Group contingencies involve providing positive and negative consequences for individual staff performance based on the overall functioning of a group of staff. In regard to absenteeism, group contingencies involve providing positive and negative consequences for all staff within a respective group based on the overall level of absences for the entire group.

An example of how a group contingency has been used to effectively reduce absenteeism pertains to a situation involving high frequency absenteeism in a residential facility, although predictable absenteeism was also addressed. The primary concern was with an excessively high frequency of staff absences across four-week work periods (staff work schedules were customarily established for each four-week pay period). A secondary concern pertained to a higher frequency of staff absences on weekends when staff were scheduled to work weekends. In this particular situation, working weekends was especially unpopular among a significant number of staff—which presumably was a reason many staff failed to report to work when scheduled for weekend duty.

The absentee-reduction approach involving a group contingency involved the following process. First, a criterion level of acceptable absences for four-week work periods was established, which represented a significantly smaller number of absences relative to what was currently occurring. The criterion was established jointly between supervisory personnel and direct support staff based on a general consensus about what seemed to be a reasonable expectation for reducing absences. Second, it was determined that if the criterion was met for a given work period, then each individual staff person would be assigned to work fewer weekends during the next four-week period. Changing the weekend work schedule could be achieved without affecting consumer services because if staff absences on the weekend were significantly reduced, the actual number of staff present on a given weekend would still be acceptable. Third, if the criterion number of absences was not met, then the group of staff for whom absences were still unacceptable would continue with the original work schedule involving more weekend duty.

The absentee-reduction program was applied with six groups of staff, representing staff working on six separate living units within the residential facility. The group-contingency strategy was accompanied by significantly less absences for five of the six groups of staff. A key part of the strategy involved letting each group of staff decide through a consensus voting procedure if they wanted to participate in the group contingency for the forthcoming work period. If they voted not to participate, which rarely occurred, then that group of staff continued on the original schedule that involved being assigned to work on more weekends each period.

The staff voting procedure as part of the overall program represented a *participative supervision* component, as did staff involvement in setting the criterion for acceptable numbers of absences each work period. The benefits of involving staff in supervisory decision-making processes that affect staff work activities have been discussed previously. It was also emphasized that staff involvement in this regard is most beneficial when supervisory actions address work issues that are particularly important to staff. Determining specific days that staff will be assigned to work, such as on weekends versus weekdays, is almost always a very important issue among staff. Consequently, essentially any new program for addressing problems with absenteeism should include staff input into how the program will work (see **Chapter 3** for elaboration of the benefits of participative supervisory processes).

Absentee-reduction programs should be designed by supervisors using a *participative supervisory* process in which staff have input into how the programs will operate.

Including group-contingency components within absentee-reduction strategies has some unique advantages and disadvantages. The most notable advantage is that it can evoke *peer pressure* among staff to reduce unacceptable absences. Staff who have good work attendance will encourage and otherwise act to convince staff with unacceptable absenteeism to improve their attendance. This can be especially useful when considering the common situation in which only a circumscribed group of staff is responsible for the primary problems with absenteeism as described earlier. Staff with good attendance can be especially motivated to convince the group with problematic absenteeism to improve their attendance because of the deleterious effects of their absenteeism on the former staff's work situation.

The peer-pressure advantage of group contingencies also represents the disadvantage of this approach to reducing absenteeism. Specifically, supervisors have little control over how some staff will exert pressure on other staff, and the means they use may not always be desirable within an agency. Again though, high absenteeism among certain staff negatively affects the work life of their staff peers who have good attendance. Hence, group contingencies are often viewed as more appropriate when dealing with unacceptable absences relative to other types of staff performance problems that may not have such pervasive effects on other staff.

Absentee-Reduction Strategies with Individual Staff. Another strategy for reducing unacceptable absenteeism involves working with staff on an individual basis instead of a group basis as just summarized. Typically this approach focuses on staff who have the most serious absentee problems, whether of a high-frequency or predictable nature. Several steps of evidence-based supervision are particularly useful for designing absentee-reduction approaches for application with individual staff.

Initially, attendance records should be carefully studied to identify those staff with the most serious absentee problems, which essentially represents the monitoring step of supervision. The absences of each staff person should be reviewed to determine if the problem consists of high-frequency or predictable absenteeism, or both. Clearly delineating why the absences are unacceptable in this regard represents the specification step of supervision. The training step then involves meeting with each individual staff person whose absenteeism is problematic to discuss precisely why the absences are unacceptable (e.g., they are too frequent or predictable).

Subsequently, supervisors should determine what will be done to support appropriate attendance among the identified staff—constituting the supportive step of supervision. Most commonly, this step involves providing individualized feedback in a face-to-face manner with a given staff person on a regular schedule such as at the end of every work period. The feedback should focus on how the staff person's performance has improved or how it is maintaining at an acceptable level, if appropriate.

In addition to providing supportive feedback, individual absentee-reduction programs essentially always need to involve the corrective step of evidence-based supervision. The corrective actions should be taken as described in **Chapter 8**, beginning with corrective feedback about the specific absences that are unacceptable. If corrective feedback is not followed by clear improvement in a staff person's attendance, then disciplinary action should be initiated immediately. Disciplinary action should continue as long as satisfactory improvement is lacking, with the ultimate action of terminating the staff member's job if warranted due to repeated absentee problems.

There are several key features of using disciplinary action effectively to reduce unacceptable absences among individual staff. In particular, how disciplinary action will be taken should be made very clear to the staff person when the supervisor first meets with the individual to begin the formal absentee-reduction process. The purpose of clearly specifying likely disciplinary action, and what exactly the action will involve, helps ensure the staff person is well aware of the consequences of unacceptable absenteeism. The process also represents a professional obligation of a supervisor; it is only fair that a staff person be informed of negative sanctions to potentially occur if the individual's problems with absenteeism are not corrected.

Another key feature of using disciplinary action effectively with absenteeism is that it must be applied in a consistent and timely manner by a supervisor. Often what happens is that a supervisor is aware of a staff person's attendance problems but does not maintain consistency in reviewing the attendance records and following up with necessary action. Rather, a number of supervisors attend only sporadically to the problems and take action inconsistently. The latter approach rarely results in improved attendance over the long run. Failure of supervisors to act quickly and consistently in response to individual absenteeism is a major reason problems with staff absenteeism tend to persist in human service agencies.

Supervisors *must* review attendance records frequently and take immediate action if problems with absenteeism are occurring. All of the other means of effective use of disciplinary action (again, refer to **Chapter 8**), such as informing agency superiors prior to taking initial action and providing timely positive feedback when improvement occurs, should also be adhered to by supervisors. Supervisors likewise should be prepared to work individually with certain staff over many weeks before satisfactory attendance results, or the staff are appropriately removed from an agency through job termination.

> **The most common reason supervisors are unsuccessful in reducing absenteeism among individual staff is they fail to consistently monitor attendance records and quickly follow up with supportive and corrective action.**

Implementing absentee-reduction procedures on an individual staff basis is advantageous because they can be used whenever a supervisor becomes aware of an absentee problem. The procedures can be applied with a single staff person or with several individuals for whom their attendance records are a concern. In this regard, most approaches for reducing staff absenteeism involve working with individual staff.

The primary disadvantage of absentee-reduction procedures used on an individual staff basis is the process can become excessively time consuming for a supervisor. This is particularly the case when problems with absenteeism involve a relatively large number of staff, such that each staff person requires specific actions by a supervisor. In the latter situation it is usually more time efficient for a supervisor to implement a reduction strategy for the entire group of staff. The strategy may involve a group contingency as described previously. Alternatively, the strategy may involve supportive and corrective procedures that are the same for all staff based on each staff person's attendance without making the consequences for individual staff contingent on the overall attendance of the entire group.

Two Final Considerations for Reducing Absenteeism

Resolving absentee problems can be a difficult and unpleasant challenge for supervisors. The difficulty exists because often supervisors must exert considerable time and effort to resolve the problems over extended time periods. Problems with absenteeism usually encompass at least several work periods, requiring supervisors to address the issues consistently over many weeks. The unpleasantness exists because most absentee-reduction approaches, and particularly those taken with individual staff, usually involve disciplinary action. Because disciplinary action by its nature involves punitive sanctions, it is usually negatively received by staff which in turn makes it a negative experience for supervisors. Nonetheless, because of the problems excessive absenteeism cause within an agency and its general pervasiveness, supervisors must be prepared and willing to work actively to both prevent and reduce problematic absenteeism.

There are two rather general considerations warranting supervisor attention that can assist in efforts to reduce staff absenteeism. One consideration pertains to the importance of *flexibility* when implementing formal absentee-reduction strategies. The second is attending to both *planned* and *unplanned* absences.

THE IMPORTANCE OF FLEXIBILITY WITHIN ABSENTEE-REDUCTION STRATEGIES

Implementing absentee-reduction strategies in an effective and fair manner usually requires a significant degree of flexibility on the part of a supervisor. Earlier the importance of clearly specifying for staff what constitutes acceptable versus unacceptable absences was stressed. However, supervisors should be prepared to be flexible in determining how such specification relates to certain situations and corresponding supervisor actions.

Flexibility is needed in considering the acceptability of certain staff absences because for every set of criteria or rules regarding what is specified as acceptable or not, there are likely to be some justifiable exceptions. Sometimes it is special circumstances within the work environment that are resulting in what appears to be unacceptable absenteeism. For example, many agencies experience budget issues at times that prohibit them from hiring new staff to fill vacant staff positions. The inability to hire new staff often results in excessive workloads for existing staff. The extra workloads may result in significant fatigue or physical discomfort for certain staff, and especially older staff or individuals with pre-existing medical conditions that are exacerbated by the increased workload. It would be inappropriate to consider the increased absenteeism in such situations to be a staff problem (i.e., it is an overall agency problem) and impose negative sanctions with those staff.

In other cases, flexibility is needed because what initially appears to be an abuse of absent time based on existing attendance criteria is really not a misuse of leave time. To illustrate, a staff member may have satisfactory attendance except for a certain time of the year. Such a pattern of absences might meet the criteria for predicable absenteeism. However, on closer evaluation it may be determined that the absences during the designated period are due to medical issues such as severe allergies that tend to be seasonal in nature. It would be inappropriate to consider absences during the predictable time period as unacceptable if the staff person was experiencing actual physical problems.

The need for flexibility in carrying out absenteeism-reduction strategies is most relevant when dealing with individual staff absences. This is one reason that the first step in implementing a strategy with a staff person to reduce absenteeism is to meet with the individual to review the pattern of absences that reflect a problem. The meeting allows the staff person an opportunity to discuss the reasons for the noted absences. In turn, such information can assist the supervisor in determining whether what initially appeared to be an abuse of leave time truly represents unacceptable absenteeism. The supervisor would then need to be appropriately flexible in determining whether to carry out the corrective action part of the strategy and especially the disciplinary action component.

ATTENDING TO PLANNED AND UNPLANNED ABSENCES

Earlier a distinction was made between *planned* and *unplanned* staff absences. It was also noted that unplanned absences have many more problematic effects within an agency. The discussion on reducing absenteeism to this point has pertained to unplanned absences—when staff are scheduled to be working but are not present on the job.

Planned absences generally refer to a staff person being absent from work with the prior approval of the supervisor. Planned absences can also pose a problem for supervisors at times, and particularly if too many staff are away from work on approved leave. Again though, the problems are less significant than those caused by unplanned absences. Because planned absences usually are approved by a supervisor prior to their occurrence, they usually are not considered within the category of problematic absenteeism.

Planned absences are noted here because such absences can be affected by unplanned absences. Sometimes absentee-reduction strategies that reduce unplanned absenteeism have an accompanying effect of increasing planned absences. Some staff who reduce their unplanned absences when an absentee-reduction program is implemented will increase their requests for approved time off from work. Supervisors should be aware of this potential impact when implementing specific procedures to reduce unplanned absences.

Generally the increase in planned absences that may accompany decreases in unplanned absences should not be considered a major concern. Supervisors usually have considerable control over whether requests for leave are approved or not. Hence, they can maintain planned absences at a level that does not involve major disruptions to the overall work routine.

In addition, planned absences typically mean that staff are using leave time that is granted by agency policy, such as vacation leave. Agencies typically limit how many approved leave days are granted for a given time period based on agency policy. Hence, if a staff person increases requests for approved leave because of reduced unplanned absences as a result of an absentee-reduction program, the staff person will eventually use all the approved leave that the agency allows. At that point, any absences the staff person has will be unplanned, and subject to the consequences within the absentee-reduction procedure.

Chapter Summary: Key Points

1. *Frequent absenteeism is a problem in many human service agencies, and one that supervisors should be prepared to address.*

2. *Supervisors must clearly specify for staff what constitutes acceptable versus unacceptable absenteeism.*

3. *Three main types of absenteeism include high frequency absences, predictable absences, and extended-duration absences, with the first two types representing performance problems supervisors should usually act to resolve.*

4. *The best way of preventing problematic absenteeism is for supervisors to consistently act to promote staff enjoyment with their work along with diligent and proficient performance.*

5. *One evidence-based strategy for reducing problematic absenteeism involves group contingencies in which consequences for individual staff are based on the average level of absences among all staff in a respective group.*

6. *The most common, evidence-based strategy for reducing absenteeism involves working with individual staff to support good attendance through positive feedback and correct unacceptable absences through corrective feedback and if necessary, disciplinary action.*

7. *To effectively reduce unacceptable absences among individual staff, supervisors must frequently review attendance records and carry out supportive or corrective action on a very timely and consistent basis.*

8. *Supervisors should be prepared to be flexible in implementing absentee-reduction programs in individual situations.*

9. *Supervisors should be aware that as unplanned (unacceptable) absences are decreased, planned absences may increase for a period of time.*

CHAPTER 12

RESOLVING PROBLEMS WITH STAFF PROVISION OF CONSUMER-TEACHING SERVICES

A primary responsibility of direct support staff in most human service agencies is *teaching*. Direct support staff frequently are charged with teaching consumers self-help and related skills of daily living. Many staff are also expected to teach various communication and social skills, vocationally related skills, leisure skills, and skills required to function in community activities.

Consumer-teaching procedures expected to be carried out by direct support staff usually are designed by agency clinicians such as teachers or behavior specialists. In other agencies, administrative personnel such as treatment team leaders write teaching plans. Regardless of who develops teaching programs for consumers though, the bulk of teaching services on a day-to-day basis is usually provided by direct support staff.

Direct support staff are generally expected to provide teaching services in two primary ways. The first way is represented in explicitly scheduled, circumscribed sessions or what is considered *formal teaching*. Most commonly, set times are established for staff to work one-on-one with a designated consumer for the explicit purpose of carrying out a teaching program. The program relates directly to a formal goal or objective as part of the consumer's overall habilitation or education plan.

The second way staff are expected to provide teaching services is to embed teaching within ongoing, daily activities of consumers. This type of *naturalistic* or *embedded teaching* involves incorporating brief instructional strategies within the daily routine to promote carry over of what is taught in formal teaching sessions. The intent also is for consumers to be actively supported in functioning as independently as possible in routine activities in their natural environments.

Implementing teaching services, both on a formal and naturalistic basis, is a critical duty of direct support staff. A primary purpose of most human service agencies is to assist consumers in developing skills to be as independent in life as possible. Because direct support staff usually are expected to carry out most of the teaching services, they must fulfill this responsibility in an effective manner. Otherwise, agency consumers are unlikely to attain desired outcomes associated with acquiring meaningful skills and increased independence.

> **A critical responsibility of direct support staff in most human service agencies is teaching meaningful skills to enhance consumer independence.**

Although providing teaching services is a common performance expectation of direct support staff, it is an area of service provision that is often problematic. Teaching services frequently are not provided in the manner in which they are intended. Correspondingly, agency consumers do not make satisfactory progress in learning and using functional skills. It is common, for example, to observe consumers receiving the same instructional program on a given skill area for weeks, months, and even years without mastering the targeted skill. Such a situation clearly represents inadequate service provision, and has detrimental effects on consumer quality of life.

There are two main reasons why implementation of teaching services is ineffective in human service agencies: either the teaching procedures are not carried out proficiently by staff or staff do not carry out assigned teaching duties as often as the duties should be performed. However, as with other performance areas of concern, these problems should not be interpreted solely as a staff issue. Rather, the inadequate performance usually relates directly to lack of effective supervision.

Effective supervision requires supervisors to accept *responsibility* for problems with staff performance (**Chapter 10**). Supervisors must act to support proficient performance—in this case appropriate implementation of teaching services—and to correct nonproficient performance. What supervisors should do to correct nonproficient teaching services must be based on why the services are not acceptable. This usually means addressing issues with the proficiency with which staff implement teaching procedures or staff failure to carry out teaching duties as frequently as expected.

Resolving problems with teaching services usually requires supervisors to take action to improve *how* staff carry out teaching procedures or to increase *how often* staff engage in teaching activities.

In addition to addressing issues relating to the quality and quantity of teaching services, supervisors must address the type of services that are of concern: either teaching provided formally in assigned teaching sessions or naturalistically during typical daily activities. This chapter focuses on what supervisors can do to resolve problems with teaching services of both a formal and naturalistic nature. However, the supervisory procedures to be discussed also relate directly to other types of therapeutic services expected to be provided by direct support staff. The latter services pertain to staff duties such as, for example, carrying out therapeutic movement exercises and mobility-enhancement procedures designed by occupational and physical therapists, and communication strategies established by speech and language pathologists.

IMPROVING FORMAL TEACHING SERVICES

As indicated earlier, formal teaching refers to when staff are assigned to carry out a teaching program with an individual consumer. The teaching is usually scheduled to occur within certain time periods of the work day and involves implementing specific instructional strategies according to a written plan. As also noted previously, when problematic performance occurs with implementation of formal teaching plans, the problems pertain to staff carrying out the teaching strategies nonproficiently or not completing the teaching sessions as often as assigned. Improving the two types of problematic teaching performance involves similar supervisory actions as well as certain actions that are idiosyncratic to each respective problem.

Before discussing how supervisors can correct problematic performance related to formal teaching, a basic prerequisite warrants attention. Specifically, it is assumed that the teaching plans staff are expected to carry out—again, typically developed and written by an agency professional—are good plans. Teaching plans must be developed and written in a quality manner with sound instructional procedures to facilitate acquisition of consumer skills. As some supervisors have experienced, however, this is not always the case.

Many supervisors are likely to have concerns at times with the quality of teaching programs that their staff are charged with carrying out. Specifically how to evaluate and subsequently alter written teaching plans when necessary is outside the scope of this text. On a general level though, if supervisors suspect that certain plans may be problematic (e.g., they lack key instructional strategies or are written in a vague or unclear manner), the supervisors should consult with whomever developed the plans to resolve the concerns.

Assuming that formal teaching plans are prepared adequately, then the plans represent in essence the first two steps of evidence-based supervision for promoting quality teaching by staff. The plans *specify the outcomes* desired for individual consumers to attain in terms of acquisition of certain skills, which represents the first step of evidence-based supervision. The plans also *specify staff performance expectations* in terms of what staff should do on the job, which constitutes the second step of evidence-based supervision. In this case the expectations pertain to staff implementing the teaching procedures as written in the plans.

Improving Staff Proficiency in Carrying Out Formal Teaching Procedures

When problems exist with the proficiency with which staff implement formal teaching plans, it means that staff are not carrying out the teaching procedures in accordance with the written plans. In turn, lack of satisfactory implementation of teaching plans usually means either staff have not been adequately trained to carry out the plans or they lack the motivation to consistently carry out the plans appropriately. Supervisors must determine which of these issues is relevant when problems with staff teaching proficiency become apparent.

The best way for supervisors to identify why teaching proficiency is problematic is to observe staff teaching performance, which represents the *monitoring* step of supervision. Observing staff carry out teaching plans usually results in supervisors determining if staff lack necessary instructional skills or are not sufficiently motivated to use their skills appropriately. For example, if supervisors observe staff carry out some teaching sessions proficiently but display nonproficient performance during other sessions, the problem is usually insufficient motivation—staff know how to teach but do not exert the effort to consistently implement teaching programs appropriately. In contrast, if supervisors observe staff consistently make the same error with a teaching program, it is likely they lack relevant skills and warrant training.

Training Staff to Teach Proficiently. Ensuring staff carry out formal teaching procedures proficiently typically requires that staff have skills in two related areas. First, staff must have skills in *basic instructional strategies* for teaching people with disabilities. Second, staff must have skills in *specific instructional strategies*. The latter skills involve teaching procedures that are individualized for respective consumers within the consumers' teaching plans.

Because teaching meaningful skills to agency consumers is a common performance expectation of direct support staff, it is recommended that all support staff receive training in basic teaching procedures early in their employment. To illustrate, a common set of teaching procedures that is trained to all support staff in some agencies includes how to assist or prompt learner responses to instructions, correct inaccurate learner responses, and support or reinforce correct learner responses. Using the performance- and competency-based training protocol described in **Chapter 4** is ideal for training staff in these types of basic teaching procedures.

Many agencies have general programs for training staff how to teach. However, as with other common training programs in human service agencies, the training-to-teach programs often are not performance- and competency-based. Many programs focus on lecturing to staff about how to teach, sometimes supplemented with readings and video- or computer-based illustrations of general teaching approaches. The programs are frequently lacking though in terms of staff trainers demonstrating desired teaching strategies and requiring staff trainees to practice the strategies with feedback until they demonstrate competence.

Supervisors should strive to ensure all of their staff receive performance- and competency-based training in basic ways to teach. Often this will entail soliciting the assistance of professional personnel who are thoroughly skilled in teaching strategies to develop a staff training program. Supervisors should likewise be involved in the development of the staff training program as well as the actual training of their staff.

Supervisor involvement in programs to train staff in basic ways to teach is particularly important because of the nature of teaching individuals who have disabilities. A vital component of such programs is the on-the-job part of training (again, see **Chapter 4**). Once staff satisfactorily complete a classroom-based program on basic teaching procedures, the training must continue in an on-the-job manner as staff actually teach consumers. Usually it is the staff supervisor's responsibility to conduct the on-the-job part of training, or at least to be integrally involved in this aspect of training with other staff trainers.

When staff initially implement teaching procedures with individual consumers, questions almost always arise regarding the instructional strategies that they are using. Additionally, teaching of actual consumers is always at least somewhat different than teaching in a role-play situation as occurs in most staff training programs. Hence, supervisors must be present when staff begin to conduct teaching sessions to answer staff questions and otherwise support and correct staffs' initial teaching efforts. In this regard, research has indicated that programs designed to train direct support staff how to teach are unlikely to be consistently effective without the on-the-job training component.

> **In most agencies, direct support staff should receive performance- and competency-based training in basic teaching procedures for people with disabilities soon after employment.**

After staff have been effectively trained in basic teaching procedures, supervisors should strive to ensure staff receive competency- and performance-based training in the specific aspects of each teaching program designed for individual consumers. Each consumer teaching plan is likely to be a little bit different, and may include some instructional strategies with which staff are not familiar. Hence, staff will need at least some training associated with each plan they are expected to implement.

In the ideal situation from a supervisor's perspective, the clinician who develops a respective teaching plan should be the person who trains staff who are expected to implement the plan. Even in this situation though, supervisors must have some involvement. Supervisors need to be familiar with all teaching plans staff are charged with carrying out to effectively supervise their routine implementation of the plans once trained.

In many cases, supervisors also need to be prepared to assume the *bulk of the responsibility* for training staff how to implement teaching plans developed by clinicians. Although from a professional perspective clinicians are expected to train staff to implement the plans they develop, supervisors will likely encounter situations in which clinicians do not adequately fulfill this responsibility. Some clinicians will not invest the necessary time to adequately train staff to carry out teaching plans. In other cases, clinicians are not skilled in conducting performance-

and competency-based staff training. Hence, the training they do provide for staff is not consistently effective. When these situations arise, supervisors must assume the responsibility of ensuring staff have the necessary skills to carry out consumer teaching plans proficiently.

Emphasizing the need for supervisors to assume responsibility for training staff how to implement teaching plans that clinicians develop may seem like an unfair expectation of supervisors. In some ways, the expectation is indeed unfair. Again however, even though clinicians are expected to train staff to implement plans they develop according to professional standards of most clinical fields, some clinicians do not meet this professional requirement very well. Consequently, whether fair or not, if supervisors are to fulfill their own responsibilities of promoting quality staff performance—in this case implementation of teaching plans—they must ensure staff are effectively trained to carry out the plans even if the supervisors have to provide the training themselves.

One factor that can reduce the time and effort of supervisors to train staff to carry out formal teaching plans is that often the amount of required training is limited. This is one reason that all direct support staff should be trained in basic instructional skills as summarized earlier. When staff are skilled in basic teaching procedures, frequently they need only a little additional training to implement a given teaching plan. This is one of the situations discussed in **Chapter 4** in which all steps of the performance- and competency-based training protocol do not have to be carried out by the supervisor. A description of specific components of the teaching plan will sometimes suffice, perhaps supplemented with a role-play demonstration (provided that on-the-job training also occurs).

Maintaining Staff Proficiency in Providing Formal Teaching Services Following Training. Ensuring staff are adequately trained, both in basic instructional procedures and strategies related to individualized teaching programs, sets the occasion for staff to conduct formal teaching sessions proficiently. However, as with other areas of staff performance, although training is a *necessary* step to promote proficient teaching, it is not *sufficient*. Training must be followed by on-the-job supervision of staff teaching performance.

Following initial training of staff in how to teach with on-the-job supervision is critical for ensuring staff conduct formal teaching sessions proficiently and effectively. A number of investigations have clearly indicated that without follow-up supervision, teaching proficiency of staff frequently deteriorates as staff conduct teaching sessions during their work routine. Lack of effective supervision in this regard is a primary reason that problems with nonproficient teaching services are prevalent in many human service agencies.

Promoting and maintaining staff teaching proficiency on a day-to-day basis involves the same basic supervisory procedures described previously for ensuring proficient staff performance in general. The component steps of evidence-based supervision should serve as a guide for what supervisors do to ensure quality teaching services provided by staff. As noted previously, the performance expectation of staff in this situation is usually clear: staff should carry out the steps specified in the written teaching plan pertaining to each consumer whom they teach.

Once staff begin their assigned teaching duties, their teaching performance should be routinely *monitored* by supervisors following the guidelines described in **Chapter 5**. Monitoring staff teaching performance is facilitated if a checklist or monitoring form is developed based on the teaching strategies within respective teaching plans for each consumer being taught. Generally, a reasonable goal for staff teaching proficiency is that across all teaching opportunities, they correctly implement at least 80%

of all specified teaching procedures (e.g., prompting, correcting learner errors, reinforcing correct learner responses) during each teaching session.

Sometimes supervisors expect staff to teach at a 100% level of proficiency. However, such a goal is usually unrealistic. Essentially no one teaches perfectly; even the most experienced and motivated teachers make some mistakes while working with different learners. In this regard, research has repeatedly indicated that perfect teaching usually is not necessary. As long as staff carry out teaching procedures at a level of at least 80% proficiency, learners with even the most severe disabilities typically acquire the skills targeted in teaching plans.

Monitoring a staff person's teaching session with a consumer should be followed by *supportive feedback* for teaching procedures implemented correctly (**Chapter 6**). Considering the importance of formal teaching sessions—in this case helping consumers learn functional skills to maximize their independence—it is also advantageous if *special recognition procedures* (**Chapter 7**) are used periodically by supervisors to support proficient teaching. One particularly effective way to specially recognize quality teaching of staff is to focus on the skill development observed among consumers whom the staff teach (again see **Chapter 7** for elaboration).

Specially recognizing staff teaching efforts by emphasizing the skill gains of the consumers they teach has several advantages. Most staff are aware of the importance of consumers learning meaningful skills and displaying increased independence in daily functioning. Recognizing that specific staff are responsible for consumer success in this regard can help staff feel quite good about their teaching accomplishments. Such recognition heightens staff awareness that they are having a significant influence on consumer quality of life.

Providing special recognition for consumer skill attainment based on staff teaching performance also has a rather unique effect on staff motivation and work enjoyment. As discussed previously, one characteristic of the job of providing direct support that decreases work motivation is that staff sometimes feel they are simply doing the same thing everyday. In turn, staff feel they are not really accomplishing anything significant but rather, simply "putting their time in" in a repetitive manner. In contrast, when consumers learn how to do something independently as a result of staff teaching performance, there is a clear outcome to staff work efforts.

When consumers acquire important skills being taught by staff, staff can experience a feeling of having finished or completed something important. Once a consumer meets a pre-specified degree of independence in performing a skill targeted by a teaching plan, staff work associated with formally carrying out the plan is concluded. Having a clear end to a work task in this regard can negate a feeling of simply doing the same thing everyday without finishing anything. It can be very motivating to staff to realize they have successfully finished an important work task.

> **A good way for supervisors to support proficient teaching services of staff is to specially recognize consumer skill development that results from staff teaching efforts.**

In addition to providing supportive feedback and periodic special recognition based on observed teaching performance of staff, supervisors will also need to provide *corrective feedback* at times. The feedback should follow the guidelines discussed in **Chapter 8**. Corrective feedback regarding inaccuracies with staff implementation of a teaching plan typically results in improved teaching.

This is particularly the case if the feedback is accompanied by supportive feedback for proficient aspects of observed teaching performance. However, in a relatively small number of cases, supervisors will likely need to follow repeated presentations of corrective feedback with disciplinary action if teaching performance does not improve.

Nonproficient teaching performance represents an area of staff work activities that usually does not result in disciplinary action in many agencies as noted in **Chapter 8**. However, failure to take disciplinary action with inadequate teaching that does not improve despite repeated presentations of corrective feedback is a serious supervisory mistake. Providing formal teaching services for consumers is a critical responsibility of most direct support staff, and should be taken seriously by staff and supervisors alike.

The best way for supervisors to impress upon staff the importance of consumer-teaching duties is to provide frequent supportive feedback for quality teaching and corrective feedback as necessary. Generally, those areas of staff performance that receive the most attention from supervisors in terms of supervisory feedback tend to be viewed by staff as their most important job responsibilities. The importance is heightened further if staff are aware that repeated occurrences of inadequate teaching will not be tolerated and will result in disciplinary action. Although disciplinary action usually will not be needed very often as just indicated, when it is required it should be provided consistently and in accordance with the other guidelines presented in **Chapter 8**. Such action should continue until either teaching performance improves or the responsible staff are removed from the agency.

Ensuring Staff Conduct Formal Teaching as Often as Expected

The second primary problem pertaining to inadequacies in formal teaching services is that some staff do not conduct teaching sessions as often as the sessions are expected to be conducted. This problem generally is not as prevalent as nonproficent teaching performance of staff but nonetheless occurs in some agencies. When staff fail to provide teaching as frequently as expected, it represents a performance problem that has serious effects on consumer welfare. Most noticeably, consumers are not receiving the quantity of teaching services they are intended to receive. Consequently, consumer skill acquisition is hindered and their ability to live as independently as possible is compromised.

The most common reason some staff do not conduct assigned teaching sessions is one of insufficient motivation; staff lack the motivation to exert the time and effort to carry out teaching programs with consumers. Before discussing supervisory actions for overcoming insufficient motivation to teach however, two other less common but nonetheless important reasons for problematic performance in this area warrant attention. One reason is other work duties required of staff conflict with their time to conduct formal teaching sessions. The other reason is that conducting teaching sessions results in challenging behavior of consumers that causes the sessions to be unpleasant for staff to conduct.

The issue of competing work duties interfering with staff completion of teaching sessions requires a degree of assessment on the part of supervisors. Sometimes this is a real issue and sometimes it is simply an excuse on the part of some staff to avoid carrying out teaching programs. As discussed in previous chapters, frequent supervisor monitoring of staff work activities—and of particular concern here, their teaching duties—will usually inform supervisors whether there is adequate time to complete assigned duties. If monitoring indicates there typically is adequate time for staff to conduct teaching sessions, then the problem is one of insufficient motivation. If monitoring reveals a true lack of sufficient time to teach due to other duties, then supervisors must re-assess the staff work schedule and make refinements as needed.

The other reason for staff failure to carry out teaching sessions as frequently as expected can be more complex. In a number of cases, individuals with disabilities will respond to teaching programs implemented by staff with various types of challenging behavior. Such behavior may involve disruption of materials or property, aggression toward the staff person who is attempting to teach, and even self-injury among some consumers. When these types of consumer behavior occur during teaching sessions, the sessions can become quite unpleasant for staff and they tend to avoid conducting subsequent sessions.

Consumer problem behavior during formal teaching represents an issue that warrants resolution both for the welfare of consumers and staff who are expected to teach the consumers. Serious problem behavior during teaching sessions can occur for a number of reasons including, for example, a history of noncompliance among some consumers that carries over into teaching sessions, consumers engaging in problem behavior to obtain increased attention from staff, and consumers disliking aspects of the teaching programs such that they will engage in problem behavior to avoid or escape participation in the programs.

When supervisors become aware that certain staff refrain from conducting teaching sessions because of consumer problem behavior, the recommended action is to seek clinical assistance to reduce the problem behavior. There are numerous evidence-based interventions to overcome problem behavior among individuals with developmental and related disabilities, and agency clinicians are expected to be well versed in the interventions. Hopefully, supervisors will have ready access to such clinicians. If not, supervisors should seek assistance from any other agency personnel who may be able to help devise procedures to overcome the problem behavior. The ultimate point is that staff should not be expected to continuously carry out teaching sessions if the sessions place either the staff or consumers in potential harm. How teaching sessions are conducted should be revised until the teaching can be conducted without problem behavior.

Motivating Staff to Conduct Teaching Sessions. Promoting staff motivation to conduct formal teaching sessions as frequently as expected involves the same general supervisory approach for maintaining staff proficiency in carrying out teaching plans. In this case the performance expectation of staff is usually well specified: teaching sessions should be conducted during the scheduled time. Subsequently, supervisors should monitor frequently to obtain accurate information regarding staff completion of assigned teaching sessions.

Monitoring staff completion of teaching sessions can also involve supervisors checking the data staff record regarding consumer responses to teaching sessions. Formal teaching sessions typically require staff to record consumer responses to various instructions or component steps of the written teaching plan on prepared forms. The completed forms represent a permanent product of staff performance in regard to having completed a designated session or not (see **Chapter 4** regarding monitoring products of staff performance). However, supervisors also need to directly monitor some of staffs' actual performance during a sample of teaching sessions to ensure the completed data forms accurately represent what occurs during teaching sessions (see later discussion on data collection issues).

Monitoring of staff teaching performance and associated recordkeeping should be followed by supervisory supportive and corrective feedback as appropriate. As with maintaining staff teaching proficiency, in some cases supervisors may also need to follow unsatisfactory completion of teaching sessions with more severe action. In this regard, a primary indicator of how frequently staff conduct assigned teaching sessions is the amount of supervisory attention directed to this area of performance. If supervisors do not routinely attend to teaching sessions as well as the resulting records, problems with staff completion of such sessions is likely to become a performance problem.

> **The more attention supervisors direct to staff completion of formal teaching sessions in terms of providing feedback for completing the sessions, the more likely it is that sessions will be conducted as often as they are expected to be conducted.**

Special Considerations for Motivating Staff to Complete Formal Teaching Sessions. There are also two special considerations warranting supervisor attention regarding staff motivation to conduct formal teaching sessions as often as desired. The first consideration pertains to the view common among some staff that in essence, they are not paid to be teachers. Such staff believe that because various clinical personnel have professional training in teaching strategies and are paid a professional salary, they should be the ones to conduct teaching sessions. These staff likewise believe they should not have to conduct formal teaching sessions unless they are paid the same as the clinical professionals.

The view of some staff as just described should be negated by supervisors immediately upon becoming aware of such a belief. Although the salary of direct support staff relative to professional personnel can be controversial in some cases, it is not an acceptable reason for supervisors to allow staff to fail to conduct assigned teaching sessions. It should be made quite clear to staff upon employment or when initially assigned to carry out consumer teaching sessions that teaching is one of their primary job responsibilities. If various staff refuse to accept that responsibility, then they should not maintain employment in a direct support capacity.

Another view of some staff that reduces their motivation to carry out teaching sessions is somewhat more difficult or at least time consuming to overcome. Specifically, some staff consider that consumers who have severe types of disabilities cannot benefit significantly from teaching programs. They believe such consumers will not learn skills that are intended to be taught and it is essentially a waste of time to conduct teaching sessions.

Many consumers do present serious challenges from a teaching perspective, and especially consumers with the most severe intellectual disabilities. Nonetheless, there is a very sound evidence base indicating that if teaching strategies are carried out in the intended manner, almost all individuals with disabilities will make progress in learning useful skills. If supervisors suspect that some staff do not believe conducting formal teaching sessions will benefit respective consumers, supervisors should clearly discuss this issue with the staff. It should be explained how current teaching technology has been shown to benefit the vast majority of people who have severe disabilities.

Although it is beneficial for supervisors to discuss with staff the proven effectiveness of existing teaching technologies, such a discussion does not warrant frequent or continued attention by supervisors. The best way for staff to acknowledge the benefits of conducting formal teaching sessions is to observe firsthand the consumer skill development that results from teaching sessions. If supervisors attend to staff teaching performances such that staff teach proficiently, the staff will usually see the effects of their efforts in terms of consumer skill acquisition. This is also a reason that staff are usually expected to maintain records on consumer responding. The records can be helpful in alerting staff regarding how consumers are becoming more independent across teaching sessions.

Promoting Naturalistic Teaching During Routine Activities

Staff implementation of formal teaching sessions is the most acknowledged means through which human service agencies assist consumers in learning new skills to increase their independence. To review briefly, formal teaching sessions focus on developing consumer skills that relate directly to goals and objectives within individual habilitation or education plans. The sessions are intended to be conducted in accordance with formally prepared teaching plans and data are maintained on consumer responses during the sessions.

Although formal teaching sessions represent a primary service component within most human service agencies, the effectiveness of this approach to enhancing consumer independence is often limited. The number of formal teaching sessions that can be provided each day for all consumers on an individual basis is frequently restricted due to other duties required of support staff. Most staff also spend the majority of their time working with groups of consumers such that available time for one-to-one teaching with individual consumers is reduced.

The best means for providing teaching services beyond what can occur through formal teaching sessions is through *naturalistic* teaching. As indicated previously, naturalistic teaching involves incorporating brief instructional trials during routinely occurring consumer activities. The highest quality agencies from a therapeutic perspective ensure that teaching is not limited to formal, circumscribed teaching sessions. The agencies promote an overall environment in which consumers are consistently being taught functional skills as they go about their daily routine.

The intent of naturalistic teaching is to maximize the amount of instruction provided for consumers that addresses skills immediately needed to function independently in daily activities. When naturalistic teaching is provided in a quality manner, staff are frequently providing brief instructions to consumers during an ongoing activity, following the instructions when necessary with the least amount of help consumers need to respond accurately to the instructions, and then reinforcing consumer responses. Naturalistic teaching in this manner should be a critical performance expectation of staff; one of the most important factors affecting consumer learning and increased independence is the number of instructional trials, or learning opportunities, consumers experience every day.

Many human service agencies espouse the importance of staff providing a continuous learning environment for consumers by incorporating teaching within daily activities. However, most agencies experience significant difficulties in consistently providing a true learning environment. Often what happens is that instead of staff instructing consumers how to perform a given activity themselves, staff perform the activity for the consumers. To illustrate, if a staff person observes a consumer having difficulty putting on a jacket prior to leaving a group home, the staff person helps the consumer put on the jacket instead of instructing the consumer at that moment in how to put on the jacket.

To effectively promote consumer skill development and independence, direct support staff should consistently embed teaching trials and learning opportunities within daily activities.

When staff perform a task for consumers instead of teaching the consumers how to do the task for themselves, staff are in essence depriving the consumers of learning important skills. Staff completion of activities for consumers is usually well intended in that staff are attempting to help support the consumers. Nonetheless, the end result is that consumers develop and maintain a dependence on staff support in contrast to acquiring increased independence in meeting their own needs.

In other cases, staff attempt to embed teaching trials within their interactions with consumers during daily activities but do so ineffectively. A common example is when a staff person observes a consumer experiencing difficulty doing something and instructs the consumer how to perform the task. However, the consumer does not have the skills to respond appropriately to the instruction. The staff person then repeats the instruction several times, without an accurate response by the consumer. Subsequently, because the task needs to be completed, the staff person ends up doing the task for the consumer. In this type of situation, the attempted teaching of the consumer is ineffective and the consumer does not acquire any new skills.

The examples just described illustrate the two main problems that prohibit an agency from providing a high-quality learning environment for consumers: staff either do not embed teaching within their interactions with consumers (i.e., they do things for consumers) or when they attempt to teach naturalistically, they do so ineffectively. Hence, to maximize the amount of teaching services provided within an agency, staff must be trained in naturalistic teaching skills and then use those skills appropriately on a daily basis. Supervisors usually must address each of these two issues.

Training Staff How to Teach During Routine Consumer Activities

Skills required of staff to embed teaching within routinely occurring activities with consumers represent a subset of basic teaching skills used during formal teaching sessions. To illustrate, earlier it was noted that a basic set of teaching skills that should be trained to all support staff involves how to provide an instruction to a consumer, provide assistance through prompting if a consumer does not respond to the instruction or correct an incorrect consumer response, and then reinforce the consumer's eventual correct response. Naturalistic teaching typically involves these same basic procedures except that instead of conducting the procedures repeatedly during a formal teaching session, the procedures are provided in one sequence whenever a teaching opportunity arises during the daily routine.

Although naturalistic teaching procedures stem directly from basic instructional strategies, staff usually need explicit training in how to embed teaching within routine activities *after* they have been trained in basic instruction. In particular, a key component of training staff to incorporate teaching within ongoing activities is to train them to recognize when a teaching opportunity exists. A useful guide in this respect is to train staff regarding two general situations in which immediate teaching opportunities are likely to arise.

One situation is when staff are repeatedly doing something for a consumer such as, for example, buttoning a shirt for a consumer, opening a door for a consumer, or fastening a vehicle safety belt for a consumer. It should be emphasized to staff that when they are repeatedly doing a given task for a consumer, a more therapeutic approach would be to teach the consumer do the task whenever the task needs to be performed.

A second situation that should be made apparent to staff as an opportune time to teach naturalistically is when they observe a consumer having difficulty doing something, such as problems in opening a bag of chips, putting batteries in a remote control for a television, or using a key to open a door. When a consumer wants to do something but is having difficulty doing it, a good teaching opportunity exists at that point for a staff person to intervene and teach the consumer how to perform the task. Teaching a consumer in such a situation is much more therapeutic relative to a staff person doing the task for the consumer.

The best way to train staff to recognize the two types of situations just noted as opportunities to teach naturalistically is to provide a lot of examples of the situations. Supervisors and other trainers should role play a number of examples of the two types of situations as part of their staff training endeavors. As each example is demonstrated, the role play should include how the exemplified activity should be interrupted by using the instruct, prompt, and reinforce process to teach naturalistically. Subsequently, following the steps of evidence-based training, each staff person should practice the naturalistic teaching strategy with feedback during several role plays with different examples.

As with all staff training programs, it is critical that supervisors follow training that involves role-play activities with training on the job. Supervisors should work with each staff person during the regular work routine to ensure they can appropriately incorporate naturalistic teaching strategies during typical daily activities. On-the-job training should be provided following the guidelines discussed previously in **Chapter 4**.

When training staff how to teach naturalistically—again using the performance- and competency-based training approach—supervisors should explicitly stress the importance of embedding teaching within daily activities as a primary performance expectation. Staff should be instructed to continuously look for things they are repeatedly doing for consumers and things consumers are trying to do but are having difficulty. It should be further emphasized that these situations are ideal times for staff to conduct brief teaching trials with consumers.

Stressing the importance to staff of incorporating teaching within daily activities should occur when beginning a program to train staff how to teach naturalistically and again at the end of the training session prior to staff leaving the training session. However, emphasizing the importance of naturalistic teaching usually will not be sufficient to ensure staff routinely teach during typically occurring activities. Supervisors must continue to stress such importance as they follow up the training with their day-to-day supervision of staff teaching performance.

> **Supervisors should ensure staff receive performance- and competency-based training in how to teach naturalistically *after* they have been effectively trained in basic teaching procedures.**

Ensuring Staff Perform Naturalistic Teaching After Receiving Training

To ensure staff consistently embed teaching within ongoing consumer activities, the same supervisory approach as described with formal teaching sessions should be employed. Supervisors should routinely monitor staff application of naturalistic teaching procedures and provide frequent feedback. The feedback should be supportive in nature when staff are frequently embedding teaching within their routine consumer interactions and are doing so proficiently. Corrective feedback should be provided if staff are not consistently teaching in a naturalistic manner—that is, when they are missing existing situational opportunities in which a teaching trial would be beneficial as described previously. Corrective feedback likewise should be provided if naturalistic teaching strategies are not provided proficiently when they are attempted by staff.

Providing feedback related to the degree to which staff are routinely embedding teaching during daily activities is especially important. The most common problem in human service agencies associated with naturalistic teaching is that staff do not provide nearly as much of this type of teaching as should be provided. Hence, supervisor attention in terms of providing feedback to staff should be especially frequent in regard to how often staff actually teach during daily activities.

Another action supervisors should take that is especially relevant for promoting naturalistic teaching by staff is *modeling.* Supervisors should frequently model or demonstrate provision of brief teaching trials within their own interactions with consumers while in the presence of staff. When supervisors model naturalistic teaching for staff to observe, the modeling can function as a prompt or reminder for staff that they should be incorporating teaching trials within their interactions with consumers.

As just indicated, in many agencies staff do not engage in naturalistic teaching nearly as frequently as desired. Some staff lack sufficient motivation to embed teaching services within daily activities. In particular, in some cases it is easier for staff to do certain things for consumers relative to exerting the effort to teach the consumers to do those things for themselves. The lack of motivation should be addressed as discussed earlier in this chapter with formal teaching sessions as well as in preceding chapters regarding motivational issues with other performance areas (see particularly **Chapter 8**).

There are also many staff who are very motivated to perform their jobs well from an overall perspective but do not consistently engage in the specific duty of teaching during routine activities. What often happens is staff become busy with numerous job duties that distract them from attending to teaching opportunities that arise. For the latter staff, the act of seeing their supervisor model brief teaching interactions with consumers as just noted can help them remember and attend to their own responsibilities in this regard. Observing their supervisor perform naturalistic teaching also helps impress upon staff the importance of this specific job responsibility.

> **Supervisors can help promote staff teaching during daily activities by *modeling* the use of naturalistic teaching strategies during their own interactions with consumers.**

SPECIAL CONSIDERATIONS FOR OVERCOMING PERFORMANCE PROBLEMS WITH TEACHING SERVICES

RESOLVING PROBLEMS WITH DATA COLLECTION AND DOCUMENTATION

It was noted earlier that formal teaching sessions involve staff recording consumer responses to the teaching. Data on consumer responses are critical for determining if the teaching procedures are having the desired effect on consumer skill acquisition. Correspondingly, the data are used to make decisions affecting the teaching processes. If the data indicate consumers are not making progress, then changes in how the teaching is conducted are warranted. In contrast, if the data show consumers are making satisfactory progress, then the teaching should continue in the same manner until consumers reach designated skill mastery. Data on consumer responses are also used in many cases to document that teaching sessions have been conducted by staff.

Because of the critical function data serve in the overall teaching process, data collection represents an important performance expectation of staff who conduct teaching sessions. However, in many agencies, staff data collection represents an area of frequent concern among supervisors and agency executives. One concern in this regard pertains to staff not completing assigned data-collection duties—some staff do not consistently record data on consumer responses to teaching programs.

Another problem with data collection that occurs in many agencies is that the data staff collect are not accurate. The most common reason data collection is not accurate is that staff do not record consumer responses when they should be recorded, which usually should happen before a formal teaching session is completed. Sometimes staff will wait until the end of their work shift to record data, or even the end of the work week. When staff delay their data recording, the resulting data almost always have problems with accuracy. Accuracy is compromised because staff cannot adequately remember consumer responses to each aspect of the teaching plans that were implemented at an earlier time.

A more significant problem with data collection that occurs in some cases pertains to staff fabricating data. That is, staff record information that has no relation to actual consumer responses during teaching sessions. An example some supervisors have experienced is when certain staff complete a week's worth of data-collection forms at the beginning of the week before conducting any teaching sessions.

Most supervisors will likely face problems with how certain staff record data and related documentation at some point in time. Hence, supervisors should be prepared to resolve this type of performance problem. The best preparation in this regard is to take steps to *prevent* problems from developing with staff data recording.

A common reason staff do not perform data-recording responsibilities in a proficient manner is that they are not sufficiently aware of why they need to record data. Often staff know it is expected to maintain records of consumer responses to teaching sessions but essentially see no reason for such recording. This situation typically occurs because staff are not aware of, or involved in, how the recorded data are used for any meaningful purpose.

In discussing supervisor monitoring of staff performance in **Chapter 5** it was emphasized that formal monitoring that involves recording of information on staff performance should not be conducted unless the recorded information is put to some meaningful use. The same situation pertains to staff collection of data on consumer responses to teaching programs. If the data staff record are not used for the purposes summarized earlier, then there really is no reason for staff to repeatedly collect such data. However, the data on consumer responses to teaching plans is vital for ensuring teaching is effective over the long run. Hence, supervisors must ensure staff are aware of how the data are used and the importance of recording data consistently and accurately.

The best way for staff to grasp the importance of collecting data on consumer responses to teaching plans is to involve them in the decision-making process for which the data are used. Specifically, staff who conduct teaching sessions and record data should be actively involved with other appropriate personnel in evaluating the effectiveness of teaching plans. Staff should likewise be involved in subsequent decision-making processes regarding actions to refine or continue the plans—which again, are based on the data staff record. In this manner, staff will be readily aware of what purpose their data recording serves. Such awareness can heighten staff acceptance of the importance of data and increase their likelihood of recording data in the appropriate manner.

> **When staff are actively involved in decision-making based on data they record as part of teaching duties, they are likely to understand the importance of data and potential problems with data collection are prevented or reduced.**

If problems with staff data collection occur even though staff are involved in decision-making based on the data, then their performance issues should be addressed with the same supervisory corrective procedures discussed in this and preceding chapters. There is one special circumstance though for which the usual supervisory process will need to be altered: when staff are clearly fabricating data as illustrated earlier.

When staff deliberately falsify data, it represents a serious performance issue. In essence, falsified data can lead to erroneous decisions regarding how teaching sessions should be conducted. In turn, the teaching sessions are not likely to be conducted in an appropriate manner and consumer learning will be compromised. Hence, fabrication of data by staff represents one of those areas of problematic staff performance discussed in **Chapter 8** that usually should result in immediate disciplinary action. In this respect, many agencies consider deliberate falsification of data by staff to be a performance problem warranting job termination.

The importance of staff responsibilities with data collection should be explained when those responsibilities are initially assigned in accordance with conducting formal teaching sessions. Such importance can be highlighted further if it is made apparent to staff at that point that falsification of data is not tolerated within the agency and represents grounds for dismissal. In this regard, it is a generally expected, professional responsibility of supervisors to inform staff beforehand regarding the serious consequences for falsifying data. It would be professionally inappropriate for supervisors, as well as being unfair to staff, if supervisors do *not* inform staff about the importance of accurate data collection and the consequences for intentionally falsifying data.

> **Supervisors should inform staff about the importance of data collection prior to assigning data-collection responsibilities and the consequences for falsifying data.**

Problematic Issues with Treatment Services for Challenging Behavior

The focus of this chapter has been on resolving problems with teaching services intended to increase independent functioning among agency consumers. Another major area of therapeutic services for which the performance of direct support staff has an important impact is treating challenging behavior displayed by agency consumers. The primary goal of such services is to prevent or otherwise decrease the occurrence of problem behavior. Essentially every human service agency is responsible to at least some degree for helping consumers overcome challenging behavior.

The core approach to treating challenging behavior among individuals with developmental and related disabilities usually involves the development and implementation of formal treatment programs to prevent or reduce the behavior, such as Behavior Support Plans (BSPs). The treatment plans usually are developed by agency clinicians such as psychologists or behavior analysts. As with formal teaching plans, programs to treat challenging behavior usually are expected to be carried out primarily by direct support staff.

The proficiency with which staff implement BSPs is a critical variable affecting the success of an agency's treatment of challenging behavior. If staff do not implement BSPs and related treatment plans consistently and proficiently, treatment services are not likely to be effective. Concerns with how BSPs are carried out on a daily basis are prevalent across many human service agencies. Consequently, this is a performance area that frequently warrants supervisor action to resolve problems and maintain quality treatment provision by support staff.

Overall, what supervisors should do to resolve problems with staff implementation of BSPs is the same as when addressing issues with problematic teaching and other performance areas discussed in preceding chapters. The desired consumer outcomes and performance expectations of staff are usually straightforward, involving reduction in challenging behavior and staff implementation of treatment plans in the manner they are written, respectively. Staff typically require performance- and competency-based training in how to implement the plans, and their implementation performance must be routinely monitored. Supportive and corrective feedback is likewise a critical supervisory action, focusing on the relative proficiency with which staff carry out the plans.

As with any important performance responsibility of staff, there are also special considerations with effectively supervising staff implementation of BSPs and related plans for challenging behavior. Actually there are many special considerations in this regard, due to the seriousness of various types of challenging behavior and the complexity of many treatment plans. Adequately addressing all of the special considerations requires a comprehensive text in its own right, such that it is beyond the scope here to provide a sufficient discussion. However, a useful text for supervisors concerned with promoting proficient implementation of treatment plans for challenging behavior is *Working with Staff to Overcome Challenging Behavior among People Who Have Severe Disabilities: A Guide for Getting Support Plans Carried Out* referred to in the **Selected Readings** at the end of this text.

The book just noted describes an evidence-based supervisory approach that is very similar to the supervisory protocol forming the basis of the current text. The former book also goes into detail regarding the numerous considerations specifically related to staff performance in preventing and reducing challenging behavior. Readers of the current text should find the information in *Working with Staff to Overcome Challenging Behavior among People Who Have Severe Disabilities* very compatible with the supervisory strategies discussed in this and preceding chapters.

Chapter Summary: Key Points

1. *A primary responsibility of most direct support staff is to teach meaningful skills to consumers both formally in structured teaching sessions and informally or naturalistically during ongoing daily activities.*

2. *Resolving problems with staff teaching performances usually requires supervisors to take action to: (1) improve how proficiently teaching is provided and, (2) how often teaching occurs.*

3. *Direct support staff usually should be trained in basic teaching procedures early in their employment and in specific procedures related to individual teaching plans prior to the plans being implemented.*

4. *Promoting and maintaining proficient teaching performance among staff on a routine basis requires use of evidence-based supervision: regularly monitoring staff teaching and providing supportive and corrective feedback.*

5. *A useful means of supporting proficient teaching by staff involves specially recognizing consumer skill development resulting from the teaching.*

6. *Training staff to teach naturalistically during routine activities with consumers should involve training in how to recognize informal teaching opportunities: (1) when staff repeatedly complete a given task for a consumer and, (2) when a consumer is having difficulty performing a desired task.*

7. *Supervisors can help promote staff teaching naturalistically during the day by modeling naturalistic teaching during their own interactions with consumers while staff are present.*

8. *Staff should be routinely involved in decision-making processes based on the data they collect as part of their teaching duties to help them recognize the importance of collecting and recording data.*

CHAPTER 13

REDUCING FREQUENT NONWORK BEHAVIOR

The preceding two chapters focused on specific areas of problematic staff performance that are common in many human service agencies. This chapter focuses on a more general area of problematic performance that almost every supervisor faces from to time: *frequent nonwork behavior.* Nonwork behavior, or what is sometimes referred to as *off-task behavior,* refers to staff engaging in activities at work that have no relation to their assigned job duties.

Nonwork behavior involves a variety of staff activities that compete with fulfillment of desired job duties. Some of the most common types involve staff socializing with each other about topics unrelated to the job, sitting with no apparent work activity, and engaging in personal activities such as phoning or texting friends. Other common types of nonwork behavior include staff using agency computers to play games or surf the internet, reading newspapers or other nonwork material, and eating a meal or snack during assigned work time.

When staff engage in nonwork behavior such as that just illustrated, by definition it means they are not completing expected duties. In turn, supports and services are not being provided for agency consumers at the desired level. In this regard, frequent or pervasive nonwork behavior among direct support staff is a well-acknowledged indicator of a poor-quality human service agency.

Excessive nonwork behavior is also a clear indication of *ineffective supervision*. When staff spend large amounts of time engaging in nonwork behavior, supervisors have not been effective in promoting and supporting quality work performance. Consequently, supervisors must change how they are going about the process of supervising staff work activities.

> **A key indicator of ineffective supervision is frequent or pervasive amounts of nonwork behavior among staff.**

In general, nonwork behavior should be approached by supervisors in an *indirect* manner. In contrast to directing supervisory strategies on nonwork behavior per se, supervisors should focus directly on what staff should be doing. Taking an indirect approach in this manner is recommended because of the nature of how nonwork behavior is typically most problematic.

Nonwork behavior often is most prevalent during relatively circumscribed periods of the work day. For example, in residential settings, it is common for support staff to be working diligently during the early morning when preparatory activities for the day take place (e.g., assisting consumers in getting dressed and having breakfast) prior to consumers leaving the residence to go to work or a day support site. In contrast, in the afternoon when consumers have returned to the residence there is frequently less structure such that staff are likely to be less busy and nonwork behavior is often more prevalent. To reduce nonwork behavior in the latter situation it is usually most effective for supervisors to focus their efforts on promoting what staff should be doing during the afternoon period (e.g., prompting and praising leisure engagement among consumers) rather than attending directly to their nonwork activities.

When it is apparent that nonwork behavior is frequent during certain situations within the work day, steps of the evidence-based supervision protocol should be implemented to promote and maintain desired work behavior. The overall approach to applying the protocol is the same as that described in preceding chapters. However, there are also special considerations in carrying out respective steps of the protocol that warrant attention when nonwork behavior is prevalent.

Special Consideration in Applying the Evidence-Based Supervision Protocol to Reduce Nonwork Behavior

Specifying Performance Expectations with Activity Schedules

One reason nonwork behavior is particularly frequent during certain situations is that what staff *should be doing* during those times has not been carefully specified. To illustrate, in the afternoon leisure situation just exemplified, staff may know they are expected to promote consumer leisure activity but precisely what they should do to enhance activity engagement is not clear. To ensure staff are sufficiently aware of their performance expectations, desired job tasks should be delineated by the supervisor as explicit work behavior such as with a specific activity schedule (**Chapter 3**). An illustration of such an activity schedule is provided on the following page.

EXAMPLE OF A WORK ACTIVITY SCHEDULE FOR PROMOTING CONSUMER LEISURE ENGAGEMENT

Place: *Hemlock Street Home*

Responsible staff: *Rose, Tanya*   **Time:** 4:00-5:30

Supper coordinator: *Rose*

Leisure coordinator: *Tanya*

Consumers: *all present in the home*

Supper coordinator duties:

1) Cook supper and prepare dining room table

2) Involve at least one consumer in assisting (prompt and reinforce consumer's assistance with at least part of cooking supper and preparing dining room table)

Leisure coordinator duties:

1) Provide at least two leisure items to each consumer and offer choice of one of the items to each consumer

2) After consumers choose a leisure item, move from consumer to consumer at least every 5 minutes and prompt each consumer to engage with the leisure item if not engaged and reinforce (with praise) the activity of each consumer who is engaged

---

The activity schedule just illustrated specifies job duties for each of two staff who would typically be working in the residence in the afternoon. One set of duties could be assigned to one staff person and the other set to the other staff member. Alternatively, the staff themselves could decide who will perform each respective set of duties.

For activity schedules to effectively promote desired work behavior, staff of course must be well familiar with the schedules. Such familiarity is best accomplished by the training step of the supervisory protocol, usually in an informal manner (**Chapter 4**). The supervisor should meet briefly with staff to describe their expected duties in accordance with the schedule, provide a written copy of the schedule to each staff person, and then quickly demonstrate how each duty should be performed. Subsequently, staff should carry out each duty during the regular job routine while the supervisor observes and provides supportive and corrective feedback as needed.

In some cases activity schedules will be sufficient for initially decreasing staff nonwork behavior and increasing completion of desired duties during certain work situations (accompanied by on-the-job training for complying with the respective schedule). However, the real benefit of activity schedules is that they facilitate the supervisor's job of implementing the remaining steps of the supervisory protocol. In turn, the latter steps significantly increase the likelihood that nonwork behavior will not occur at unacceptable levels in the future.

THE CRITICAL ROLE OF SUPERVISOR MONITORING IN PREVENTING AND DECREASING NONWORK BEHAVIOR

Once performance expectations have been made clear in terms of desired work behavior, and particularly through activity schedules, supervisors can then formally monitor staff performance during situations in which nonwork behavior has been frequent. The monitoring should center on the duties that staff should be performing, and conducted in accordance with guidelines discussed in **Chapter 5**. The prepared activity schedule can be used to help the supervisor focus the monitoring on the designated duties that each staff person should be performing.

Formally monitoring staff work behavior (and indirectly nonwork behavior) during times in which nonwork behavior has been problematic provides the supervisor with critical information regarding the quality of staff performance. In turn, such information allows the supervisor to provide supportive and corrective feedback to staff based on the quality of their observed work activities (see later discussion). Supervisor monitoring is also important because it makes the supervisor *visible* during times when nonwork behavior has been a concern.

Supervisor visibility has a number of benefits in regard to promoting proficient staff performance as discussed previously (again see **Chapter 5**). Of particular concern here is the effect on nonwork behavior. Nonwork behavior of staff tends to occur in an inverse fashion with supervisor visibility: the more often staff see their supervisor during times in which nonwork behavior previously has been frequent, the less likely nonwork behavior will continue to occur. Conversely, the less often staff see their supervisor (i.e., the supervisor is not frequently present in the workplace to monitor staff performance), the more likely nonwork behavior will continue to be a concern.

The effect of supervisor visibility on increasing desired work performance and decreasing nonwork behavior should be considered with a qualification. Specifically, desired work behavior is likely to increase only if staff are sufficiently aware of what they should be doing during a designated time period. Again, written activity schedules, provided with training of staff in how to perform the duties addressed by the schedules, leave little doubt that staff will be well aware of their expected duties during targeted situations.

Nonwork behavior of staff tends to vary inversely with supervisor presence; the more often a supervisor is present and visible in the staff workplace, nonwork behavior is less likely to be a problem.

Focusing Feedback on Desired Work Behavior

As just alluded to, feedback provided to staff following formal monitoring of their performance should focus on what they should be doing during a respective situation in which nonwork behavior has been prevalent. Sometimes supervisors fall into the trap of focusing the feedback on the nonwork behavior. A common scenario is that a supervisor observes staff to be sitting with no apparent work activity and then criticizes staff for their lack of work. Although in one sense this supervisory action seems logical—staff should not be engaging in nonwork behavior—it is often ineffective for promoting desired performance.

Research has indicated that providing criticism or otherwise negative comments when observing staff to be engaged in nonwork behavior can result in staff changing what they are doing—they get busy. However, such comments alone do not consistently result in staff getting busy doing the specific duties that they should be doing in the given situation. To ensure staff disengage from nonwork behavior *and* then engage in the desired duties that should occur, supervisors should provide feedback to staff that specifies what should be occurring. One generally recommended way for supervisors to provide the latter specification is to refer staff to the activity schedule and point out what duties the schedule instructs staff to be performing.

Whenever supervisors respond to apparent nonwork behavior by directing staff to what they should be doing, the supervisors should return to the work site relatively quickly to again monitor staff performance in accordance with the activity schedule. In many cases, more desirable performance will be observed at that time such that supervisors can then provide supportive feedback to staff. If more desirable performance is not observed however and nonwork behavior is still prevalent, then corrective feedback should be provided again. If nonwork behavior continues to be observed frequently during subsequent observations by the supervisor, then it is likely that disciplinary action will need to be initiated (**Chapter 8**).

> **When supervisors provide staff with feedback regarding nonwork behavior, the feedback should focus on what staff should be doing and not on the nonwork behavior per se.**

General Considerations for Reducing Frequent Nonwork Behavior

In addition to special considerations when implementing respective steps of the evidence-based supervision protocol to reduce nonwork behavior, there are also some more general considerations warranting attention. These include establishing reasonable goals relating to nonwork behavior, maintaining flexibility in addressing nonwork behavior, and responding to subtle types of nonwork behavior.

Reasonable Goals for Nonwork Behavior

Nonwork behavior is a natural phenomenon within all jobs. No one, staff or supervisors, spends every minute at work performing job duties. Hence, there essentially will always be some amount of nonwork behavior among staff. Supervisors must determine what constitutes acceptable and unacceptable amounts of nonwork behavior among the staff they supervise.

There is no hard and fast rule for determining acceptable versus unacceptable amounts of nonwork behavior, or goals that supervisors should strive to attain in this regard. In an absolute sense, decisions about whether nonwork behavior is problematic should be based on the degree to which agency consumers are attaining specified outcomes as a function of staff work performance. If consumers are attaining the desired outcomes within expected timelines, then existing levels of nonwork behavior generally would not be considered problematic. However, it is difficult to precisely align what staff are doing on a daily basis with consumer outcome attainment, which often takes many days to achieve. Hence, other considerations are also warranted when establishing goals for acceptable levels of nonwork behavior.

One means for considering whether nonwork behavior is sufficiently pervasive to represent a significant problem is to address specific situations in which nonwork behavior is most prevalent. As indicated earlier, frequent nonwork behavior often is associated with certain work periods or times of day. In these cases, the recommended strategy as described earlier is to focus on the work that staff should be performing in the respective situations. If staff are spending the vast majority of their time in those situations performing assigned duties, albeit not necessarily 100% of the time, then generally nonwork behavior is not overly problematic.

In situations as just referred to, a general guideline is that if staff are spending around 80% or more of their time performing assigned duties, then nonwork behavior is usually not considered a serious issue. The 80% figure is a *guideline* and not a hard and fast rule. Because some amount of nonwork behavior will essentially always occur—and as described below, sometimes necessary for the welfare of staff—supervisors must be attentive to why nonwork behavior is occurring. Supervisors should also be flexible in deciding whether nonwork behavior represents a serious problem.

SUPERVISOR FLEXIBILITY IN ADDRESSING NONWORK BEHAVIOR IN CERTAIN SITUATIONS

Nonwork Behavior Following Challenging Situations. Many direct support staff engage in work activities, both scheduled and unscheduled as part of the job routine, that can be physically challenging. A common example is when one or more staff have to intervene physically with a consumer to prevent the consumer from harming someone, which may include restraining the individual for a period of time. Using physical restraint for protective purposes can be physically demanding for staff, often resulting in shortness of breath and elevated heart rate. Once the challenging situation is resolved, the staff need a period of inactivity to regain their composure.

When staff rest for a period of time following a physically challenging activity, such as restraining an individual, their activity appears as nonwork behavior (e.g., sitting quietly with no other activity). However, it would be unwise to consider such behavior as inappropriate given the circumstances—the rest period is necessary for the welfare of the staff. If a supervisor entered the staff workplace during the rest period, it would be inadvisable to immediately redirect the staff to duties as specified in the work activity schedule for that time period. It would be highly inappropriate to criticize or provide other negative comments for the ongoing staff activity.

In the type of situation just illustrated, a supervisor must have adequate knowledge of what has occurred in the workplace, either based on observation or brief interaction with staff. Such information is necessary to prevent the supervisor from taking inappropriate action with staff for what appears on the surface to be nonwork behavior but actually is quite justified. This is yet another reason for the importance of a supervisor frequently monitoring staff work activities. If a supervisor is routinely present in the staff workplace, the supervisor usually becomes quickly aware upon entering the work site that an unusual incident has occurred. Such awareness should prompt the supervisor to then obtain relevant information from staff about what has taken place. The supervisor subsequently is less likely to take inappropriate action with the involved staff.

> **Supervisors should acknowledge that staff may need a break following very challenging physical activities and not consider the break as inappropriate nonwork behavior.**

Consideration of Staff Break Times. The daily job routine of direct support staff includes break periods during which no work activities are expected of staff. Break times may be scheduled for highly specific time periods, or more loosely on a daily basis as determined by staff needs as long as the breaks occur within a generally assigned time frame. Break periods are needed for the physical and mental well being of staff and usually required by policy and work or union contracts. Activities staff engage in during break times usually represent nonwork behavior, at least in terms of what the staff are observed to be doing.

Nonwork behavior during break periods is appropriate as just described, provided the breaks occur within the time parameters allowed within the agency. Hence, break periods represent another situation for which it would be inappropriate for supervisors, upon entering the staff work area, to redirect staff to specific work duties (i.e., because a supervisor observes apparent nonwork behavior that usually constitutes staff activity during breaks). Supervisors must have adequate knowledge about when breaks are occurring so they can respond accordingly if they enter the area in which staff are on break and not performing work duties.

One factor that can facilitate a supervisor's awareness of when staff are taking an appropriate work break versus engaging in inappropriate nonwork behavior is to ensure staff have a designated area specifically for break times. Ideally the area would be a specially designated break room. If such a room is not available, then there should be at least a specific area within a room. In this manner, when staff are in the break area, it will be readily apparent to a supervisor that they are taking a break and engaging in acceptable nonwork behavior that otherwise would be considered inappropriate. It is also helpful if supervisors maintain awareness of when breaks are expected to be taken by staff.

In contrast, if there is not a designated break area and staff must take their breaks in the same location in which they regularly work, it can be difficult for supervisors to discriminate when staff are taking an appropriate break versus engaging in inappropriate nonwork behavior. Additionally, at times some staff take advantage of not having a designated break area. To illustrate, certain staff may be engaging in nonwork activity in the work area when they should be working. When the latter staff see the supervisor enter the area, they misleadingly inform the supervisor that they are on their scheduled break time. This type of situation, which can be difficult for a supervisor to resolve, can be avoided if supervisors ensure that staff have a specially designated area that is used exclusively for taking work breaks.

There is an additional advantage of providing special break areas for staff that pertains to staff work enjoyment. Having an area away from the routine work site for break time makes it easier for staff to disassociate from their work responsibilities, and truly relax or engage in another desired activity for a period of time. In turn, staff tend to enjoy their breaks more if the breaks are totally separate from all work expectations and ongoing events in the workplace that may require their attention. Staff also often appreciate a supervisor who ensures that they have a break area that allows them to be away from the regular work environment for their break activities. Such appreciation enhances staff enjoyment associated with working for a particular supervisor, as well as with their overall work enjoyment.

> **Providing specified locations for staff work breaks facilitates a supervisor's job of determining when staff are on an appropriate break versus engaging in inappropriate nonwork behavior.**

Consideration of Nonwork Exceptions to Typically Diligent Work. Previous chapters have emphasized the importance of supervisors routinely interacting with staff in a pleasant and respectful manner to help motivate staff to work diligently and enjoy their work. One means of interacting pleasantly and respectfully pertains to supervisor observations of a staff person's occasional nonwork behavior that represents an exception to the individual's typically diligent work. That is, a supervisor usually observes the staff person to be performing expected job duties but on occasion, observes nonwork behavior to be occurring.

When a supervisor enters the work area and observes a staff member to be engaged in nonwork behavior that represents an exception to the individual's usually diligent performance, the supervisor generally should not attend to the nonwork behavior. Rather, the supervisor should briefly interact in a courteous manner with the staff person and then go about other supervisory duties. This action is often well appreciated by staff.

Staff know when they are not performing expected duties and they usually realize that the supervisor is likely to be aware of their ongoing, nonwork activities. When the supervisor does not respond or otherwise bring attention to the occasional nonwork behavior, it indicates that the supervisor trusts the staff person's judgment and is not concerned with what the staff person is currently doing. Having the supervisor's trust can help the staff person enjoy working for the supervisor, and increase enjoyment with the job overall.

The rationale for the supervisor action just noted is based on the fact that some nonwork behavior is to be expected. Sometimes an individual has to return an important phone call that should not wait until break time, for example, or simply gets caught up in a personal conversation with another staff member. As long as these activities are infrequent and not characteristic of a staff person's usual work performance, they rarely interfere with completion of necessary job duties. If a supervisor does not recognize or accept this characteristic of the world of work and attends to every instance of nonwork behavior, the impact on staff tends to be quite negative. Such supervisory action reduces staff enjoyment associated with working for the supervisor as well as enjoyment with the job itself.

In recommending that supervisors not attend to occasional observations of staff nonwork behavior, it should be emphasized that the recommendation pertains to those staff whom the supervisor usually observes to be very diligent with their work performance. Disregard for nonwork behavior should not be based on any other factor, and particularly not on any special friendship or other nonwork relationship a supervisor has with a staff person. Also, if a supervisor observes over time that a staff person who previously appeared very diligent is spending increasing amounts of time engaging in nonwork behavior, then the latter activities should become a concern for the supervisor. In turn, the supervisor should then address the problematic nonwork behavior in the manner discussed previously.

REDUCING SUBTLE TYPES OF FREQUENT NONWORK BEHAVIOR

Sometimes supervisors must address nonwork behavior among certain staff that is more subtle than sitting with no work activity and other more apparent types of nonwork activities described to this point. The most common example is when a staff member avoids completing important job duties by spending excessive amounts of time on other, perhaps less important work activities. To illustrate, some staff intentionally avoid direct contact work with consumers for teaching or promoting leisure engagement, for example, by maximizing their time spent on paper work or computer activities. The latter work may be important to complete but the staff extend the amount of time spent on the duties beyond what should be necessary to complete them.

When staff avoid important duties by continuously engaging in other work activities beyond what is reasonable, the situation can be difficult for supervisors to resolve. The problem is not what staff are doing per se, but that they are spending too much time doing it. The excessive amount of time spent on certain tasks interferes with completion of other important duties.

When staff spend excessive amounts of time on certain tasks that detract from completion of other work duties, the process also can have a negative effect on other staff. Staff are usually aware when one of their peers is avoiding certain duties by overly attending to other tasks, which often are less demanding that the former tasks. Staff can become seriously disgruntled with their peer in this situation, due in part to having to work harder to perform the duties that the peer is not completing. Such a situation erodes work enjoyment among the former staff.

To resolve problems with staff avoiding important duties by needlessly expanding their time spent on other tasks, supervisors need to have a good awareness of how much time should be necessary to complete respective work tasks. The best way for supervisors to maintain sufficient knowledge in this regard is to have staff job expectations well specified (e.g., with activity schedules) and frequently monitor staff performance in their work area (see **Chapter 5** for elaboration). When supervisors do have good evidence that some staff are avoiding respective duties by overly attending to selected work tasks, they should respond to the situation in the same manner as described earlier with less subtle types of nonwork behavior. In some cases, supervisors will also have to provide more explicit time frames for staff regarding the amount of allowable time to complete certain tasks.

Chapter Summary: Key Points

1. *Frequent nonwork behavior among staff is usually associated with circumscribed situations during the work day and warrants supervisor attention during those situations.*

2. *Supervisors generally should address frequent nonwork behavior indirectly by focusing their interactions with staff on what should be occurring rather than the nonwork behavior per se.*

3. *Frequent nonwork behavior during certain situations is most readily prevented or reduced by supervisors providing work activity schedules regarding what staff should be doing during the situations, being frequently present in the staff work area to monitor staff performance, and providing feedback that focuses on the duties that staff should be performing.*

4. *Everyone engages in some nonwork behavior on the job; supervisors must determine if the amount of nonwork behavior is problematic on a situation-by-situation basis by focusing on whether duties expected during each situation are being completed satisfactorily or not.*

5. *Supervisors must be flexible in deciding to intervene to reduce nonwork behavior, and realize that such behavior can be appropriate in some situations such as immediately after staff have been involved in physically demanding work activities and during agency-approved break times.*

SECTION IV

SELECTED READINGS

Selected Readings

The readings referenced in this section provide supplemental information for topics covered in **Chapters 1-13**. To facilitate selection of those readings most relevant to particular topics of interest, readings are grouped according to the following content areas.

- Training Staff to Teach People with Intellectual and Developmental Disabilities
- Training Other Work Skills to Staff
- Improving and Maintaining Ongoing Areas of Staff Performance (Varying Job Duties)
- Promoting Supportive Social Interactions with Consumers
- Promoting Treatment Services Specific to Groups of Consumers
- Promoting Quality Personal Care and Support for Consumers
- Promoting Quality Documentation and Record Keeping by Staff
- Preventing and Reducing Absenteeism
- Promoting Work Enjoyment
- Review and Discussion Papers Related to Evidence-Based Supervision
- Books Related to Evidence-Based Supervision
- A Training Curriculum for Supervisors

The first nine sections presented above provide references to research articles that represent the evidence base for the information presented throughout the preceding chapters. The next two sections provide references pertaining to overviews and discussions regarding specific areas of evidence-based supervision, and the final section provides a reference for a curriculum designed to train supervisors in evidence-based supervision. It should also be noted, however, that information provided in individual readings often covers several different content areas. The groupings of the readings into the above categories represent the primary topic addressed within each reading.

TRAINING STAFF TO TEACH PEOPLE WITH INTELLECTUAL AND DEVELOPMENTAL DISABILITIES

Catania, C.N., Almeida, D., Liu-Constant, B., & Reed, F.D.D. (2009). Video modeling to train staff to implement discrete-trial instruction. *Journal of Applied Behavior Analysis, 42,* 387-392.

Ducharme, J.M., & Feldman, M.A. (1992). Comparison of staff training strategies to prompt generalized teaching skills. *Journal of Applied Behavior Analysis, 25,* 165-179.

Engleman, K.K., Altus, D.E., Mosier, M.C., & Mathews, R.M. (2003). Brief training to promote the use of less intrusive prompts by nursing assistants in a dementia care unit. *Journal of Applied Behavior Analysis, 36,* 129-132.

Fabry, P.L. & Reid, D.H. (1978). Teaching foster grandparents to train severely handicapped persons. *Journal of Applied Behavior Analysis, 11,* 111-123.

Hundert, J. (1982). Training teachers in generalizing writing of behavior modification programs for multi-handicapped deaf children. *Journal of Applied Behavior Analysis, 15,* 111-122.

Kissel, R.C., Whitman, T.L., & Reid, D.H. (1983). An institutional staff training and self-management program for developing multiple self-care skills in severely/profoundly retarded individuals. *Journal of Applied Behavior Analysis, 16,* 395-415.

Lerman, D.C., Tetreault, A., Hovanetz, A., Strobel, M., & Garro, J. (2008). Further evaluation of a brief, intensive teacher-training model. *Journal of Applied Behavior Analysis, 41*, 243-248.

MacDuff, G.S., Krantz, P.J., MacDuff, M.A., & McClannahan, L.E. (1988). Providing incidental teaching for autistic children: A rapid training procedure for therapists. *Education and Treatment of Children, 11*, 205-217.

McGuire, P.S., Vanburen, P., Alger, K., & Thomas, D.R. (1987). Assessing teaching opportunities in a residential treatment facility. *Behavioral Residential Treatment, 2*, 199-210.

Miles, N.I., & Wilder, D.A. (2009). The effects of behavioral skills training on caregiver implementation of guided compliance. *Journal of Applied Behavior Analysis, 42*, 405-410.

Morch, W.T., & Eikeseth, S. (1992). Some issues in staff training and improvement. *Research in Developmental Disabilities, 13*, 43-55.

Nigro-Bruzzi, D., & Sturmey, P. (2010). The effects of behavioral skills training on mand training by staff and unprompted vocal mands by children. *Journal of Applied Behavior Analysis, 43*, 757-761.

Parsons, M.B., & Reid, D.H. (1999). Training basic teaching skills to paraeducators of students with severe disabilities: A one-day program. *Teaching Exceptional Children, 31*, 48-54.

Parsons, M.B., Reid, D.H., & Green, C.W. (1993). Preparing direct service staff to teach people with severe disabilities: A comprehensive evaluation of an effective and acceptable training program. *Behavioral Residential Treatment, 8*, 163-185.

Parsons, M.B., Reid, D.H., & Green, C.W. (1996). Training basic teaching skills to community and institutional support staff for people with severe disabilities: A one-day program. *Research in Developmental Disabilities, 17*, 467-485.

Parsons, M.B., Reid, D.H., & Lattimore, L. P. (2009). Increasing independence of adults with autism in community activities: A brief, embedded teaching strategy. *Behavior Analysis in Practice, 2,* 40-48.

Sarokoff, R.A., & Sturmey, P. (2004). The effects of behavioral skills training on staff implementation of discrete-trial teaching. *Journal of Applied Behavior Analysis, 37,* 535-538.

Schepis, M.M., Ownbey, J.B., Parsons, M.B., & Reid, D.H. (2000). Training support staff to teach young children with disabilities in an inclusive preschool setting. *Journal of Positive Behavior Interventions, 2,* 170-178.

Schepis, M.M., Reid, D.H., Ownbey, J., & Parsons, M.B. (2001). Training support staff to embed teaching within natural routines of young children with disabilities in an inclusive preschool. *Journal of Applied Behavior Analysis, 34,* 313-327.

Schwartz, I.S., Anderson, S.R., & Halle, J.W. (1989). Training teachers to use naturalistic time delay: Effects on teacher behavior and on the language use of students. *The Journal of the Association for the Severely Handicapped, 14,* 48-57.

Singer, G., Sowers, J., & Irvin, L.K. (1986). Computer-assisted video instruction for training paraprofessionals in rural special education. *Journal of Special Education Technology, 8,* 27-34.

Vonderen, A.V., Duker, P., & Didden, R. (2010). Instruction and video feedback to improve staff's trainer behaviour and response prompting during one-to-one training with young children with severe intellectual disability. *Research in Developmental Disabilities, 31,* 1481-1490.

TRAINING OTHER WORKS SKILLS TO STAFF

Adams, G.L., Tallon, R.J., & Rimell, P. (1980). A comparison of lecture versus role-playing in the training of the use of positive reinforcement. *Journal of Organizational Behavior Management, 2*(3), 205-212.

Anderson, T.K., Kratochwill, T.R., & Bergan, J.R. (1986). Training teachers in behavioral consultation and therapy: An analysis of verbal behaviors. *Journal of School Psychology, 24,* 229-241.

Baker, D.J. (1998). Effects of video-based staff training with manager-led exercises in residential support. *Mental Retardation, 36,* 198-204.

Blaxall, M.C.D., Parsonson, B.S., & Robertson, N.R. (1993). The development and evaluation of a sexual harassment contact person training package. *Behavior Modification, 17,* 148-163.

Bowles, P.E., Jr., & Nelson, R.O. (1976). Training teachers as mediators: Efficacy of a workshop versus the bug-in-the-ear technique. *Journal of School Psychology, 14,* 15-26.

Brown, F., & Esquith, D. (1983). Effects of two grading contingencies on practicum assignments with trainees in a severely multiply handicapped program. *Education and Training of the Mentally Retarded, 18,* 287-292.

Collins, S., Higbee, T.S., & Salzberg, C.L. (2009). The effects of video modeling on staff implementation of a problem-solving intervention with adults with developmental disabilities. *Journal of Applied Behavior Analysis, 42,* 849-854.

Cooper, K.J., & Browder, D.M. (2001). Preparing staff to enhance active participation of adults with severe disabilities by offering choice and prompting performance during a community purchasing activity. *Research in Developmental Disabilities, 22,* 1-20.

Cotnoir-Bichelman, N.M., Thompson, R.H., McKerchar, P.M., & Haremza, J.L. (2006). Training student teachers to reposition infants frequently. *Journal of Applied Behavior Analysis, 39,* 489-494.

Dancer, D.D., Braukmann, C.J., Schumaker, J.B., Kirigin, K.A., Willner, A.G., & Wolf, M.M. (1978). The training and validation of behavior observation and description skills. *Behavior Modification, 2,* 113-133.

Delameter, A.M., Connors, C.K., & Wells, K.C. (1984). A comparison of staff training procedures: Behavioral applications in the child psychiatric inpatient setting. *Behavior Modification, 8,* 39-58.

Demchak, M.A., & Browder, D.M. (1990). An evaluation of the pyramid model of staff training in group homes for adults with severe handicaps. *Education and Training in Mental Retardation, 25,* 150-163.

Digennaro-Reed, F.D., Codding, R., Catania, C.N., & Maguire, H. (2010). Effects of video modeling on treatment integrity of behavioral interventions. *Journal of Applied Behavior Analysis, 43,* 291-295.

Edwards, G., & Bergman, J.S. (1982). Evaluation of a feeding training program for caregivers of individuals who are severely physically handicapped. *Journal of the Association for the Severely Handicapped, 7,* 93-100.

Embregts, P.J.C.M. (2002). Effect of resident and direct-care staff training on responding during social interactions. *Research in Developmental Disabilities, 23,* 353-366.

Finn, L.L., & Sturmey, P. (2009). The effect of peer-to-peer training on staff interactions with adults with dual diagnoses. *Research in Developmental Disabilities, 30,* 96-106.

Fitzgerald, J.R., Reid, D.H., Schepis, M.M., Faw, G.D., Welty, P.A., & Pyfer, L.M. (1984). A rapid training procedure for teaching manual sign language skills to multidisciplinary institutional staff. *Applied Research in Mental Retardation, 5,* 451-469.

Ford, J.E. (1983). Application of a personalized system of instruction to a large, personnel training program. *Journal of Organizational Behavior Management, 5(3/4),* 57-65.

Fox, C.J., & Sulzer-Azaroff, B. (1989). The effectiveness of two different sources of feedback on staff teaching of fire evacuation skills. *Journal of Organizational Behavior Management, 10(2),* 19-35.

Gage, M.A., Fredericks, H.D.B., Johnson-Dorn, N., & Lindley-Southard, B. (1982). Inservice training for staffs of group homes and work activity centers serving developmentally disabled adults. *The Journal of the Association for Persons with Severe Handicaps, 7,* 60-70.

Gardner, J.M. (1972). Teaching behavior modification to non-professionals. *Journal of Applied Behavior Analysis, 5,* 517-521.

Green, C.W., Parsons, M.B., & Reid, D.H. (1993). Integrating instructional procedures into traditional congregate care situations for people with severe disabilities. *Behavioral Residential Treatment, 8,* 243-262.

Green, C.W., & Reid, D.H. (1994). A comprehensive evaluation of a train-the-trainers model for training education staff to assemble adaptive switches. *Journal of Mental and Physical Disabilities, 6,* 219-238.

Inge, K.J., & Snell, M.E. (1985). Teaching positioning and handling techniques to public school personnel through inservice training. *The Journal of the Association for Persons with Severe Handicaps, 10,* 105-110.

Jensen, J.M., Parsons, M.B., & Reid, D.H. (1998). Supervisory training for teachers: Mulitple, long-term effects in an education program for adults with severe disabilities. *Research in Developmental Disabilities, 19,* 449-463.

Johnson, M.D., & Fawcett, S.B. (1994). Courteous service: Its assessment and modification in a human service organization. *Journal of Applied Behavior Analysis, 27,* 145-152.

Jones, F.H., & Eimers, R.C. (1975). Role playing to train elementary teachers to use a classroom management "skill package". *Journal of Applied Behavior Analysis, 8,* 421-433.

Jones, F.H., Fremouw, W., & Carples, S. (1977). Pyramid training of elementary school teachers to use a classroom management "skill package". *Journal of Applied Behavior Analysis, 10,* 239-253.

Katz, R.C., & Lutzker, J.R. (1980). A comparison of three methods for training timeout. *Behavior Research of Severe Developmental Disabilities, 1,* 123-130.

Koegel, R.L., Russo, D.C., & Rincover, A. (1977). Assessing and training teachers in the generalized use of behavior modification with autistic children. *Journal of Applied Behavior Analysis, 10,* 197-205.

Lavie, T., & Sturmey, P. (2002). Training staff to conduct a paired-stimulus preference assessment. *Journal of Applied Behavior Analysis, 35,* 209-211.

Macurik, K.M., O'Kane, N.P., Malanga, P., & Reid, D.H. (2008). Video training of support staff in intervention plans for challenging behavior: Comparison with live training. *Behavioral Interventions, 23,* 143-163.

Maher, C.A. (1984). Training educational administrators in organizational behavior management: Program description and evaluation. *Journal of Organizational Behavior Management, 6*(1), 79-97.

Maloney, D.M., Phillips, E.L., Fixsen, D.L., & Wolf, M.M. (1975). Training techniques for staff in group homes for juvenile defenders: An Analysis. *Criminal Justice and Behavior, 2,* 195-215.

Mansdorf, I.J., & Burstein, Y. (1986). Case manager: A clinical tool for training residential treatment staff. *Behavioral Residential Treatment, 1,* 155-168.

McKeown, Jr., D., Adams, H.E., & Forehand, R. (1975). Generalization to the classroom of principles of behavior modification taught to teachers. *Behavior Research & Therapy, 13,* 85-92.

Moore, J.W., & Fisher, W.W. (2007). The effects of videotape modeling on staff acquisition of functional analysis methodology. *Journal of Applied Behavior Analysis, 40,* 197-202.

Moser, A.J. (1973). Training nonprofessional behavioral change agents. *Journal of School Psychology, 11,* 251-255.

Neef, N.A., Trachtenberg, S., Loeb, J., & Sterner, K. (1991). Video-based training of respite care providers: An interactional analysis of presentation format. *Journal of Applied Behavior Analysis, 24,* 473-486.

Page, T.J., Christian, J.G., Iwata, B.A., Reid, D.H., Crow, R.E., & Dorsey, M.F. (1981). Evaluating and training interdisciplinary teams in writing IPP goals and objectives. *Mental Retardation, 19,* 25-27.

Page, T.J., Iwata, B.A., & Reid, D.H. (1982). Pyramidal training: A large-scale application with institutional staff. *Journal of Applied Behavior Analysis, 15,* 335-351.

Panyan, M.C., & Patterson, E.T. (1974). Teaching attendants the applied aspects of behavior modification. *Mental Retardation, 12,* 30-32.

Parsons, M.B., McCarn, J.E., & Reid, D.H. (1993). Evaluating and increasing meal-related choices throughout a service setting for people with severe disabilities. *Journal of the Association for Persons with Severe Handicaps, 18,* 253-260.

Parsons, M.B., & Reid, D.H. (1995). Training residential supervisors to provide feedback for maintaining staff teaching skills with people who have severe disabilities. *Journal of Applied Behavior Analysis, 28,* 317-322.

Quilitch, H.R., Miller, S.M., McConnell, M.A., & Bryant, S. (1975). Teaching personnel to implement behavioral programs. *Educational Technology,* 27-31.

Realon, R.E., Wheeler, A.J., Spring, B., & Springer, M. (1986). Evaluating the quality of training delivered by direct-care staff in a state mental retardation center. *Behavioral Residential Treatment, 1,* 199-212.

Reid, D.H., Rotholz, D.A., Parsons, M.B., Braswell, B.A., Green, C.W., et al. (2003). Training human service supervisors in aspects of positive behavior support: Evaluation of a statewide, performance-based program. *Journal of Positive Behavior Interventions, 5,* 35-46.

Rosales, R., Stone, K., & Rehfeldt, R.A. (2009). The effects of behavioral skills training on implementation of the Picture Exchange Communication system. *Journal of Applied Behavior Analysis, 42,* 541-549.

Roscoe, E.M., & Fisher, W.W. (2008). Evaluation of an efficient method for training staff to implement stimulus preference assessments. *Journal of Applied Behavior Analysis, 41,* 249-254.

Roscoe, E.M., Fisher, W.W., Glover, A.C., & Volkert, V.M. (2006). Evaluating the relative effects of feedback and contingent money for staff training of stimulus preference assessments. *Journal of Applied Behavior Analysis, 39,* 63-77.

Rosen, H.S., Yerushalmi, C.J., & Walker, J.C. (1986). Training community residential staff: Evaluation and follow-up. *Behavioral Residential Treatment, 1,* 15-38.

Sanson-Fister, R.W., Seymour, F.W., & Baer, D.M. (1976). Training institutional staff to alter delinquents' conversation. *Journal of Behavior Therapy & Experimental Psychiatry, 7,* 243-247.

Schepis, M.M., & Reid, D.H. (1993). Training direct service staff in congregate settings to interact with people with severe disabilities: A quick, effective, and acceptable program. *Behavioral Interventions, 1,* 13-26.

Schinke, S.P. & Wong, S.E. (1977). Evaluation of staff training in group homes for retarded persons. *American Journal of Mental Deficiency, 82,* 130-136.

Schinke, S.P., & Wong, S.E. (1978). Teaching child care workers: A Behavioral approach. *Child Care Quarterly, 7,* 45-61.

Shane, H. (1974). Command performance: A behavior modification technique in a game format. *Mental Retardation, 12,* 18-20.

Shore, B.A., Iwata, B.A., Vollmer, T.R., Lerman, D.C., & Zarcone, J.R. (1995). Pyramidal staff training in the extension of treatment for severe behavior disorders. *Journal of Applied Behavior Analysis, 28,* 323-332.

Sigafoos, J., Roberts, D., Couzens, D., & Caycho, L. (1992). Improving instruction for adults with developmental disabilities: Evaluation of a staff training package. *Behavior Residential Treatment, 7,* 283-297.

Sloat, K.C.M., Tharp, R.G., & Gallimore, R. (1977). The incremental effectiveness of classroom-based teacher-training techniques. *Behavior Therapy, 8*, 810-818.

Smth, T., Parker, T., Taubman, M., & Lovass, O.I. (1992). Transfer of staff training from workshops to group homes: A failure to generalize across settings. *Research in Developmental Disabilities, 13*, 57-71.

Speidel, G.E., & Tharp, R.G. (1978). Teacher-training workshop strategy: Instructions, discrimination training, modeling, guided practice, and video feedback. *Behavior Therapy, 9*, 735-739.

Stein, T.J. (1975). Some ethical considerations of short-term workshops in the principles and methods of behavior modification. *Journal of Applied Behavior Analysis, 8*, 113-115.

Stoddard, L.T., McIlvane, W.J., McDonagh, E.C., & Kledaras, J.B. (1986). The use of picture programs in teaching direct care staff. *Applied Research in Mental Retardation, 7*, 349-358.

Stumphauzer, J.S., & Davis, L.C. (1983). Training Mexican American mental health personnel in behavior therapy. *Journal of Behavior Therapy & Experimental Psychiatry, 14*, 215-217.

Templeman, T.P., Fredericks, H.D.B., Bunse, C., & Moses, C. (1983). Teaching research in-service training model. *Education and Training of the Mentally Retarded, 28*, 245-252.

Tynam, W.D., & Gengo, V. (1992). Staff training in a pediatric rehabilitation hospital: Development of behavioral engineers. *Journal of Developmental and Physical Disabilities, 4*, 299-306.

van den Pol, R.A., Reid, D.H., & Fuqua, R.W. (1983). Peer training of safety-related skills to institutional staff: Benefits for trainers and trainees. *Journal of Applied Behavior Analysis, 16*, 139-156.

Watson, L.S., Jr., Gardner, J.M., & Sanders, C. (1971). Shaping and maintaining behavior modification skills in staff members in a MR institution: Columbus State Institute Behavior Modification Program. *Mental Retardation, 9,* 39-42.

Watson, L.S., Jr., & Uzzell, R. (1980). A program for teaching behavior modification skills to institutional staff. *Applied Research in Mental Retardation, 1,* 41-53.

Willner, A.G., Braukmann, C.J., Kirigin, K.A., Fixsen, D.L., Phillips, E.L., & Wolf, M.M. (1977). The training and validation of youth-preferred social behaviors of child-care personnel. *Journal of Applied Behavior Analysis, 10,* 219-230.

Ziarnik, J.P., & Bernstein, G.S. (1982). A critical examination of the effect of inservice training on staff performance. *Mental Retardation, 20,* 109-114.

Zlomke, L.C., & Benjamin, V.A., Jr. (1983). Staff in-service: Measuring effectiveness through client behavior change. *Education and Training of the Mentally Retarded, 18,* 125-130.

IMPROVING AND MAINTAINING ONGOING AREAS OF STAFF PERFORMANCE (VARYING JOB DUTIES)

Andrasik, F., & McNamara, J.R. (1977). Optimizing staff performance in an institutional behavior change system: A pilot study. *Behavior Modification, 1,* 235.

Aragon, A., & Holmes, P.A. (1990). Engagement of patients and staff on a psychiatric hospital ward. *Journal of Organizational Behavior Management, 11*(2), 171-188.

Azrin, N.H., Jammer, J.P., & Besalel, V.A. (1989). Student learning as the basis for reinforcement to the instructor. *Behavioral Residential Treatment, 4,* 159-170.

Azrin, N.H., & Pye, G.E. (1989). Staff management by behavioral contracting. *Behavioral Residential Treatment, 4,* 89-98.

Barrowclough, C., & Fleming, I. (1986). Training direct care staff in goal planning with elderly people. *Behavioral Psychotherapy, 14,* 192-209.

Bible, G.H., & Sneed, T.J. (1976). Some effects of an accreditation survey on program completion at a state institution. *Mental Retardation, 14,* 14-15.

Bourdon, R. (1982). Measuring and tracking management performance for accountability. *Journal of Organizational Behavior Management, 4*(3/4), 101-112.

Brackett, L., Reid, D.H., & Green, C.W. (2005). Effects of reactivity to observations on staff performance. *Journal of Applied Behavior Analysis, 40,* 191-195.

Bricker, W.A., Morgan, D.G., & Grabowski, J.G. (1972). Development and maintenance of a behavior modification repertoire of cottage attendants through TV feedback. *American Journal of Mental Deficiency, 77,* 128-136.

Byrd, G.R., Sawyer, B.P., & Locke, B.J. (1983). Improving direct care via minimal changes in conventional resources: An empirical analysis. *Mental Retardation, 21,* 164-168.

Calpin, J.P., Edelstein, B., & Redmon, W.K. (1988). Performance feedback and goal setting to improve mental health center staff productivity. *Journal of Organizational Behavior Management, 9*(2), 35-58.

Codding, R.S., Feinberg, A.B., Dunn, E.K., & Pace, G.M. (2005). Effects of immediate performance feedback on implementation of behavior support plans. *Journal of Applied Behavior Analysis, 38,* 205-219.

Codding, R.S., Livanis, A., Pace, G.M., & Vaca, L. (2008). Using performance feedback to improve treatment integrity of classwide behavior plans: An investigation of observer reactivity. *Journal of Applied Behavior Analysis, 41,* 417-422.

Cook, T., & Dixon, M.R. (2005). Performance feedback and probabilistic bonus contingencies among employees in a human service organization. *Journal of Organizational Behavior Management, 25*(3), 45-63.

Dib, N., & Sturmey, P. (2007). Reducing student stereotypy by improving teachers' implementation of discrete-trial teaching. *Journal of Applied Behavior Analysis, 40,* 339-343.

DiGennaro, F.D., Martens, B.K., & Kleinmann, A.E. (2007). A comparison of performance feedback procedures on teachers' treatment implementation integrity and students' inappropriate behavior in special education classrooms. *Journal of Applied Behavior Analysis, 40*, 447-461.

Durward, L., & Whatmore, R. (1976). Testing measures of the quality of residential care: A pilot study. *Behavior Research & Therapy, 14*, 149-157.

Dyer, K., Schwartz, I.S., & Luce, S.C. (1984). A supervision program for increasing functional activities for severely handicapped students in a residential setting. *Journal of Applied Behavior Analysis, 17*, 249-259.

Faw, G.D., Reid, D.H., Schepis, M.M., Fitzgerald, J.R., & Welty, P.A. (1981). Involving institutional staff in the development and maintenance of sign language skills with profoundly retarded persons. *Journal of Applied Behavior Analysis, 14*, 411-423.

Fleming, R.K., & Sulzer-Azaroff, B. (1989). Enhancing quality of teaching by direct care staff through performance feedback on the job. *Behavioral Residential Treatment, 4*, 377-395.

Fleming, R.K., & Sulzer-Azaroff, B. (1992). Reciprocal peer management: Improving staff instruction in a vocational training program. *Journal of Applied Behavior Analysis, 25*, 611-620.

Ford, J.E. (1984). A comparison of three feedback procedures for improving teaching skills. *Journal of Organizational Behavior Management, 6*(1), 65-77.

Gladstone, B.W., & Spencer, C.J. (1977). The effects of modeling on the contingent praise of mental retardation counselors. *Journal of Applied Behavior Analysis, 10*, 75-84.

Green, C.W., Canipe, V.C., Way, P.J., & Reid, D.H. (1986). Improving the functional utility and effectiveness of classroom services for students with profound multiple handicaps. *The Journal of the Association for Persons with Severe Handicaps, 11*, 162-170.

Green, C.W., Reid, D.H., Perkins, L.I., & Gardner, S.M. (1991). Increasing habilitative services for persons with profound handicaps: An application of structural analysis to staff management. *Journal of Applied Behavior Analysis, 24,* 459-471.

Green, C.W., Rollyson, J.H., Passante, S.C., & Reid, D.H. (2002). Maintaining proficient supervisor performance with direct support personnel: An analysis of two management approaches. *Journal of Applied Behavior Analysis, 35,* 205-208.

Greene, B.F., Willis, B.S., Levy, R., & Bailey, J.S. (1978). Measuring client gains from staff-implemented programs. *Journal of Applied Behavior Analysis, 11,* 395-412.

Gross, A.M., & Ekstrand, M. (1983). Increasing and maintaining rates of teacher praise: A study using public posting and feedback fading. *Behavior Modification, 7,* 126-135.

Hagan, R.L., Craighead, W.E., & Paul, G.L. (1975). Staff reactivity to evaluative behavioral observations. *Behavior Therapy, 6,* 201-205.

Hall, R.V., Panyan, M., Rabon, D., & Broden, M. (1968). Instructing beginning teachers in reinforcement procedures which improve classroom control. *Journal of Applied Behavior Analysis, 1,* 315-322.

Harchick, A.E., Sherman, J.A., Sheldon, J.B., & Strouse, M.C. (1992). Ongoing consultation as a method of improving performance of staff members in a group home. *Journal of Applied Behavior Analysis, 25,* 599-610.

Hawkins, A.M., Burgio, L.D., Langford, A., & Engel, B.T. (1992). The effects of verbal and written feedback on staff compliance with assigned prompted voiding in a nursing home. *Journal of Organizational Behavior Management, 13*(1), 137-150.

Hollander, M.A., & Plutchik, R. (1972). A reinforcement program for psychiatric attendants. *Journal of Behavior Therapy & Experimental Psychiatry, 3,* 297-300.

Hollander, M.A., Plutchik, R., & Horner, V. (1973). Interaction of patient and attendant reinforcement programs: The "piggyback" effect. *Journal of Consulting and Clinical Psychology, 41,* 43-47.

Horner, R.H., Thompsen, L.S., & Storey, K. (1990). Effects of case manager feedback on the quality of individual habilitation plan objectives. *Mental Retardation, 28,* 227-231.

Horton, G.O. (1975). Generalization of teacher behavior as a function of subject matter specific discrimination training. *Journal of Applied Behavior Analysis, 8,* 311-319.

Hrydowy, E.R., & Martin, G.L..(1994). A practical staff management package for use in a training program for persons with developmental disabilities. *Behavior Modification, 18,* 66-88.

Ingham, P., & Greer, R.D. (1992). Changes in student and teacher responses in observed and generalized settings as a function of supervisor observations. *Journal of Applied Behavior Analysis, 25,* 153-164.

Katz, R.C., Johnson, C.A., & Gelfand, S. (1972). Modifying the dispensing of reinforcers: Some implications for behavior modification with hospitalized patients. *Behavior Therapy, 3,* 579-588.

Kolko, D.J., McCanna, M.W., & Donaldson, L. (1989). Sequential assessment of staff administration of contingency management procedures on a child psychiatric unit. *Behavior Modification, 13,* 216-244.

Kreitner, R., Reif, W.E., & Morris, M. (1977). Measuring the impact of feedback on the performance of mental health technicians. *Journal of Organizational Behavior Management, 1*(1), 105-109.

Langone, J., Koorland, M., & Oseroff, A. (1987). Producing changes in the instructional behavior of teachers of the mentally handicapped through inservice education. *Education and Treatment of Children, 10,* 146-164.

Leach, D.J., & Dolan, N.K., (1985). Helping teachers increase student academic engagement rate: The evaluation of a minimal feedback procedure. *Behavior Modification, 9,* 55-71.

Marshall, B.D., Jr., Banzett, L., Keuhnel, T., & Moore, J. (1983). Maintaining nursing staff performance on an intensive behavior therapy unit. *Analysis and Intervention in Developmental Disabilities, 3,* 193-204.

McGimsey, J.F., Greene, B.F., & Lutzker, J.R. (1995). Competence in aspects of behavioral treatment and consultation: Implications for service delivery and graduate training. *Journal of Applied Behavior Analysis, 28,* 301-315.

Methot, L.L., Williams, W.L., Cummings, A., & Bradshaw, B. (1996). Measuring the effects of a manager-supervisor training program through the generalized performance of managers, supervisors, front-line staff and clients in a human service setting. *Journal of Organizational Behavior Management, 16(2),* 3-34.

Neef, N.A., Shafer, M.S., Egel, A.L., Cataldo, M.R., & Parrish, J.M. (1983). The class specific effects of compliance training with "do" and "don't" requests: Analogue analysis and classroom application. *Journal of Applied Behavior Analysis, 16,* 81-99.

O'Reilly, M.F., Renzaglia, A., Hutchins, M., Koterba-Buss, L., Clayton, M., Halle, J.W., & Izen, C. (1992). Teaching systematic instruction competencies to special education student teachers: An applied behavioral supervision model. *Journal of the Association for Persons with Severe Handicaps, 17,* 104-111.

Panyan, M., Boozer, H., & Morris, N. (1970). Feedback to attendants as a reinforcer for applying operant techniques. *Journal of Applied Behavior Analysis, 3,* 1-4.

Parsons, M.B., Rollyson, J.H., & Reid, D.H. (2004). Improving day-treatment services for adults with severe disabilities: A norm-referenced application of outcome management. *Journal of Applied Behavior Analysis, 37,* 365-377.

Parsons, M.B., Schepis, M.M., Reid, D.H., McCarn, J.E., & Green, C.W. (1987). Expanding the impact of behavioral staff management: A large-scale, long-term application in schools serving severely handicapped students. *Journal of Applied Behavior Analysis, 20,* 139-150.

Parsonson, B.S., Baer, A.M., & Baer, D.M. (1974). The application of generalized correct social contingencies: An evaluation of a training program. *Journal of Applied Behavior Analysis, 7,* 427-437.

Patterson, R., Cooke, C., & Liberman, R.P. (1972). Reinforcing the reinforcers: A method of supplying feedback to nursing personnel. *Behavior Therapy, 3,* 444-446.

Patterson, E.T., Griffin, J.C., & Panyan, M.C. (1976). Incentive maintenance of self-help skill training programs for nonprofessional personnel. *Journal of Behavior Therapy & Experimental Psychiatry, 7,* 249-253.

Petscher, E.S., & Bailey, J.S. (2006). Effects of training, prompting, and self-monitoring on staff behavior in a classroom for students with disabilities. *Journal of Applied Behavior Analysis, 39,* 215-226.

Plavnick, J.B., Ferreri, S.J., & Maupin, A.N. (2010). The effects of self-monitoring on the procedural integrity of a behavioral intervention for young children with developmental disabilities. *Journal of Applied Behavior Analysis, 43,* 315-320.

Pomerleau, O.F., Bobrove, P.H., & Smith, R.H. (1973). Rewarding psychiatric aides for the behavioral improvement of assigned patients. *Journal of Applied Behavior Analysis, 6,* 383-390.

Pommer, D.A., & Streedbeck, D. (1974). Motivating staff performance in an operant learning program for children. *Journal of Applied Behavior Analysis, 7,* 217-221.

Prue, D.M., Krapfl, J.E., Noah, J.C., Cannon, S., & Maley, R.F. (1980). Managing the treatment activities of state hospital staff. *Journal of Organizational Behavior Management, 2*(3), 165-181.

Quilitch, H.R. (1975). A comparison of three staff-management procedures. *Journal of Applied Behavior Analysis, 8,* 59-66.

Quilitch, H.R., de Longchamps, G.D., Warden, R.A., & Szczepaniak, C.J. (1977). The effects of announced health inspections upon employee cleaning performance. *Journal of Organizational Behavior Management, 1*(1), 79-88.

Repp, A.C., & Barton, L.E. (1980). Naturalistic observations of institutionalized retarded persons: A comparison of licensure decisions and behavioral observations. *Journal of Applied Behavior Analysis, 13,* 333-341.

Repp, A.C., Barton, L.E., & Brulle, A.R. (1981). Correspondence between effectiveness and staff use of instructions for severely retarded persons. *Applied Research in Mental Retardation, 2,* 237-245.

Realon, R.E., Lewallen, J.D., & Wheeler, A.J. (1983). Verbal feedback vs. verbal feedback plus praise: The effects on direct care staff's training behaviors. *Mental Retardation, 21,* 209-212.

Reid, D.H., Green, C.W., & Parsons, M.B. (2003). An outcome management program for extending advances in choice research into choice opportunities for supported workers with severe multiple disabilities. *Journal of Applied Behavior Analysis, 36,* 575-578.

Reid, D.H., Parsons, M.B., Lattimore, L.P., Towery, D.L., & Reade, K.K. (2005). Improving staff performance through clinician application of outcome management. *Research in Developmental Disabilities, 26,* 101-116.

Reid, D.H., Parsons, M.B., McCarn, J.E., Green, C.W., Phillips, J.F., & Schepis, M.M. (1985). Providing a more appropriate education for severely handicapped persons: Increasing and validating functional classroom tasks. *Journal of Applied Behavior Analysis, 18,* 289-301.

Reinoehl, R.B., & Halle, J.W. (1994). Increasing the assessment probe performance of teacher aides through written prompts. *Journal of the Association for Persons with Severe Handicaps, 19,* 32-42.

Richman, G.S., Riordan, M.R., Reiss, M.L., Pyles, D.A.M., & Bailey, J.S. (1988). The effects of self-monitoring and supervisor feedback on staff performance in a residential setting. *Journal of Applied Behavior Analysis, 21*, 401-409.

Sanson-Fisher, R.W., Poole, A.D., & Harker, J. (1979). Behavioral analysis of ward rounds within a general hospital psychiatric unit. *Behavior Research & Therapy, 17*, 333-348.

Seys, D., & Duker, P. (1988). Effects of staff management on the quality of residential care for mentally retarded individuals. *American Journal on Mental Retardation, 93*, 290-299.

Seys, D.M. & Duker, P.C. (1993). Staff management procedures and changes in the distribution of nontargeted activities by residential staff members: A secondary analysis. *Behavioral Residential Treatment, 8*, 21-28.

Seys, D., Kersten, H., & Duker, P. (1990). Evaluating a ward staff program for increasing spontaneous and varied communicative gesturing with individuals who are mentally retarded. *Behavioral Residential Treatment, 5*, 247-257.

Sneed, T.J., & Bible, G.H. (1979). An administrative procedure for improving staff performance in an institutional setting for retarded persons. *Mental Retardation, 17*, 92-94.

Van Houton, R., & Sullivan, K. (1975). Effects of an audio-cueing system on the rate of teacher praise. *Journal of Applied Behavior Analysis, 8*, 197-201.

Wallace, C.J., Davis, J.R., Liberman, R.P., & Baker, V. (1973). Modeling and staff behavior. *Journal of Consulting and Clinical Psychology, 41*, 422-425.

Welsch, W.V., Ludwig, C., Radiker, J.E., & Krapfl, J.E. (1973). Effects of feedback on daily completion of behavior modification projects. *Mental Retardation, 11*, 24-26.

Whatmore, R., Durward, L., & Kushlick, A. (1975). Measuring the quality of residential care. *Behavior Research & Therapy, 13*, 227-236.

Whyte, R.A., Van Houten, R., & Hunter, W. (1983). The effects of public posting on teachers' performance of supervision duties. *Education and Treatment of Children, 6*, 21-28.

Williams, W.L., Vittorio, T.D., & Hausherr, L. (2002). A description and extension of a human services management model. *Journal of Organizational Behavior Management, 22(1)*, 47-71.

Wilson, P.G., Reid, D.H., & Korabek-Pinkowski, C.A. (1991). Analysis of public verbal feedback as a staff management procedure. *Behavioral Residential Treatment, 6*, 263-277.

Promoting Supportive Social Interactions with Consumers

Baldwin, S. & Hattersley, J. (1984). Use of self-recording to maintain staff-resident interaction. *Journal of Mental Deficiency Research, 28*, 57-66.

Brown, K.M., Willis, B.S., & Reid, D.H. (1981). Differential effects of supervisor verbal feedback and feedback plus approval on institutional staff performance. *Journal of Organizational Behavior Management, 3(1)*, 57-68.

Burg, M.M., Reid, D.H., & Lattimore, J. (1979). Use of a self-recording and supervision program to change institutional staff behavior. *Journal of Applied Behavior Analysis, 12*, 363-375.

Burgio, L.D., Whitman, T.L. & Reid, D.H. (1983). A participative management approach for improving direct-care staff performance in an institutional setting. *Journal of Applied Behavior Analysis, 16*, 37-53.

Coles, E., & Blunden R. (1981). Maintaining new procedures using feedback to staff, a hierarchical reporting system, and a multidisciplinary management group. *Journal of Organizational Behavior Management, 3(2)*, 19-33.

Doerner, M., Miltenberger, R.G., & Bakken, J. (1989). The effects of staff self-management on positive social interactions in a group home setting. *Behavioral Residential Treatment, 4*, 313-330.

Hile, M.G., & Walbran, B.B. (1991). Observing staff-resident interactions: What staff do, what residents receive. *Mental Retardation, 29*, 35-41.

Montegar, C.A., Reid, D.H., Madsen, C.H., Jr., & Ewell, M.D. (1977). Increasing institutional staff to resident interactions through in-service training and supervisor approval. *Behavior Therapy, 8,* 533-540.

Seys, D.M., & Duker, P.C. (1986). Effects of a supervisory treatment package on staff-mentally retarded resident interactions. *American Journal of Mental Deficiency, 90,* 388-394.

Spreat, S., Piper, T., Deaton, S., Savoy-Paff, D., Brantner, J., Lipinski, D., Dorsey, M., & Baker-Potts, J.C. (1985). The impact of supervisory feedback on staff and client behavior. *Education and Training of the Mentally Retarded. 20,* 196-203.

Suda, K.T., & Miltenberger, R.G. (1993). Evaluation of staff management strategies to increase positive interactions in a vocational setting. *Behavioral Residential Treatment, 8,* 69-88.

Venn, M.L., & Wolery, M. (1992). Increasing day care staff members' interactions during caregiving routines. *Journal of Early Intervention, 16,* 304-319.

Promoting Treatment Services Specific to Groups of Consumers

Arco, L (1991). Effects of outcome performance feedback on maintenance of client and staff behavior in a residential setting. *Behavioral Residential Treatment, 6,* 231-247.

Breuning, S.E., Davis, V.J., & Lewis, J.R. (1981). Examination of methods of selecting goal-directed activities for institutionalized retarded adults. *Education and Training of the Mentally Retarded, 16,* 5-12.

Burch, M.R., Reiss, M.L., & Bailey, J.S. (1987). A competency-based "hands-on" training package for direct care staff. *Journal of the Association for Persons with Severe Handicaps, 12,* 67-71.

Cowen, R.J., Jones, F.H., & Bellack, A.S. (1979). Grandma's rule with group contingencies—A cost-efficient means of classroom management. *Behavior Modification, 3,* 397-418.

Dowrick, P.W., & Johns, E.M. (1976). Video feedback effects on therapist attention to on-task behaviors of disturbed children. *Journal of Behavior Therapy & Experimental Psychiatry, 7,* 255-257.

Green, C.W., Parsons, M.B., & Reid, D.H. (1993). Integrating instructional procedures into traditional congregate care situations for people with severe disabilities. *Behavioral Residential Treatment, 8,* 243-262.

Kaprowy, E.A., Norton, G.R., & Melnychuk, E.E. (1986). Parametric reinforcement effects in a programmed activities environment for the severely retarded. *Behavior Modification, 10,* 19-36.

LeLaurin, K., & Risley, T.R. (1972). The organization of day care environments: "zone" versus "man-to-man" staff assignments. *Journal of Applied Behavior Analysis, 5,* 225-232.

Mansell, J., Felce, D., de Kock, U., & Jenkins, J. (1982). Increasing purposeful activity of severely and profoundly mentally-handicapped adults. *Behavior Research & Therapy, 20,* 593-604.

McCormick, L., Cooper, M., & Goldman, R., (1979). Training teachers to maximize instructional time provided to severely and profoundly handicapped children. *AAESPH Review, 4,* 301-310.

Parsons, M.B., Cash, V.B., & Reid, D.H. (1989). Improving residential treatment services: Implementation and norm-reference evaluation of a comprehensive management system. *Journal of Applied Behavior Analysis, 22,* 143-156.

Parsons, M.B., & Reid, D.H. (1993). Evaluating and improving residential treatment during group leisure situations: A program replication and refinement. *Research in Developmental Disabilities, 14,* 67-85.

Porterfield, J., Blunden, R., & Blewitt, E. (1980). Improving environments for profoundly handicapped adults using prompts and social attention to maintain high group engagement. *Behavior Modification, 4,* 225-241.

Quilitch, H.R., & Gray, J.D. (1974). Purposeful activity for the PMR: A demonstration project. *Mental Retardation, 12,* 28-29.

Seys, D.M., & Duker, P.C. (1978). Improving residential care for the retarded by differential reinforcement of high rates of ward-staff behavior. *Behavioral Analysis and Modification, 2,* 203-210.

Spangler, P.F., & Marshall, A.M. (1983). The unit play manager as facilitator of purposeful activities among institutionalized profoundly and severely retarded boys. *Journal of Applied Behavior Analysis, 16,* 345-349.

Sturmey, P., & Crisp, A.G. (1989). Organizing staff to provide individual teaching in a group: A critical review of room management and related procedures. *Australia and New Zealand Journal of Developmental Disabilities, 15,* 127-142.

Ward, M.H., & Baker, B.L. (1968). Reinforcement therapy in the classroom. *Journal of Applied Behavior Analysis, 1,* 323-328.

PROMOTING QUALITY PERSONAL CARE AND SUPPORT FOR CONSUMERS

Alavosious, M.P., & Sulzer-Azaroff, B. (1986). The effects of performance feedback on the safety of client lifting and transfer. *Journal of Applied Behavior Analysis, 19,* 261-267.

Alavosious, M.P., & Sulzer-Azaroff, B. (1990). Acquisition and maintenance of health-care routines as a function of feedback density. *Journal of Applied Behavior Analysis, 23,* 151-162.

Babcock, R.A., Sulzer-Azaroff, B., Sanderson, M., & Scibak, J. (1992). Increasing nurses' use of feedback to promote infection-control practices in head-injury treatment. *Journal of Applied Behavior Analysis, 25,* 621-627.

Casella, S.E., Wilder, D.A., Neidert, P., Rey, C., Compton, M., & Chong, I. (2010). The effects of response effort on safe performance by therapists at an autism treatment facility. *Journal of Applied Behavior Analysis, 43,* 729-734.

Ivancic, M.T., Reid, D.H., Iwata, B.A., Faw, G.D., & Page, T.J. (1981). Evaluating a supervision program for developing and maintaining therapeutic staff-resident interactions during institutional care routines. *Journal of Applied Behavior Analysis, 14*, 95-107.

Iwata, B.A., Bailey, J.S., Brown, K.M., Foshee, T.J., & Alpern, M. (1976). A performance-based lottery to improve residential care and training by institutional staff. *Journal of Applied Behavior Analysis, 9*, 417-431.

Kneringer, M., & Page, T.J. (1999). Improving staff nutritional practices in community-based group homes: Evaluation, training, and management. *Journal of Applied Behavior Analysis, 32*, 221-224.

Korabek, C.A., Reid, D.H., & Ivancic, M.T. (1981). Improving needed food intake of profoundly handicapped children through effective supervision of institutional staff performance. *Applied Research in Mental Retardation, 2*, 69-88.

Kunz, G.G.R., Lutzker, J.R., Cuvo, A.J., Eddleman, J., Lutzker, S.Z., Megson, D., & Gulley, B. (1982). Evaluating strategies to improve careprovider performance on health and developmental tasks in an infant care facility. *Journal of Applied Behavior Analysis, 15*, 521-531.

Lattimore, J., Stephens, T.E., Favell, J.E., & Risley, T.R. (1984). Increasing direct care staff compliance to individualized physical therapy body positioning prescriptions: Prescriptive checklists. *Mental Retardation, 22*, 79-84.

McMorrow, M.J., Sheeley, R., Levinson, M., Maedke, J., Treworgy, S., Tripp, T., Casey, M., & Hunter, R. (1991). The use of publicly-posted performance feedback in an inpatient psychiatric treatment setting. *Behavioral Residential Treatment, 6*, 165-181.

Nabeyama, B., & Sturmey, P. (2010). Using behavioral skills training to promote safe and correct staff guarding and ambulation distance of students with multiple physical disabilities. *Journal of Applied Behavior Analysis, 43*, 341-345.

Nielsen, D., Sigurdsson, S.O., & Austin, J. (2009). Preventing back injuries in hospital settings: The effects of video modeling on safe patient lifting by nurses. *Journal of Applied Behavior Analysis, 42,* 551-561.

PROMOTING QUALITY DOCUMENTATION AND RECORD KEEPING BY STAFF

Christian, W.P., Norris, M.B., Anderson, S.R., & Blew, P.A. (1983). Improving the record-keeping performance of direct service personnel. *Journal of Mental Health Administration, 11,* 4-7.

Egan, P., Luce, S.C., & Hall, R.V. (1988). Use of a concurrent treatment design to analyze the effects of a peer review system in a residential setting. *Behavior Modification, 12,* 35-56.

Epstein, L.H., & Wolff, E. (1978). A multiple baseline analysis of implementing components of the problem-oriented medical record. *Behavior Therapy, 9,* 85-88.

Farmer, R., Wolery, M., Gast, DL., & Page, J.L. (1988). Individual staff training to increase the frequency of data collection in an integrated preschool program. *Education and Treatment of Children, 11,* 127-142.

Feldstein, S., & Feldstein, J.H. (1990). Positive reinforcement for submission of timely reports by professional staff in a residential facility. *Education and Training in Mental Retardation, 25,* 188-192.

Hutchison, J.M., Jarman, P.H., & Bailey, J.S. (1980). Public posting with habilitation teams: Effects on attendance and performance. *Behavior Modification, 4,* 57-70.

Jones, H.H., Morris, E.K., & Barnard, J.D. (1986). Increasing staff completion of civil commitment forms through instructions and graphed group performance feedback. *Journal of Organizational Behavior Management, 7*(3/4), 29-43.

Lovett, S.B., Bosmajian, C.P., Frederiksen, L.W., & Elder, J.P. (1983). Monitoring professional service delivery: An organizational level intervention. *Behavior Therapy, 14,* 170-177.

Mozingo, D.B., Smith, T., Riordan, M.R., Reiss, M.L., & Bailey, J.S. (2006). Enhancing frequency recording by developmental disabilities treatment staff. *Journal of Applied Behavior Analysis, 39,* 253-256.

Quilitch, H.R. (1978). Using a simple feedback procedure to reinforce the submission of written suggestions by mental health employees. *Journal of Organizational Behavior Management, 1*(2), 155-163.

Repp, A.C., & Deitz, D.E.D. (1979). Improving administrative-related staff behaviors at a state institution. *Mental Retardation, 17,* 185-192.

Shook, G.L., Johnson, C.M., & Uhlman, W.F. (1978). The effect of response effort reduction, instructions, group and individual feedback, and reinforcement of staff performance. *Journal of Organizational Behavior Management, 1*(3), 206-215.

Smith, D.W., & Wells, M.E. (1983). Use of a microcomputer to assist staff in documenting resident progress. *Mental Retardation, 21,* 111-115.

Thompson, T.J., Thornhill, C.A., Realon, R.E., & Ervin, K.M. (1991). Improving accuracy in documentation of restrictive interventions by direct-care personnel. *Mental Retardation, 29,* 201-205.

Welsh, T.M., Miller, L.K., & Altus, D.E. (1994). Programming for survival: A meeting system that survives 8 years later. *Journal of Applied Behavior Analysis, 27,* 423-433.

PREVENTING AND REDUCING ABSENTEEISM

Boudreau, C.A., Christian, W.P., & Thibadeau, S.F. (1993). Reducing absenteeism in a human service settings: A low cost alternative. *Journal of Organizational Behavior Management, 13*(2), 37-50.

Briggs, R.M. (1990). Reducing direct-care staff absenteeism: Effects of a combined reinforcement and punishment procedure. *Mental Retardation, 28,* 163-168.

Brown, N., & Redmon, W.K. (1989). The effects of a group reinforcement contingency on staff use of unscheduled sick leave. *Journal of Organizational Behavior Management, 10*(2), 3-17.

Durand, V.M. (1983). Behavioral ecology of a staff incentive program: Effects on absenteeism and resident disruptive behavior. *Behavior Modification, 7,* 165-181.

Durand, V.M. (1985). Employee absenteeism: A selective review of antecedents and consequences. *Journal of Organizational Behavior Management, 7*(1/2), 135-167.

Ford, J.E. (1981). A simple punishment procedure for controlling employee absenteeism. *Journal of Organizational Behavior Management, 3*(2), 71-78.

Gardner, J.M. (1970). Effects of reinforcement conditions on lateness and absence among institutional personnel. *Ohio Research Quarterly, 3,* 315-316.

Pierce, P.S., Hoffman, J.L., & Pelletier, L.P. (1974). The 4-day work week versus the 5-day work week: Comparative use of sick time and overtime by direct care personnel in an institutional facility for the severely and profoundly retarded. *Mental Retardation, 12,* 22-24.

Reid, D.H., Schuh-Wear, C.L., & Brannon, M.E. (1978). Use of a group contingency to decrease staff absenteeism in a state institution. *Behavior Modification, 2,* 251-266.

Shoemaker, J., & Reid, D.H. (1980). Decreasing chronic absenteeism among institutional staff: Effects of a low-cost attendance program. *Journal of Organizational Behavior Management, 2*(4), 317-328.

Strouse, M.C., Carroll-Hernandez, T.A., Sherman, J.A., & Sheldon, J.B. (2003). Turning over turnover: The evaluation of a staff scheduling system in a community-based program for adults with developmental disabilities. *Journal of Organizational Behavior Management, 23* (2/3), 45-63.

Zaharia, E.S., & Baumeister, A.A. (1978). Technician turnover and absenteeism in public residential facilities. *American Journal of Mental Deficiency, 82,* 580-593.

PROMOTING WORK ENJOYMENT

Davis, J.R., Rawana, E.P., & Capponi, D.R. (1989). Acceptability of behavioral staff management techniques. *Behavioral Residential Treatment, 4,* 23-44.

Davis, J.R., & Russell, R.H. (1990). Behavioral staff management: An analogue study of acceptability and its behavioral correlates. *Behavioral Residential Treatment, 5,* 259-270.

Green, C.W., & Reid, D.H. (1991). Reinforcing staff performance in residential facilities: A survey of common managerial practices. *Mental Retardation, 29,* 195-200.

Green, C.W., Reid, D.H., Passante, S., & Canipe, V. (2008). Changing less-preferred duties to more-preferred: A potential strategy for improving supervisor work enjoyment. *Journal of Organizational Behavior Management, 28(2),* 90-109.

Miltenberger, R.G., Larson, J., Doerner, M., & Orvedal, L. (1992). Assessing the acceptability of staff management procedures to direct care and supervisory staff. *Behavioral Residential Treatment, 7,* 23-34.

Parsons, M.B. (1998). A review of procedural acceptability in organizational behavior management. *Journal of Organizational Behavior Management, 18(2/3),* 173-190.

Parsons, M.B., Reid, D.H., & Crow, R.E. (2003). The best and worst ways to motivate staff in community agencies: A brief survey of supervisors. *Mental Retardation, 41,* 96-102.

Reid, D.H., & Parsons, M.B. (1995). Comparing choice and questionnaire measures of the acceptability of a staff training procedure. *Journal of Applied Behavior Analysis, 28,* 95-96.

Reid, D.H., & Parsons, M.B. (1996). A comparison of staff acceptability of immediate versus delayed verbal feedback in staff training. *Journal of Organizational Behavior Management, 16(2),* 35-47.

Wilder, D.A., Therrien, K., & Wine, B. (2005). A comparison between survey and verbal choice methods of identifying potential reinforcers among employees. *Journal of Organizational Behavior Management, 25(4),* 1-13.

REVIEW AND DISCUSSION PAPERS RELATED TO EVIDENCE-BASED SUPERVISION

Adkins, V.K. (1996). Discussion: Behavioral procedures for training direct care staff in facilities serving dependent populations. *Behavioral Interventions, 11,* 95-100.

Arco, L. (1993). A case for researching performance pay in human service management. *Journal of Organizational Behavior Management, 14(1),* 117-136.

Arco, L., & Birnbrauer, J.S. (1990). Performance feedback and maintenance of staff behavior in residential settings. *Behavioral Residential Treatment, 5,* 207-217.

Balcazar, F., Hopkins, B.L., & Suarez, Y. (1986). A critical, objective review of performance feedback. *Journal of Organizational Behavior Management, 7(3/4),* 65-89.

Bell, C. & Zemki, R. (1992). How do employees in service jobs find out how they're doing? Good feedback systems. *Training,* 36-44.

Bernstein, G.S. (1982). Training behavior change agents: A conceptual review. *Behavior Therapy, 13,* 1-23.

Bernstein, G.S, & Karan, O.C. (1978). Preservice training of professionals as behavior managers: A review. *Behavior Therapy, 9,* 124-126.

Christian, W.P. (1983). A case study in the programming and maintenance of institutional change. *Journal of Organizational Behavior Management, 5(3/4),* 99-153.

Davis, M. (1986). Systematic staff training. *Mental Health and Mental Retardation Quarterly Digest, 5.* (Available from Mental Health and Mental Retardation Services, Topeka, Kansas).

Demchak, M.A. (1987). A review of behavioral staff training in special education settings. *Education and Training in Mental Retardation, 22,* 205-217.

Egelston, J.D. (1986). Organizational behavior management in public residential facilities. *Mental Retardation Systems, 3,* 35-48.

Favell, J.E., Favel, J.E., Riddle, J.I., & Risley, T.R. (1984). Promoting change in mental retardation facilities: Getting services from the paper to the people. In W.P. Christian, G.T. Hannah, & T.J. Glahn (Eds.), *Programming effective human services: Strategies for institutional change and client transition:* (pp.15-37). New York: Plenum.

Flanagan, S.G., Cray, M.E., & Meter, D.V. (1983). A facility-wide consultation and training team as a catalyst in promoting institutional change. *Analysis and Intervention in Developmental Disabilities, 3,* 151-169.

Fleming, R.K., & Reile, P.A. (1993). A descriptive analysis of client outcomes associated with staff interventions in developmental disabilities. *Behavioral Residential Treatment, 8,* 29-43.

Ford, J.E. (1980). A classification system for feedback procedures. *Journal of Organizational Behavior Management, 2*(3), 183-191.

Frazier, T.W. (1972). Training institutional staff in behavior modification principles and techniques. In R.D. Ruben, H. Fensterheim, J.D. Henderson & L.P. Ullmann (Eds.), *Advances in behavior therapy: Proceedings of the fourth conference of the association for advancement of behavior therapy* (pp. 171-178). New York: Academic Press.

Gardner, J.M. (1973). Training the trainers. A review of research on teaching behavior modification. In R.D. Rubin, J.P. Brady, & J.D. Henderson (Eds.), *Advances in behavior therapy, Vol. 4* (pp.145-158). New York: Academic Press.

Harchik, A.E., Sherman, J.A., Hopkins, B.L., Strouse, M.C., & Sheldon, J.B. (1989). Use of behavioral techniques by paraprofessional staff: A review and proposal. *Behavioral Residential Treatment, 4,* 331-357.

Hastings, R.P., & Reminton, B. (1994). Rules of engagement. Toward an analysis of staff responses to challenging behavior. *Research in Developmental Disabilities, 15,* 279-298.

Loeber, R., & Weisman, R.G. (1975). Contingencies of therapist and trainer performance: A review. *Psychological Bulletin, 82,* 660-688.

Mayhew, G.L., Enyart, P., & Cone, J.D. (1979). Approaches to employee management: Policies and preferences. *Journal of Organizational Behavior Management, 2*(2), 103-111.

Mazza, J., & Pumroy, D.K. (1975). A review of evaluation of behavior modification programs. *The Psychological Record, 25,* 111-121.

McInnis, T. (1978). Training and motivating staff members. In D. Marholin (Ed.), *Child behavior therapy* (pp. 434-445). New York: Gardner Press.

Miller, R., & Lewin, L.M. (1980). Training and management of the psychiatric aide: A critical review. *Journal of Organizational Behavior Management, 2*(4), 295-315.

Neef, N.A. (1995). Research on training trainers in program implementation: An introduction and future directions. *Journal of Applied Behavior Analysis, 28,* 297-299.

Oorsouw, W.M.W.J., Embregts, P.J.C.M., Bosman, A.M.T., & Jahoda, A. (2009). Training staff serving clients with intellectual disabilities: A meta-analysis of aspects determining effectiveness. *Research in Developmental Disabilities, 30,* 503-511.

Pollack, M.J., Fleming, R.K., & Sulzer-Azaroff, B. (1994). Enhancing professional performance through organizational change. *Behavioral Interventions, 9,* 27-42.

Prue, D.M., & Fairbank, J.A. (1981). Performance feedback in organizational behavior management: A review. *Journal of Organizational Behavior Management, 3*(1), 1-16.

Quilitch, H.R. (1979). Applied behavior analysis studies for institutional management. In L.A. Hamerlynck (Ed.), *Behavioral systems for the developmentally disabled: II. Institutional, clinic and community environments* (pp.70-81). New York: Brunner/Mazel.

Rapp, S.R., Carstensen, L.L., & Prue, D.M. (1983). Organizational Behavior Management 1978-1982: An annotated bibliography. *Journal of Organizational Behavior Management, 5*(2), 5-50.

Reid, D.H. (2004). Training and supervising direct support personnel to carry out behavioral procedures. In J.L. Matson, R.B. Laud, & M.L. Matson (Eds.), *Behavior modification for persons with developmental disabilities: Treatments and supports* (pp. 73-99). Kingston, NY: NADD Press.

Reid, D.H., & Fitch, W.H. (in press). Training staff and parents: Evidence-based approaches. In J.L. Matson & P. Sturmey (Eds.), *International handbook of autism and pervasive developmental disorders.* New York: Springer.

Reid, D.H., & Green, C.W. (1990). Staff training. In J.L. Matson (Ed.), *Handbook of behavior modification with the mentally retarded* (2nd Edition) (pp.71-90). New York: Plenum Press.

Reid, D.H., McCarn, J.M., & Green, C.W. (1988). Staff training and management in school programs for severely developmentally disabled students. In M.D. Powers (Ed.), *Severe developmental disabilities: Expanded systems of interactions.* Baltimore: Brookes.

Reid, D.H., O'Kane, N.P., & Macurik, K.M. (2011). Staff training and management. In W.W. Fisher, C.C. Piazza, & Roane, H.S. (Eds.), *Handbook of applied behavior analysis.* New York: Guilford Press.

Reid, D.H., & Parsons, M.B. (2000). Organizational behavior management in human service settings. In J. Austin & J.E. Carr (Eds.), *Handbook of applied behavior analysis* (pp. 275-294). Reno, NV: Context Press.

Reid, D.H., Parsons, M.B., & Green, C.W. (1989). Treating aberrant behavior through effective staff management: A developing technology. In E. Cipani (Ed.), *AAMR Monograph: The treatment of severe behavior disorders: Behavior analysis approaches* (pp.175-190). Washington, D.C.: American Association on Mental Retardation.

Reid, D.H., Parsons, M.B., & Schepis, M.M. (1990). Management practices that affect the relative utility of aversive and nonaversive procedures. In S.L. Harris & J.S. Handleman (Eds.), *Life threatening behavior: Aversive and nonaversive interventions*. Newark, NJ: Rutgers University Press.

Reid, D.H., & Schepis, M.M. (1983). Training institutional staff in the treatment of severe behavior disorders of the mentally retarded. In R.P. Barrett & S.E. Breuning (Eds.), *Treatment of severe behavior disorders: Contemporary approaches with the mentally retarded.* New York: Plenum.

Reid, D.H., & Schepis, M.M. (1986). Direct care staff training. In R.P. Barrett (Ed.), *Severe behavior disorders in the mentally retarded: Nondrug approaches to treatment* (pp. 297-322). New York: Plenum Press.

Reid, D.H., Schepis, M.M., & Fitzgerald, J.R., (1984). Innovations in organizational behavior management in institutions for the developmentally disabled. In S.E. Breuning, J.L. Matson, & R.P. Barrett (Eds.), *Advances in mental retardation and developmental disabilities* (Vol. 2) (pp. 181-204), Greenwich, CT: JAI Press.

Reid, D.H., & Shoemaker, J. (1984). Behavioral supervision: Methods of improving institutional staff performance. In W.P. Christian, G.T. Hannah, & T.J. Glahn (Eds.), *Programming effective human services: Strategies for institutional change and client transition* (pp. 39-61). New York: Plenum Press.

Reid, D.H., & Whitman, T.L. (1983). Behavioral staff management in institutions: A critical review of effectiveness and acceptability. *Analysis and Intervention in Developmental Disabilities, 3,* 131-149.

Risley, T.R., & Favell, J. (1979). Constructing a living environment in an institution. In L.A. Hamerlynck (Ed.), *Behavioral systems for the developmentally disabled: II. Institutional, clinic, and community environments* (pp. 3-24). New York: Brunner/Mazel.

Slama, K.M., & Bannerman, D.J. (1983). Implementing and maintaining a behavioral treatment system in an institutional setting. *Analysis and Intervention in Developmental Disabilities, 3,* 171-191.

Sulzer-Azaroff, B., Pollack, M.J., Hamad, C., & Howley, T. (1998). Promoting widespread, durable service quality via interlocking contingencies. *Research in Developmental Disabilities, 19,* 39-61.

Williams, W.L., Vittorio, T.D., & Hausherr, L. (2002). A description and extension of a human services management model. *Journal of Organizational Behavior Management, 22(1),* 47-71.

BOOKS RELATED TO EVIDENCE-BASED SUPERVISION

Christian, W.P., Hannah, G.T., & Glahn, T.J. (Eds.). (1984). *Programming effective human services: Strategies for institutional change and client transition.* New York: Plenum.

Daniels, A.C. (1994). *Bringing out the best in people: How to apply the astonishing power of positive reinforcement.* New York: McGraw-Hill.

Daniels, A.C., & Daniels, J. E. (2005). *Measure of a leader: An actionable formula for legendary leadership.* Atlanta: Performance Management Publications.

LaVigna, G.W., Willis, T.J., Shaull, J.F., Abedi, M., & Sweitzer, M. (1994). *The periodic service review: A total quality assurance system for human services and education.* Baltimore: Paul H. Brookes.

Miller, L.M. (1978). *Behavior management: The new science of managing people at work.* New York: John Wiley & Sons.

Reid, D.H. (Ed.), (1998). *Organizational behavior management and developmental disabilities services: Accomplishments and future directions.* Binghamton, NY: Haworth Press.

Reid, D.H., & Parsons, M.B. (2006). *Motivating human service staff: Supervisory strategies for maximizing work effort and work enjoyment. 2nd Edition.* Morganton, NC: Habilitative Management Consultants, Inc.

Reid, D.H., & Parsons, M.B. (2002). *Working with staff to overcome challenging behavior among people who have severe disabilities: A guide for getting support plans carried out.* Morganton, NC: Habilitative Management Consultants.

Reid, D.H., Parsons, M.B., & Green, C.W. (1989). *Staff management in human services: Behavioral research and application.* Springfeild IL: Charles C Thomas.

Wetzel, R.J., & Hoschoer, R.L. (1984). *Residential teaching communities: Program development and staff training for developmentally disabled persons.* Glenview IL: Scott, Foresman and Company.

A Training Curriculum for Supervisors

Reid, D.H., Parsons, M.B., & Green, C. W. (2011). *The supervisor training curriculum: Evidence-based ways to promote work quality and enjoyment among support staff.* Washington, DC: American Association on Intellectual and Developmental Disabilities.

INDEX

absenteeism 4, 6, 7, 41, 44, 66, 72, 179, 182, 228, 243-264
abuse 48, 98, 179, 194
acceptability (among staff) 42-44
    of general supervisor interactions 5, 6, 20-21, 101, 103, 116, 121, 123, 192
    of monitoring procedures 20, 84, 98-107, 144
    of training procedures 75-79
activity schedules 36, 39-46, 64, 74, 86-87, 91, 303-305
awards (see special recognition)
behavioral skills training (see also training) 52
behavior support plans 37, 49, 54-55, 61, 72, 146, 229, 296-297
break times 174, 310-313
burnout 4, 110
challenging behavior 15, 146, 147, 210, 220, 229, 280-282, 296-298, 310
choice 34, 35, 53
clinicians 55, 57, 65, 67, 111, 220, 267, 274, 275, 281-283, 296
compensatory time 245
corrective supervision 13, 18, 179-203, 258
data collection 84, 282, 283, 292-296
disciplinary action 190, 193, 194-201, 234, 243, 254, 258, 259, 260, 279, 295, 296, 308
documentation (see also data collection) 132, 209-212, 216, 292-296
evaluation 19, 82, 85, 102, 139
evidence-based (definition) 7, 8, 81, 227
executive personnel 57, 127, 138, 170-174, 198, 199, 220, 223, 233-235
feedback 59, 63-64, 68, 70, 72, 76, 79, 88, 92, 109-150, 157, 159, 164, 184, 190-193, 258, 307, 308
    corrective 115, 118, 119, 143, 190-193, 278, 279, 290, 291, 307
    evidence-based protocol 114-130, 191
    formal 116, 125, 129, 130, 136, 149-150, 153
    group 140-144, 150, 153
    immediate vs. delayed 144, 145, 150, 153
    individual 140, 150
    informal 116, 130-133, 149, 150, 153, 154
    negative (see also corrective) 172, 192, 193
    outcome-based 145-149
    positive (see also supportive) 113-115, 131-133, 140-144, 153, 166, 167, 171, 205, 238, 239
    private 129, 130, 143
    public (see also group) 129, 130, 142-144, 171
    publicly posted (see also group) 142-144, 150, 153
    supportive 114, 277, 290, 307
    vocal 134, 135-137, 149, 150
    written 130, 134-139, 153

goals (for consumers) 14, 25, 285
goal setting 239, 240, 276, 277, 308, 309
group contingencies 254-257
group homes 28, 36, 37, 147, 286
injuries 210, 250
interactions (with consumers) 4, 7, 26, 27, 87, 88, 95, 149
Intermediate Care Facilities (ICFs) 69
job retention 6, 112, 113, 182, 209, 210
job termination 197-200, 232, 279, 284, 295, 296
leisure activities 37, 184, 185, 303, 304
merit pay 175-177
mission statements 13, 15, 25
modeling 291, 292
monitoring (of staff performance) 13, 17, 19, 33, 76, 81-107, 109, 121-122, 180, 186, 196, 212, 215, 231, 252, 257, 259, 271, 276, 280-283, 290, 294, 297, 315
    formal 82-91, 96, 104, 107, 305
    forms 86-88, 91
    frequency recording 87-88
    informal 82, 91-94, 103, 132
    overt vs. covert 97, 98
motivation
    of staff 4, 5, 11, 18, 79, 110-112, 122, 155, 175, 182, 189-201, 212-220, 231, 244, 271, 275, 280-285, 313
    of supervisors 238-241
negative supervisory styles 105, 106, 111, 113, 165, 181-183, 233, 235
nonwork behavior 228, 301-316
off task (see also nonwork behavior) 301
outcome management 14, 25
outcomes (among consumers) 13-15, 31, 32, 43, 90, 156, 229, 308, 309
overtime 44, 45, 245
participative supervision 42-44, 120, 222, 223, 256, 294, 295
pay raises 175-177
peer pressure 256, 257
performance checklists (see also monitoring) 36-38, 53, 54, 86, 87, 91
performance lotteries 161-163
praise (see also supportive feedback) 114, 128-130
professional staff 270, 283
reactivity (to monitoring) 94-97
record keeping (see also data collection) 91, 221, 285
reinforcement 239-241
residential agencies 13, 31, 94, 195, 207, 243, 245, 254-256, 302, 303
role playing 56, 62, 63, 70, 78, 79, 273, 275, 289
schools 156
self-motivation 238-241
self-reinforcement 240, 241
sick leave (see also absenteeism) 247-250, 253
special recognition 153-177, 205, 277
    activities 154, 155, 163-175
    appreciation events 159-161
    awards 153-163
supported work 61, 62, 65
supportive supervision 13, 18, 254, 258, 269
task analysis 36

Task Enjoyment Motivation Protocol (TEMP) 206, 207, 212-220, 222
teaching (of consumers by staff) 39, 49, 54, 61, 65, 73-75, 95, 117-119, 134, 146, 156, 161, 195, 210, 228, 267-298
    formal 267-269, 270-285
    naturalistic 181-186, 268, 269, 285-292
team process 14
training 13, 16, 47-79, 88, 109, 180, 183, 196, 207-209, 215, 251-252, 257, 272-276, 288, 297
    competency-based 16, 51, 52, 59, 60, 68, 69, 70, 77, 184, 273-275
    media-based 71-73
    on-the-job 58, 60, 66-68, 70, 208, 273, 274, 289, 304, 305
    orientation 48-50
    peer training 73-76
    performance-based 16, 51, 52, 57-60, 68, 69, 70-72, 177, 184, 273-275
    pyramidal training 73-76
turnover 6, 112, 113
unusual incidents 210, 211
visibility (of supervisor) 92-94, 238, 306
work privileges 161